Wirtschaftsinformatik-Wörterbuch

Deutsch-Englisch · Englisch-Deutsch
German-English · English-German

von

Dipl.-Ing. Dr. rer. pol. Lutz J. Heinrich

o. Universitätsprofessor für Betriebswirtschaftslehre
und Wirtschaftsinformatik an der Universität Linz,
derzeit: Guest Professor for Business Administration,
Emory University, Atlanta/Georgia, USA

und

Mag. Dr. rer. soc. oec. Friedrich Roithmayr

o. Universitätsprofessor für Wirtschaftsinformatik
an der Universität Innsbruck

unter Mitarbeit von
Dipl.-Ing. Mag. Dr. Martin Lamprecht, MSc.
Victoria University of Wellington, New Zealand

und
Dipl.-Kfm. Dr. Dietrich Splettstößer
CURTIN University of Technology Perth, Australia

Mit über 7000 deutschen Begriffen der Wirtschaftsinformatik
und ihren englischen Bezeichnungen sowie umgekehrt einschließlich
wichtiger deutsch- und englischsprachiger Abkürzungen mit ihren
Langbezeichnungen

2., korrigierte und erweiterte Auflage

R. Oldenbourg Verlag München Wien

CIP-Titelaufnahme der Deutschen Bibliothek

Heinrich, Lutz J.:
Wirtschaftsinformatik-Wörterbuch : Deutsch-Englisch, Englisch-Deutsch / von Lutz J. Heinrich u. Friedrich Roithmayr. Unter Mitarb. von Martin Lamprecht u. Dietrich Splettstösser. – 2., korr. u. erw. Aufl. – München ; Wien : Oldenbourg, 1990
ISBN 3-486-21620-1

NE: Roithmayr, Friedrich:; HST

© 1990 R. Oldenbourg Verlag GmbH, München

Das Werk einschließlich aller Abbildungen ist urheberrechtlich geschützt. Jede Verwertung außerhalb der Grenzen des Urheberrechtsgesetzes ist ohne Zustimmung des Verlages unzulässig und strafbar. Das gilt insbesondere für Vervielfältigungen, Übersetzungen, Mikroverfilmungen und die Einspeicherung und Bearbeitung in elektronischen Systemen.

Gesamtherstellung: Rieder, Schrobenhausen

ISBN 3-486-21620-1

Inhalt

Vorwort zur zweiten Auflage VII

Aus dem Vorwort zur ersten Auflage VIII

Preface to the Second Edition IX

Deutsch-Englisch 1

Englisch-Deutsch 107

Französischsprachige Abkürzungen 207

Aus dem Vorwort zur ersten Auflage

Mit diesem ersten Wörterbuch der Wirtschaftsinformatik Deutsch-Englisch und Englisch-Deutsch wollen die Autoren einen Beitrag dazu leisten, Studierenden der Wirtschaftsinformatik und Praktikern, insbesondere Informationsmanagern und Informationssystem-Planern, englischsprachige Texte leichter zugänglich zu machen. Bereits ein kurzer Blick in die bisher vorliegenden Fachwörterbücher der Datenverarbeitung, der EDV usw. zeigt, daß sie diesem Anspruch nicht gerecht werden können, weil sie einerseits für den Wirtschaftsinformatiker viel Überflüssiges oder sogar Überholtes enthalten (so in einem Beispiel über einhundert Begriffe von Lochband bis Lochzange), andererseits aber viele Lücken aufweisen.

Das Überflüssige und die Lücken erklären sich insbesondere daraus, daß die bisher publizierten Fachwörterbücher die besondere Sichtweise der Wirtschaftsinformatik nicht berücksichtigen. Überflüssiges entsteht, weil die Informations- und Kommunikationstechnologie für die Wirtschaftsinformatik nicht als Mittel zum Zweck, sondern als Gegenstand angesehen wird; technische Details zur Informations- und Kommunikationstechnologie interessieren den Wirtschaftsinformatiker in der Regel nicht, und sie werden in den für ihn relevanten englischsprachigen Texten auch kaum verwendet. Lücken entstehen, weil die Autoren der vorliegenden Fachwörterbücher Information und Kommunikation nicht als wirtschaftliches Gut betrachten; die Informationsfunktion von Organisationen als das Erklärungs- und Gestaltungsobjekt der Wirtschaftsinformatik wird von ihnen also nicht berücksichtigt.

Linz, im Februar 1989
L. J. Heinrich
F. Roithmayr

Vorwort zur zweiten Auflage

Die im Frühjahr 1989 erschienene 1. Auflage des Wirtschaftsinformatik-Wörterbuchs war bereits nach wenigen Monaten vergriffen. Dies bestätigt die im Vorwort zur 1. Auflage von den Autoren geäußerte Vermutung, daß ein erheblicher Bedarf an einem fachspezifischen Wörterbuch besteht, also ein Bedarf, der durch die bislang angebotenen Wörterbücher allein nicht abgedeckt werden kann.

Der Bestand der 1. Auflage wurde von den Autoren und ihren Mitarbeitern gründlich überarbeitet. Insbesondere wurden Fehler ausgemerzt und an verschiedenen Übersetzungen Verbesserungen durchgeführt; der Bestand wurde um mehr als 1.500 Einträge, sowohl im deutsch-englischen als auch im englisch-deutschen Teil, erweitert. Einige französischsprachige Abkürzungen, die sowohl in deutschsprachigen als auch in englischsprachigen Texten häufig verwendet werden, wurden angefügt. Die Autoren sind daher zuversichtlich, daß die 2. Auflage - noch besser als die 1. Auflage - sowohl Praktikern als auch Studierenden helfen wird, englischsprachige Texte der Wirtschaftsinformatik ins Deutsche zu übertragen und umgekehrt.

Herr Dr. M. Lamprecht, der bereits bei der Bearbeitung der 1. Auflage hilfreich war, wurde bei seiner Arbeit für die 2. Auflage von Prof. I. F. Jackson und Mrs. M. Smith (alle Victoria University, Wellington/New Zealand) unterstützt. Mit Herrn Dr. D. Splettstößer (CURTIN University of Technology, Perth/Australia) haben die Autoren einen weiteren Mitarbeiter gewonnen. Beide Mitarbeiter waren bei der Überarbeitung des Bestands der 1. Auflage hilfreich; sie haben aber auch dazu beigetragen, den Bestand für die 2. Auflage zu erweitern. Die Fachkompetenz dieser Mitarbeiter, die sie in mehrjähriger Tätigkeit an einschlägigen Lehr- und Forschungseinrichtungen englischsprachiger Universitäten erworben haben, war für die Autoren von großem Nutzen.

Bezüglich der lexikographischen Ordnung der Begriffe im deutsch-englischen Teil ist folgendes zu beachten: Die Umlaute ä, ö, ü und äu werden wie die Vokale a, o, u und au behandelt. Begriffe mit den Zeichen " " (Leerzeichen), "-" (Bindestrich), "/" (Schrägstrich) und "´" (Apostroph) werden - in dieser Reihenfolge - vor dem Alphabet eingeordnet.

Die Autoren danken Frau Dr. E. Heinrich für das mehrmalige Korrekturlesen und Frau M. Edtbauer für die Erfassung der Texte und die Durchführung der Korrekturen.

Atlanta und Innsbruck, im Februar 1990   L. J. Heinrich
                                                                                                         F. Roithmayr

Preface to the Second Edition

The Economic Informatics Dictionary, German - English and English - German, was first published in Spring 1989. Main motive for the authors to publish an Economic Informatics Dictionary was the strong need for a widely accepted source giving translations from German into English and from English into German of the principal terms used in Economic Informatics.

The term "Economic Informatics" is used as the english synonym for "Wirtschaftsinformatik", a quite new and dynamic field of scientific research and academic teaching in German speaking countries (Austria, Germany, Switzerland). Economic Informatics, especially its main part discipline Business Informatics, is primarily concerned with the application of information and communications technology to organizational needs. Therefore, it can be seen as integration of essential parts of both Computer Science and Business Administration. Economic Informatics covers research and teaching areas like Management Information Systems, Information Analysis and Design, Information Engineering, Software Engineering, Information Resource Management, Computer Auditing, Privacy, and Security as well as fundamentals of information and communications technology.

The second edition of the Dictionary represents a significant revision of the first edition. The authors, with help of Dr. M. Lamprecht (who was supported by Prof. I. F. Jackson and Mrs. Monika Smith, Victoria University, Wellington/New Zealand) and Dr. D. Splettstößer (CURTIN University of Technology, Perth/Australia), have updated the entries by a process of adjustment, insertion and sometimes elimination. In the end, the second edition has about 1.500 entries more than the first edition, both in the German - English and in the English - German part.

The authors appreciate the contribution of M. Lamprecht and D. Splettstößer. They also wish to thank Dr. E. Heinrich for repeated proofreading, and M. Edtbauer for edeting and typing.

Atlanta, Georgia, and Innsbruck, February 1990   L. J. Heinrich
                                                     F. Roithmayr

Deutsch - Englisch

German - English

A

Abbilden imaging
Abbildungsmodus image mode
Abbildungsspeicher image storage
Abbildungsverarbeitung image processing
abbrechen cancel (to)
Abbruch abnormal end
ABC-Analyse ABC classification
abfangen intercept (to)
abfertigen dispatch (to)
Abfrage query
Abfrage-/Antwort Kommunikation query/reply communications
Abfrage mit Fortschreibung query with update
Abfragemodus query mode
Abfragesprache query language
Abfragezeichen prompting character
Abfühlstation sensing station
Abgangskontrolle leaving check
abgehender Ruf call request
abgeleitet derived
abgerufene Nachricht solicited message
Abgleichcode match code
abgleichen match (to)
abhängig dependent
abhängige Auftragskontrolle dependent job control
abhängige Auftragssteuerung dependent job control
abhängige Variable dependent variable
Abhängigkeit dependability
Abheftloch filing hole
Abheftlochung filing holes
abhören listen in (to), tap (to)
Abhören einer Leitung wire tapping
Abhörmethode listening technique, tapping
abhörsicheres Telephon tap-proof telephone set
Abhörsicherheit listening security
Abhörvorrichtung listening device
abklemmen cripple (to), pinch off (to)
Ablagefach stacker
Ablauf flow, sequence
Ablaufbeobachtung run monitoring
ablaufbezogenes Testen structured testing
Ablaufdiagramm flowchart, dataflow diagram
ablauffähiges Programm executable program
Ablaufintegration process integration
ablaufgesteuerter Ansatz process-driven approach
Ablauflinie flow line
Ablaufmodell process model
Ablauforganisation process organization
ablauforientierter Ansatz process-oriented approach
Ablaufplaner scheduler
Ablaufplanung scheduling
Ablaufrückverfolgung backtracking
Ablaufsprung transfer of control
Ablaufsteuerung flow control
Ablaufunterbrechung flow interrupt
Ablaufverfolger tracer
Ablaufverfolgung tracing
ableitbar deducible
Ableitung deduction, derivation, inference
abmelden log-out (to), log-off (to)
Abmeldung log-off, sign-off
Abnahme acceptance
Abnahmeprotokoll acceptance protocol
Abnahmetest acceptance test
abnehmen accept (to)
abnormale Bedingung abnormal condition
abnormales Ende abnormal end
Abrechnung account
Abrechnungseinheit accounting unit
Abrechnungsroutine accounting routine
Abrechnungssystem accounting system
Abrißkarte stub card
abrollen rollover (to)
Abrollgerät scrolling device
Abrufauftrag call order
Abrufbetrieb polling mode, selecting mode
abrufen call (to), fetch (to)
Abruftechnik polling technique
Absatz marketing, sales
Absatzförderung sales promotion
Absatzgestaltung text-line grouping
Absatzmenge sales volume
Absatzweg distribution channel
abschalten disable (to), turn off (to)
Abschalten der Leitung disable the line
abschätzen assess (to)
Abschätzung assessment, estimation
abschirmen shield (to)
Abschirmung shielding
Abschlußtest final test
abschneiden truncate (to)
Abschnitt segment
abschreibbare Kosten depreciable costs
Abschreibungsmethode depreciation method
Absicht intention
absolute Häufigkeit absolute frequency
absolute Programmierung absolute programming

absolutes Recht absolute right
Absolutwert absolute value
Abstand distance
absteigende Folge descending order
absteigende Reihenfolge descending sequence
absteigender Sortierbegriff descending key
abstimmen tune (to)
Abstimmsumme hash total
Abstimmung tuning
abstrakte Maschine abstract machine
abstrakter Datentyp abstract data type
abstraktes Modell abstract model
abstraktes Programm abstract program
Abstraktion abstraction
Abstraktionsebene level of abstraction
Abstraktionsprinzip principle of abstraction
Abstraktionssystem abstraction system
abstreichen truncate (to)
Absturz unusual end, crash
Absturzprogramm crash program
absuchen scan (to)
Abtastbereich scanning field
abtasten sense (to), scan (to)
Abtaster scanner
Abtastung scanning
Abtastverfahren scanning technique
Abteilung Datenverarbeitung/Organisation information systems department
Abteilung Informations- und Kommunikationssysteme information systems department
Abteilungsebene department level, hierarchical level of department
Abteilungskoordinator department coordinator
abteilungsorientierte Feinstudie departmental detailed analysis
Abwärtskommunikation downward communication
Abweichung deviation, variance
Abweichung vom Normalen out of line
Abweichungsanalyse deviation analysis, variance analysis
Abweichungsbericht deviation report, variance report
Abzweigung branch
ACE = Animated Computer Education
ACE = Automatic Calling Equipment
ACE = Automatic Circuit Exchange
ACIA = Asynchronous Communications Interface Adapter
Acknowledge = Acquisition of Knowledge
ACL = Application Control Language

ACL = Association for Computational Linguistics
ACM = Association for Computing Machinery
ACS = Advanced Communications Services
ACS = Australian Computer Society
ACS = Auxiliary Core Storage
ACTS = Automatic Computer Telex Services
adaptierbare Benutzerschnittstelle adaptible interface
adaptive Benutzerschnittstelle adaptive user interface
ADC = Analog/Digital-Converter
Ad-hoc-Abfrage ad-hoc query
Add-on-Strategie add-on strategy
Addiermaschine adding machine, totalizer
adi = Anwenderverband Deutscher Informationsverarbeiter
Adjazenzmatrix adjacent matrix
ADL = Arbeitsgemeinschaft für Informationsverarbeitung
administrative Datenverarbeitung administrative data processing
administratives Informationsmanagement administrative information management
administratives Ziel administrative goal
ADP = Automatic Data Processing
Adreßbus address bus
Adresse address
Adressenleser postal scanner
adressierbarer Speicher adressable memory
adressieren address (to)
Adressiermaschine addressing machine, mailer
Adressierungsart adressing mode
Adreßverkettung address chaining
ADU = Analog/Digital-Umsetzer
AD-Umsetzer = Analog/Digital-Umsetzer
ADV = Automatisierte Datenverarbeitung
ADV-System = Automatisches Datenverarbeitungssystem
AED = Abfrageeinrichtung für Datenverkehr
AGC = Automatic Gain Control
Aggregierung aggregation
agressive Strategie agressive strategy
AHP = Analytic Hierarchy Process
AI = Artificial Intelligence
AID = Automatic Interaction Detector
AIDA = Apparate zur Identifikation und Autorisierung
Akkummulator accummulator

4

Aktion action
Aktionsanzeiger action entry
Aktionsbezeichner action stub
Aktionscode-Technik action code technique
Aktionsdiagramm action diagram
Aktionsnachricht action message
aktionsorientierte Datenverarbeitung trigger-oriented data processing
Aktionsplan action plan, tactical plan
Aktionsspielraum action scope
Aktivationsfehler activation error
aktive Beobachtung active observation
aktive Datei active file, current file
aktive Zeile active line, current line
aktiver Fehler active fault, current fault
aktiver Status active state
aktives Hilfesystem active help system
aktivieren activate (to)
aktualisieren update (to)
Aktualität topicality
Aktualparameter actual argument
aktuelles Inhaltsverzeichnis current directory
Akustikcursor acoustic cursor
Akustikmuff acoustic muff, coupler
akustische Anzeige audible alarm
akustischer Alarmgeber acoustic alarm device
akustischer Koppler acoustic coupler
akustisches Warnsignal audible alarm
Akzeptanz acceptance
Akzeptanzanalyse acceptance analysis
Akzeptanzforschung acceptance research
Akzeptanztest acceptance test
akzeptiertes System accepted system
Alarmeinrichtung alarm system
Alarmgeber alarm device
Alarmplan alarm guide
Album scrapbook
ALGOL = Algorithmic Language
Algorithmik algorithmics
algorithmische Programmiersprache algorithmic programming language
algorithmische Programmierung algorithmic programming
Algorithmus algorithm
Aliasname alias name
allgemeine Benutzerklasse public domain category
allgemeine EDV-Vergaberichtlinien general guidelines for EDP contracts
allgemeine Vertragsbedingungen general conditions of contract
allgemeine Verweisung auf Normen general reference to standards

Allgemeine Wirtschaftsinformatik General Economic Informatics
allgemeines Betriebssystem general purpose operating system
Allgemeingültigkeit generality
Alpha-Veränderung alpha change
Alphabet alphabet
alphabetische Daten alphabetic data
alphabetisches Zeichen alphabetic character
alphanumerisch alphanumeric
alphanumerische Daten alphanumeric data
alphanumerische Tastatur alphanumeric keyboard
alphanumerisches Zeichen alphanumeric character
Altern der Priorität priority aging
Alternative alternative
Alternativenbewertung evaluation of alternatives
Alternativenmenge choice-set
Alternativlösung alternative solution
Altpapier waste paper
Amtsleitung subscriber line
analog analog
Analog/Digital-Umsetzer analog/digital converter
Analogaufzeichnung analog recording
analoge Darstellung analog representation
analoge Daten analog data
analoge Steuerung analog control
Analogie analogy
Analogieschließen analogy reasoning
Analogieschluß analogism
Analogrechner analog computer
Analogsignal analog signal
Analogwert analog quantity
Analysator analyzer
Analyse analysis
Analyse der Arbeitsorganisation analysis of work organization
Analyse des Istzustands analysis of current system
Analysemethode analysis method
Analysewerkzeug analysis tool
Analysezyklus analysis cycle
analysieren analyze (to)
Analytiker analyst
analytische Arbeitsplatzbewertung analytic job evaluation
analytisches Denken analytic thinking
analytisches Modell analytic model
analytisches Schlußfolgern analytic inferencing
Anbieter bidder

Anbieterunterstützung

Anbieterunterstützung supplier's support
Änderbarkeit changeability, modifyability
ändern change (to), modify (to), update (to)
Änderungsanforderung change request
Änderungskennzeichen change code
Änderungsmanagement change management
Änderungsrate rate of change
Anfängermodus novice mode
Anfangskennsatz header label
Anfangsseitennummer start page number
Anfangswert initial value
Anforderung requiry, requirement
Anforderungsanalyse requirements analysis, requirements engineering
Anforderungsbeschreibung requirements specification
Anforderungsbetrieb requiry mode
Anforderungsdefinition requirements definition
Anforderungsprofil requirements profile
Anforderungstest requirements validation
Anforderungszeichen prompter, cursor
Anfrage request
Anfrage-Technik request technique
Anführungszeichen quotation mark
Angebot bid, tender, proposal
Angebotsanalyse bid analysis, tender analysis
Angebotsbewertung bid evaluation, tender evaluation
Angebotseinholung bidding, tendering
Angemessenheit adequacy, appropriateness
angenommenes Dezimalkomma assumed decimal point
angepaßt customized
Angewandte Informatik applied informatics
angrenzend contiguous
Anhang appendix
Anhäufung cluster
Anlage equipment, facility
Anlagenauswahl equipment selection, hardware selection
Anlagenbediener operator
Anlagenbuchhaltung fixed assets accounting
Anlageninstandhaltung equipment maintenance
Anlagenmiete leasing
Anlagenplanung facilities planning
Anlagevermögen fixed assets
anlaufen initiate (to), start (to)

Anlaufkosten launching costs, start up expense
Anlaufzeit initiate time, start time
anleiten instruct (to)
Anlieferungszeit delivery time
Anmeldemodus log-on mode
anmelden log-on (to), sign-on (to)
Anmeldung log-on, sign-on
Anmerkung comment, remark, narrative (in DFD)
Annahme assumption
annehmen accept (to), assume (to)
annullieren cancel (to)
Anomalie anomaly
anpassen adapt (to), customize (to)
Anpassung adaptation
Anpassungseinrichtung adapting device, adaptor
Anpassungsfähigkeit adaptability
Anpassungsmethode customizing method
Anpassungsprotokoll adaption protocol
Anpassungsrechner protocol converter
Anpassungsschaltung gateway
Anpassungswartung adaptive maintenance
Anrufbeantworter answering machine, answerphone
Anrufumleitung call diversion
Anrufwartung call service
Ansatz approach
Anschlagdrucker impact printer
anschlagfreier Drucker non-impact printer
Anschlußzeit connect time
Anschriftfeld address field
ANSI = American National Standards Institute
Ansprechzeit reaction time
anthropozentrisch anthropocentric
anthropozentrischer Ansatz anthropocentric approach
Antrag proposition
Antwort reply, response
antworten respond (to)
Antwortzeit response time
Antwortzeitverhalten response time distribution
anwählen dial (to)
anweisen direct (to)
Anweisung instruction, statement
Anweisungs-Technik instruction technique
Anwendbarkeit applicability
anwenden apply (to)
Anwender user
Anwenderbetrieb user factory
Anwendergruppe user group

Anwendersoftware application software, user software
Anwendersoftware-Paket application software package, user software package
Anwendung application
Anwendungsanalyse application analysis
Anwendungsaufgabe application task
Anwendungsentwicklung application development
Anwendungsentwurf application design
Anwendungsinformatik application informatics
Anwendungsintegration integration of application
Anwendungskennwort application password
Anwendungsprogramm application program
Anwendungsprogrammierer application programmer
Anwendungsrückstau application backlog
Anwendungsschicht application layer
Anwendungssoftware application software
Anwendungssoftware-System application software system
anwendungsspezifische integrierte Schaltung application dependent integrated circuit
Anwendungssystem application system
Anwendungssystem-Administrator application systems administrator
Anwendungssystem-Generation application systems generation
Anwendungssystem-Lebenszyklus application systems life-cycle
Anwendungssystem-Management application systems management
Anwendungssystem-Planung application systems planning
Anwendungssystem-Portfolio application systems portfolio
Anwesenheitserfassung attendance reporting
Anwesenheitszeit attendance time
Anzahl Testläufe number of tests performed
Anzahl Vorgänger predecessor count
anzapfen tap (to)
Anzeichen symptom
Anzeige display
anzeigen display (to)
Appetenzkonflikt appetence conflict
APL = A Programming Language
APLG = A Programming Language for Graphics
APSE = ADA Programming Support Environment

APT = Automatic Programming for Tools
Äquivalenz equivalence
Arbeitsablauf process flow, sequence of operations, working process
Arbeitsanalyse job analysis
Arbeitsanforderung job requirement
Arbeitsauftrag job order
Arbeitsbeanspruchung working strain
Arbeitsbedingung work condition, working condition
Arbeitsbelastung workload
Arbeitsbereich work area
Arbeitsbereicherung job enrichment
Arbeitsbewertung job evaluation, job grading
Arbeitsblatt spreadsheet, worksheet
Arbeitsdatei work file
Arbeitserweiterung job enlargement
Arbeitsfolge job sequence
Arbeitsgang operation step
Arbeitsgangdauer operation duration
Arbeitsgemeinschaft joint venture
Arbeitsgestaltung job design
Arbeitsgruppe task force, workgroup
Arbeitsgruppen-Verarbeitung workgroup computing
Arbeitshypothese working hypothesis
Arbeitsinformation job information
Arbeitsinhalt job content
Arbeitsintensität working intensity
Arbeitskapazität working capacity
Arbeitskosten labor costs
Arbeitslast workload
Arbeitslast-Prognose workload projection
Arbeitsmethode working style
Arbeitsmotivation job motivation
Arbeitsorganisation organization of work
Arbeitsorganisationsanalyse work organization analysis
Arbeitsplan job plan, production schedule
Arbeitsplaner scheduler
Arbeitsplanung operations scheduling
Arbeitsplatz work area, workplace
Arbeitsplatzbeschreibung job description, job specification
Arbeitsplatzbewertung work area evaluation
Arbeitsplatzbezeichnung job designation
Arbeitsplatzcomputer workplace computer, workstation
Arbeitsplatzebene hierarchical level of position, workplace level
Arbeitsplatzergonomie ergonomics of work area

Arbeitsplatzgestaltung

Arbeitsplatzgestaltung human engineering, job design, workplace layout
Arbeitsplatzsystem work station system
Arbeitsplatzumgebung workplace environment
Arbeitsprinzip operation principle
Arbeitsproduktivität job productivity
Arbeitsprogramm work program
Arbeitsprozeß working process
Arbeitspsychologie industrial psychology
Arbeitsqualität quality of work
Arbeitsrechner host
Arbeitsrecht industrial law, labor law
Arbeitsregister accumulator
Arbeitssituation job situation
Arbeitssitzung work session
Arbeitssoziologie industrial sociology
Arbeitsspeicher working memory
Arbeitsstation workstation
Arbeitsstrukturierung job structuring
Arbeitsstudie work study
Arbeitssystem working system
Arbeitstagebuch time analysis report
Arbeitstechnik job technique, time management
Arbeitsteilung job partitioning
Arbeitstisch workbench
Arbeitsüberlastung overwork
Arbeitsumgebung work environment
Arbeitsumgebungsanalyse analysis of work environment
Arbeitsunzufriedenheit job dissatisfaction, work dissatisfaction
Arbeitsverfahren working method, working technique
Arbeitsverfassungsgesetz labor law
Arbeitsvergrößerung job enlargement
Arbeitsvorbereitung job preparation, operations scheduling
Arbeitsvorgang step operation
Arbeitswechsel job rotation
Arbeitsweise functioning
Arbeitswissenschaft labor science
Arbeitszeiterfassung work measurement, working time measuring
Arbeitszeitvorgabe work standard
Arbeitszufriedenheit job satisfaction, work satisfaction
Arbeitszuordnung assignment of tasks
ArbVG = Arbeitsverfassungsgesetz
Architektur architecture
Architekturmodell model of architecture
Archiv archive
Archivierung archiving
Archivierungsmedium archival medium
Arithmetikprozessor arithmetic processor
arithmetische Operation arithmetic operation
arithmetischer Operator arithmetic operator
ARPANET = Advanced Research Project Agency Network
Art der Datenstation terminal type
Artikelbestandssatz inventory record
Artikelnummer product code
ASA = American Standards Association
ASA = Austrian Smart Card Association
ASCII = American Standard Code for Information Interchange
ASIC = Application Specific Integrated Circuit
ASLT = Advanced Solid Logic Technology
ASME = American Society of Mechanical Engineers
ASME-Symbolik ASME symbolics
ASR = Automatic Send Receive
Assemblersprache assembler language
assemblieren assemble (to)
Assemblierer assembler
Assoziationstyp association type
Assoziativspeicher content addressable memory, associative memory
ASU = Asynchron/Synchron-Umsetzer
ASW = Anwendersoftware
asymmetrische Störung random interference
asynchron asynchronous
Asynchronbetrieb asynchronous mode
asynchrone Übertragung asynchronous transmission
ATM = Automated Teller Machine
Attribut attribute
Attribute-Spezifikationstabelle attribute specification list
Attribute-Verwendungsmatrix attribute usage matrix
Attribute-Wertebereich domain of attribute
Attributtyp attribute type
Attributverwendung attribute usage
Attributwert attribute value
audiovisuelle Kommunikation audiovisual communications
auditive Rückmeldung auditive feedback
Aufbauorganisation organizational structure
Aufbereiter editor
Aufbewahrungsfrist retention period
Aufbewahrungspflicht retention obligation
auffordern request (to)
Aufforderungszeichen prompter
auffrischen refresh (to)

Auffrischungsrate refreshing rate
Auffüllen (mit Zeichen) padding
Aufgabe task
Aufgaben der Systemplanung tasks of systems planning
Aufgabenanalyse analysis of tasks
Aufgabenbereicherung job enrichment
Aufgabenbeschreibung task description
Aufgabenbezogenheit relevance to tasks
Aufgabenerweiterung job enlargement
Aufgabeninhalt job content
Aufgabenintegration integration of tasks
Aufgabenmerkmal task characteristic
aufgabenorientiertes Testen black box testing
Aufgabenplanung task planning
aufgabenspezifisch task specific
Aufgabenstrukturierung task structuring
Aufgabenumfang task scope
Aufgabensynthese task synthesis
Aufgabensystem system of tasks
Aufgabenträger bearer of tasks
Aufgabentyp task type
Aufgabenwandel task modification
Aufgabenwechsel job rotation
Aufgabenzuordnung task assignment
Aufgabenzuweisung job assignment
aufgeteilte Datenhaltung partitioned data base
Aufklebezettel sticker
Auflösung explosion, resolution
Auflösungsvermögen resolving power
Aufrollung scrolling
Aufruf call
aufrufen call (to)
Aufrüstung upgrade
aufschlüsseln allocate (to)
Aufschlüsselung allocation
aufsteigende Folge ascending order
aufsteigende Reihenfolge ascending order
aufsteigender Sortierbegriff ascending key
aufstellen install (to)
Aufstellung installation
Aufteilung partitioning
Auftrag job, order
Auftraggeber orderer
Auftragnehmer contractor
Auftragsabrechnung job accounting
Auftragsabwicklung order processing
Auftragsannahme taking the order
Auftragsauswahl job selection
Auftragsbearbeitung order servicing
Auftragsbestätigung order acknowledgement, order confirmation
Auftragsdaten order data
Auftragsdurchführung executing the order
Auftragsdurchlaufzeit lead time
Auftragseingang order entry
Auftragseinplanung dispatching, job scheduling
Auftragserteilung giving the order
Auftragsferneingabe remote job entry
Auftragsfreigabe job release
Auftragsinformationssystem order processing subsystem
Auftragskennzeichen job identification
Auftragskette job chain
Auftragskontrollsprache job control language
Auftragsname job name
Auftragsnummer job number, order number
Auftragspriorität job priority, order priority
Auftragsrechnung job calculation
Auftragsrückstand order backlog
Auftragsschritt job step
Auftragssprache job control language
Auftragssteuerung job control, order control
Auftragsverarbeitung order processing
Auftragsvergabe allocating the order, order placement
Auftragsverwaltung job management
Auftragswarteschlange job queue
Aufwand effort
Aufwand in Mannjahren man year's effort
Aufwandschätzung effort estimate
Aufwärtskommunikation upward communication
Aufwärtsübersetzung upward compilation
aufwärtsverträglich upward compatible
Aufwärtsverträglichkeit upward compatibility
Aufzeichnung logging, recording
Aufzeichnung von Sicherheitsvergehen security event logging
Aufzeichnungsdichte recording density
Aufzeichnungsformat recording format
ausbauen expand (to)
Ausbaufähigkeit expandability
Ausdruck expression
Ausdruck im Querformat landscape printing
ausdrückliche Garantie explicit warranty
Ausfall breakdown, failure, outage
Ausfallhäufigkeit failure frequency
Ausfallrate failure rate, fault rate
Ausfallschaden-Versicherung downtime insurance

Ausfallsicherheit

Ausfallsicherheit fault security
Ausfallwahrscheinlichkeit probability of failure
Ausfallzeit downtime, outage time
Ausfügeoperation pop
ausführbar executable
ausführbares Programm executable program
ausführen execute (to)
Ausführungsfehler execution error
Ausführungsinformation execution information
Ausführungszeit execution time
Ausgabe output
Ausgabe am Bildschirm soft copy
Ausgabe von Geld expenditure
Ausgabeaufbereiter editor
Ausgabeaufbereitung editing
Ausgabebefehl output command
Ausgabebeleg output document
Ausgabedatei output data set
Ausgabedaten output data
Ausgabeeinheit output unit
Ausgabefehler output error
Ausgabegerät output device
Ausgabegeschwindigkeit output rate
Ausgabeklasse output class
Ausgabemedium output medium
Ausgabeoperation output operation
Ausgaberate output transfer rate
Ausgabesatz output record
Ausgabeschutz output protection
Ausgabestrom output stream
Ausgabetechnik output technology
Ausgabewarteschlange output queue
Ausgabewerk output unit
Ausgang exit
Ausgangswert default value
ausgeben display (to), output (to)
Aushang bulletin, notice
Aushangbrett bulletin board, notice board
Auskunftsgebühr information fee
Auskunftsrecht information right
Auskunftssystem retrieval system
auslagern swap out (to)
Auslagerung swapping
Auslastung capacity utilization
auslesen read (to)
Auslieferung delivery, distribution
auslösendes Ereignis trigger event
Ausnahmebedingung exception condition
Ausnahmebehandlung exception handling
ausrichten align (to)
Ausrichtung alignment
Ausrüstung configuration, kit
Aussagenanalyse content analysis

ausschließliches Nutzungsrecht exclusive right of use
ausschneiden cut (to)
Ausschreibung request for proposal, invitation to tender
Ausschuß committee
Außenkonflikt external conflict
außerplanmäßig unscheduled
Ausstoß output
Austastlücke TV blank
Austauschbarkeit exchangeability, compatibility
Austauschformat interchange standard
austesten debug (to)
Austrittsbarriere exit barrier
Auswahl selection
Auswählbarkeit selectivity
auswählen pick (to), select (to)
Auswahlkriterium selection criterion
Auswahlmethode selection method
Auswahlmöglichkeit option
Auswahlprozeß selection process
Auswahlregel selection rule
Auswahlverfahren selection procedure
Ausweich-Rechenzentrum backup computing center
Ausweichbetrieb backup
Ausweichcomputer backup computer, standby computer
Ausweichverfahren backup procedure
Ausweis badge, identity card
Ausweisleser badge reader
Auswerteprogramm postprocessor
Auswertung analyzing, interpretation
Auswirkung impact
Auswirkungsanalyse impact analysis
Autarkie self-sufficiency
AUTEX = Automatische Telex- und Teletexauskunft
Authentizität authenticity
Autokorrelation autocorrelation
Automat automat
Automatenmißbrauch abuse of automatic device
Automation automation
automatische Antwort auto answer
automatische Betriebsart automatic mode
automatische Datenerfassung automatic data capturing
automatische Datenverarbeitung automatic data processing
automatische Fertigung automatic manufacturing
automatische Optimierungssteuerung automatic gain control
automatische Preiszuordnung price look-up

automatische Rufbeantwortungseinrichtung automatic answering equipment, auto answer equipment
automatische Schrifterkennung automatic character recognition
automatische Spracherkennung automatic speech recognition
automatische Telephonnummernwahl auto dialing
automatische Wähleinrichtung automatic calling equipment
automatische Wählvermittlung automatic circuit exchange
automatische Wissensdarstellung automatic knowledge representation
automatischer Anrufbeantworter automatic answering set, automatic answerphone
automatischer Fernschreibdienst automatic computer telex services
automatischer Wagenrücklauf auto carriage return
automatischer Zeilenvorschub auto line feed
automatisches Datenverarbeitungssystem automatic data processing system
automatisches Programmieren automatic programming
automatisierbar automatable
Automatisierung automation
Automatisierung der Fertigung automation of manufacturing
Automatisierungsgrad degree of automation
Autonomie autonomy
Autor author
Autor-Kritiker-Zyklus author-reviewer cycle
Autor-Lektor-Prinzip author-instructor principle
Autorenrecht author's right
Autorensoftware author's software
Autorensprache author's programming language
Autorenunterstützungssystem author support system
autorisieren authorize (to)
Autorisieren authorizing
autorisierter Benutzer authorized user
AV = Arbeitsvorbereitung
AV = Audiovision
Aversionskonflikt aversion conflict
AVR = Allgemeine EDV-Vergaberichtlinien
Axiom axiom

B

Bachmann-Diagramm Bachmann diagram
Backtracking-Verfahren back tracking
Bahn sheet
Bahnbreite sheet width
bakterizides Papier bactericide paper
Balken bar
Balkencode bar code
Balkencode-Leser bar code scanner
Balkendiagramm bar chart
Ballroller tracker ball
BAM = Block Availability Map
Band tape
Bandarchiv tape archive
Bandbreite bandwidth
Banddatenbestand tape file
Banddichte tape density
Bandende end of tape
Bandfehler tape error
Bandgeschwindigkeit tape speed
Bandkapazität tape capacity
Bandkennsatz end of volume label
Bandspule tape spool
Bankautomat automated bank machine
Bankautomation automated banking
Bankgeschäft am Verkaufspunkt point of sale banking
Bankomat automated teller machine
Bankschalter-Terminal bank counter terminal
BAO = Belastungsorientierte Auftragsfreigabe
Barcode bar code
Barcode-Abtastung bar code scanning
Barcode-Leser bar code scanner
Barriere barrier, threshold
BASIC = Beginners All Purpose Symbolic Instruction Code
BASICA = BASIC Advanced
Basis base
Basis bildend basic
Basisanwendung basic application
Basisband baseband
Basisbandnetz baseband network
Basisbandübertragung baseband transmission
Basisereignis basic event
Basissoftware basic software
Basissystem basic system
Basistechnologie basic technology
Batchbetrieb batch mode
Batchverarbeitung batch processing
Baubestimmung constructional requirement
Baud baud

Baueinheit physical unit
Baugruppe assembly
Baukastenprinzip module principle
Baum tree
Baumrechner tree computer
Baumstruktur tree structure
Baumtopologie tree topology
Baustein module
Baustein-Korrespondenz module correspondence
BBA = Bachelor of Business Administration
BBK = Breitbandkommunikation
bbn = bundeseinheitliche Betriebsnummer
BC = Binärcode
BCD = Binary Coded Decimal
BCS = British Computer Society
Bd = Baud
BDE = Betriebsdatenerfassung
BDSG = Bundesdatenschutzgesetz
Beanspruchung stress
Beantwortungszeit response time
bearbeiten handle (to), work on (to)
Bearbeitungsgebühr fee for administrative handling
Bearbeitungsreihenfolge operating sequence
Bearbeitungszeit operating time, run time
Bearbeitungszeit je Einheit operating time per unit
Bearbeitungszeitgrenze run time limit
Bearbeitungszentrum manufacturing center
Bedarf need, requirement
Bedarfsbericht report on need
Bedarfsvorhersage forecasting of need, need forecast
Bedeutungsanalyse content analysis
bedienen operate (to), serve (to)
Bediener operator
Bedienerbefehl operator command
Bedienerfreundlichkeit operator convenience
Bedienerführung prompting, operational guidance
Bedienerführungsanzeige operational guidance indicator
Bedienerkonsole operator console
bedienerloses Drucken unattended printing
Bedienernachricht operator message
Bedieneroberfläche operator interface
Bedienungsanleitung operating instruction
Bedienungseinheit service unit

Bedienungshandbuch operations manual
Bedienungspult control panel
Bedienungstafel control panel
bedingte Anweisung conditional statement
bedingter Sprungbefehl conditional jump
Bedingung condition
Bedingungsanzeiger condition entry
Bedingungsbezeichner condition stub
Bedrohung threat
Bedrohungsanalyse threat analysis
Bedürfnis need
Bedürfnishierarchie need hierarchy
Beendigung termination
Befehl command, instruction
Befehlsdatei command file
Befehlssatz instruction set
Befehlssprache instruction language, command language
Befehlstaste command key
Befehlstyp instruction type
Befehlsvorrat instruction set
Befehlswort instruction word
Befehlszähler address counter
Befragung questioning, interrogation
Befragungsexperiment questioning experiment
Befragungsgespräch questioning interview
Befugnis authority
Befund finding
beginnen start (to), begin (to)
Beginntermin starting date
Beglaubigung authentication
Begrenzer delimiter
Begriffskalkül conception calculus
Begriffssystem system of terms
Behälter-Rechenzentrum container computing center
Behälterkarte bin card
Beherrschbarkeit manageability
beherrschter Prozeß process under control
beinahe Briefqualität near letter quality
Belastbarkeit load carrying ability, power rate, stress stability
Belastung load, stress
Belastung mit Kosten, mit Gebühren chargeout
Belastungsdiagramm load chart
belastungsorientierte Auftragsfreigabe load-dependent job release
Belastungsprogramm stress program
Beleg document
Belegaufbereitung document preparation
Belegdrucker document printer
Belegdurchlauf document transport

Beleggestaltung document design
Belegleser document reader
Belegsystem document system
belegt busy
Belegungszeit elapsed time
Belegverarbeitung document processing
Beleuchtungsstärke illuminance
Bemerkung comment, remark
benachbart contiguous
Benachrichtigung notification
benannt named
Benchmark benchmark
Benchmarking benchmarking
Benchmarktest benchmark test
Benutzbarkeit ease of usage, usability
benutzen use (to)
Benutzer end-user, user
Benutzerabfrage user query
Benutzeradäquanz user adequance
Benutzerakzeptanz user acceptance
Benutzeranalyse user analysis
Benutzeranforderung user requirement
Benutzeranzahl user load
Benutzerausgang user exit
Benutzerberatung user consulting
Benutzerberechtigung user authority
Benutzerbericht user report
Benutzerbeteiligung user involvement, user participation
Benutzerdatei user file
Benutzerdaten user data
Benutzerdialog user dialog
Benutzerdokumentation user's documentation
Benutzerentwurf user design
Benutzerfehler user error
Benutzerfeld user field
Benutzerfertigkeit user's skill
Benutzerforschung user research
Benutzerfreundlichkeit user friendliness
Benutzerführung user guidance
benutzergesteuert user controlled, user driven
benutzergesteuerte Datenverarbeitung user driven computing, end-user computing
benutzergesteuerter Dialog user controlled dialog
Benutzergruppe user group
Benutzerhandbuch user's manual, user's guide
Benutzeridentifizierung user identification
Benutzeridentifizierung und -überprüfung user identification and verification
Benutzerillusion user illusion
Benutzerkatalog user dictionary

Benutzerklasse

Benutzerklasse category of users
Benutzerkontrolle user monitoring
Benutzermodell user model
Benutzernachricht user message
Benutzeroberfläche user interface
Benutzerorientierung user orientation
Benutzerprofil user profile
Benutzerprogramm user program
Benutzerschnittstelle man-machine interface, user interface
Benutzerschulung user training
Benutzerservice user support service
Benutzerservice-Zentrum user service center, information center
Benutzersicht user view
Benutzerspeicher user area
Benutzersprache user language
Benutzerstation user terminal
Benutzersystem end-user system
Benutzertransaktion user transaction
Benutzertyp type of end-user
Benutzerunabhängigkeit end-user independence
Benutzerunterstützung end-user support
Benutzerverhalten end-user behavior
Benutzerzeit up-time
Benutzerziel user objective
Benutzerzufriedenheit user satisfaction
benutzungsfreundlich easy to use
Benutzungsfreundlichkeit usage convenience, ease of use
Benutzungsmöglichkeit usage capability
Benutzungsrecht usage regulation
Beobachtung observation
Beobachtungsexperiment observation experiment
Beobachtungsinterview observation interview
beraten advise (to), consult (to)
Berater advisor, consultant
Beratungsfirma consulting firm
Beratungsservice consulting service
Beratungssystem advisory system, consulting system
Beratungsunternehmen consulting company
berechnen calculate (to)
Berechnung calculation
Berechnungsexperiment calculation experiment
Berechnungsprogramm calculation program
berechtigen authorize (to)
Berechtigung authority, authorization
Berechtigungsnummer authority number
Bereich area, domain, range

Bereich einer Variablen range of a variable
Bereichsprüfung range check
Bereichsüberschreitung overload
Bereitliste ready list
Bereitschaftsrechner standby computer
Bereitschaftswarteschlange dispatching queue
Bericht report
Berichterstattung reporting, report writing
Berichtigungsrecht correction right
Berichtsdatei report file
Berichtsgenerator report program generator
Berichtsspezifikation report specification
Berichtssystem report system
Berichtstermin report date
Berufsbild career
berührungsempfindlicher Bildschirm touch sensitive screen
Beschaffung procurement
Beschaffungskosten procurement costs
Beschaffungsplanung procurement planning
Beschaffungsrichtlinie procurement guideline
beschäftigen employ (to)
Beschäftigung employment
beschleunigter Datenfluß expedited data flow
beschreiben describe (to)
beschreibende Daten descriptive data
Beschreiber descriptor
Beschreibung description
Beschreibungsfehler description error
Beschreibungsmerkmal descriptive feature
Beschreibungsmittel description tool
Beschreibungsmodell description model
Beschreibungsregel description rule
Beschreibungssprache description language
Beschreibungstechnik description technique
Beschriftungsstelle inscription position
Besichtigungsanalyse analysis by inspection
besondere Helligkeit special brightness
besondere Vertragsbedingungen special conditions of contract
Besondere Wirtschaftsinformatik Special Economic Informatics
Bestand inventory
Bestandsdaten inventory data
Bestandssenkung reduction of stock
Bestandsüberwachung inventory control

Beweglichkeit

bestätigen confirm (to)
Bestätigung acknowledgement, confirmation
bestehendes Problem current problem
bestehendes System current system
Bestellauftrag order
Bestelldatum order date
Bestelldaten order data
Bestelldisposition order disposition
bestellen order (to)
Besteller orderer
Bestellformular order form
Bestellmenge order quantity
Bestellnummer purchase order number
Bestellpunkt order point
Bestellpunktverfahren standing order procedure
Bestellrhythmusverfahren periodic procedure order
Bestellüberwachung order control
Bestellung order
Bestellverfahren order procedure
Bestimmungsort destination
Bestreitungsvermerk notice of contestation
Beta-Veränderung beta change
beteiligen participate (to)
Beteiligter participant
Beteiligung participation
Beteiligungsbereitschaft commitment for involvement
Beteiligungsfähigkeit ability of user involvement
Beteiligungsmotiv motive for user involvement
Beteiligungsorganisation organizing user involvement
Betrag amount
Betrieb (Werk) plant
betriebliche Datenverarbeitung business data processing
betrieblicher Funktionalbereich business function
betriebliches Informationssystem business information system
Betriebsanweisung operating instruction
Betriebsanzeige operating indicator
Betriebsart operational mode
Betriebsberater management advisor, management consultant
betriebsbereit ready for operation
Betriebsbereitschaft operational readiness
Betriebsbuchhaltung cost accounting, factory accounting
Betriebsdatenerfassung factory data collection, shop-floor data collection

Betriebsdaten-Erfassungsgerät factory terminal
Betriebsform operational mode
Betriebsgemeinkosten factory overhead costs
Betriebsinformatik Business Informatics
Betriebskosten operating costs, production costs, running costs
Betriebsleiter production manager
Betriebsmittel resource, facility
Betriebsmittel-Zugriffsschutz resource access security
Betriebsmittelaufteilung resource sharing
Betriebsmittelnutzung resource utilization
Betriebsmittelplanung resource scheduling
Betriebsmittelverbund resource sharing
Betriebsmittelzuteilung resource allocation
Betriebsorganisation plant organization
Betriebsrat labor council, shop steward, staff association
Betriebssicherheit safety of operation
Betriebssoziologie industrial sociology
Betriebssystem operating system
Betriebssystem laden loading operating system
Betriebstemperaturbereich working temperature range
Betriebstest operational test
betriebsübergreifendes Informationssystem interorganizational information system
Betriebsunterbrechung breakdown, interrupt of operation
Betriebsunterbrechungs-Versicherung breakdown insurance
Betriebsvereinbarung labor agreement
Betriebsverfassung labor constitution
Betriebsverfassungsgesetz Labor Constitution Act
Betriebsvergleich comparison of organizations
Betriebsvorschrift operating instruction
betriebswirtschaftliche Datenverarbeitung business data processing
Betriebswirtschaftslehre Business Administration
Betriebszeit production time, operating time, running time
Betriebszustand operational status
Betroffener affected individual
Betrug abuse, fraud
BetrVG = Betriebsverfassungsgesetz
beurteilen rate (to), assess (to)
bevorzugen prioritize (to)
Beweglichkeit flexibility

Bewegtbild video
Bewegtbild-Aufbereitung video editing
Bewegtbild-Digitalisierer video digitizer
Bewegtbild-Fernsprecher video phone
Bewegtbild-Konferenz video conference
Bewegtbild-Kommunikation video communications
Bewegtbild-Sichtgerät video screen
Bewegtbild-Speicher video memory
Bewegtbild-Telekonferenz video teleconference
Bewegtbild-Übertragung video transmission
Bewegung animation, transaction
Bewegungsdatei transaction file
Bewegungsdaten transaction data, amendment data
Bewegungshäufigkeit activity rate
bewerten evaluate (to), assess (to)
Bewertung evaluation, assessment
Bewertungskriterium evaluation criterion
Bewertungsmethode evaluation technique
Bewertungsprozeß evaluation process
Bewertungsverfahren evaluation procedure
bezeichnen identify (to)
Bezeichner identifier
Beziehung relation, relationship
Beziehungsanalyse relationship analysis
Beziehungsgrad degree of relationship
Beziehungsintegrität referential integrity
Beziehungsmappe relationship map
Beziehungstyp relationship type
Beziehungszahl relative figure
Bezug reference
BIAIT = Business Information Analysis and Integration Technique
Bibliometrie bibliometry
Bibliothek library
Bibliotheksverwaltungsprogramm library management program
BICS = Business Information Control Study
bidirektional bidirectional
bidirektionaler Drucker bidirectional printer
BIGFERN = Breitbandiges Integriertes Glasfaser-Fern-Netz
BIGFON = Breitbandiges Integriertes Glasfaser-Fernmelde-Ortsnetz
Bild picture, image
Bildabtaster scanner
Bildauflösung image resolution
Bildbearbeiter image grabber
Bildelement picture element, pixel
Bildfenster picture window
Bildkompression white line skipping

Bildmenge image set, picture set
Bildplatte optical disk
Bildpunkt picture element, pixel
Bildschirm screen
Bildschirmarbeit screen working
Bildschirmarbeitsplatz screen work area
Bildschirmausgabe screen display, soft copy
Bildschirmeinheit display unit
Bildschirmfenster display window
Bildschirmformular display table, display form
Bildschirmformular-Generator screen form generator
Bildschirmgerät display device
Bildschirmgraphik display graphics
Bildschirmgröße screen size, display size
Bildschirminhalt screen content
Bildschirminhalt drucken print screen (to)
Bildschirmmaske display mask, screen layout
Bildschirmrecorder instant camera for screen
Bildschirmtext interactive videotex
Bildschirmtext-Gesetz interactive videotex law
Bildschirmtext-Staatsvertrag interactive videotex treaty
Bildspeicher video memory
Bildsymbol icon, iconograph
Bildtelephon picture phone
Bildung literacy
Bildverarbeitung image processing, picture processing
Bildverstehen image recognition
Bildwiederholfrequenz refresh frequency
Bildwiederholrate refresh rate
Bildwiederholspeicher video refresh memory
Bildwiederholung refresh
Bildzeichen visual symbol, pictograph
binär binary
binäre synchrone Datenübertragung binary synchronous communications
binäres Menü binary menu
binäres Suchen binary search
Binärmuster bit pattern
Binärzeichen binary character
Bindelader linkage loader
Binder linkage editor
Bio-Computer bio computer
biometrische Daten biometric data
Bionik bionics
BIP = Business Information Planning
bipolarer Transistor bipolar transistor
Bit = binary digit

Büroinformationssystem

Bit/s bps
Bit-Fehlerrate bit transmission error rate
Bit-Fehlerwahrscheinlichkeit bit transmission error probability
Bitbreite bit width
Bitmuster bit pattern
bitparallel bit parallel
Bitrate bit rate
bitseriell bit serial
BIU = Bus Interface Unit
Black-Box-Prinzip black box principle
Blasenspeicher bubble memory
Blatt sheet
Blattanfang top of forms
blättern page (to)
Blattleser page reader
Blindenschrift braille
Blindkopie blind copy
blinken blink (to)
Blinkfunktion blinking output option
Blitzschaden damage by lightning
Blitzschutzvorrichtung lightning arrester
Block block
Block-Fehlerwahrscheinlichkeit block error rate
Blockchiffre block chiffre
Blockdiagramm block diagram
Blockende end of block
Blockgraphik block graphics
Blockkonzept block concept
Blockprüfung block check
Blockprüfzeichen block check character
Blocksatz justified text
Blockschaltbild block diagram
Blocktastatur numeric keypad
Blockungsfaktor blocking factor
Blockverfügbarkeitsliste block availability map
Blockzwischenraum interblock gap
Boole'sche Algebra Boolean algebra
Boole'sche Funktion Boolean function
BOSP = Business Office Systems Planning
Botschaft communication, message, news
Bottom-up-Strategie bottom-up strategy
Bottom-up-Test bottom-up test
Box-Jenkins-Methode Box-Jenkins method
bpi = bits per inch
bps = bits per second
BPU = Basic Processing Unit
Braille-Terminal Braille terminal
Branch-and-Bound-Verfahren branch and bound procedure
Branche industry
Branchensoftware industry-specific standard software

Brandmelder fire warning device
Brandursache source of fire
Brandverhütung fire prevention
Brandversicherung fire insurance
Breitband broadband, wideband
Breitbandkommunikation broadband communications
Breitbandnetz broadband network
Breitbandübertragung broadband transmission
Breitensuche breadth-first search
Brief letter
Briefkasten mailbox
Brieföffnungsmaschine letter opening machine
Briefqualität letter quality
Bringsystem push system
Brook'sches Gesetz Brook's law
Brücke bridge
Brückenprogramm bridging program, linkage program
Bruttolohn gross pay
BSC = Binary Synchronous Communications
BSI = British Standards Institution
BSP = Business Systems Planning
BTx = Bildschirmtext
BTx-Dienst BTx service
BTx-Gesetz BTx act
BTx-Recht BTx law
BTx-Staatsvertrag BTx treaty
BTx-Telex-Dienst BTx telex service
Buchhaltungsprogramm accounting program
Buchstabe letter
Buchung bookkeeping entry
Buchungsbeleg accounting voucher
Buchungsdaten accounting data
Buchungsschnitt accounting deadline
Bündelung bundling
Bundesdatenschutzbeauftragter federal data protection officer
Bundesdatenschutzgesetz federal data protection law
Büro office
Büro der Zukunft office of the future
Büroarbeit office work
Büroarbeit außer Haus telecommuting
Büroarbeitsanalyse office work analysis
Büroarbeitsplatz office work area
Büroausstattung office equipment
Büroautomation office automation
Bürocomputer office computer
Bürofernschreiben office telewriting
Büroinformationssystem office information system

Bürokommunikation

Bürokommunikation office communications
Bürokommunikationssystem office communications system
Büromöbel office furniture
Büropersonal clerical staff
Bürosatz office composition
Bürotechnik office technology
Bürovorgangssystem office trigger system
Bussystem bus system
Bustopologie bus topology
BVB = Besondere Vertragsbedingungen
Byte byte

C

CA-Technologie = Computer Aided Technology
CAA = Computer Aided Assembling
Cache-Speicher cache memory
CAD = Computer Aided Design
CADD = Computer Aided Design and Drafting
CAE = Computer Aided Engineering
CAI = Computer Aided Industry
CAI = Computer Assisted Instruction
CAL = Computer Aided Learning
CAM = Computer Aided Manufacturing
CAO = Computer Aided Office
CAP = Computer Aided Planning
CAP = Computer Aided Publishing
CAQ = Computer Aided Quality Assurance
CAR = Computer Aided Retrieval
CAR = Computer Aided Robotics
CAS = Computer Aided Strategy and Sales Controlling
CASE = Computer Aided Software Engineering
CASE = Computer Aided Systems Engineering
CAT = Computer Aided Testing
CAT = Computer Aided Training
CAT = Computer Aided Translation
CAUSE = Computer Automated Software Engineering
CBA = Cost/Benefit Analysis
CBMS = Computer Based Message System
CBT = Computer Based Training
CBX = Computerized Branch Exchange
CC = Cable Connector
CCD = Charge Coupled Device
CCIA = Computer and Communications Industry Association
CCT = Cognitive Complexity Theory
CCTA = Central Computing and Telecommunications Agency
CD = Cash Dispenser
CD = Compact Disk
CD-RAM = Compact Disk Random Access Memory
CD-ROM = Compact Disk Read Only Memory
CD-Technologie CD technology
CDE = Compact Disk Erasable
CeBIT = Centrum Büro- und Informationstechnik
CECUA = Confederation of European Computer Users Associations
CECUA-Modellvertrag CECUA model contract
Centronics-Schnittstelle centronics interface
CEO = Chief Executive Officer
CEP = Corporate Electronic Publishing
CGS = Computer Graphics Society
Charakteristik characteristic
charakteristisches Merkmal feature
Checkliste check list
Chefprogrammierer chief programmer
Chef-Programmierer-Team chief programmer team
chiffrieren encode (to), cipher (to)
Chiffrierschlüssel cryptographic key
Chiffrierung ciphering
Chipkarte smart card
CIM = Computer Input from Microfilm
CIM = Computer Integrated Manufacturing
CIO = Chief Information Officer
CIO = Computer Integrated Office
CISC = Complex Instruction Set Computer
CLG = Command Language Grammar
Clusteranalyse cluster analysis
CMOS = Complementary Metal-Oxide Semiconductor
CMV = Computermißbrauch-Versicherung
CNC = Computerized Numerical Control
COBOL = Common Business Oriented Language
COCOMO = Constructive Cost Model
CODASYL = Conference on Data Systems Languages
Code code
Code-Inspektion code inspection
Code-Optimierung code optimization
Code-Prüfung code checking
code-transparente Datenübermittlung code transparent data transmission
CODIC = Computer Directed Communications
codierte Daten coded data
Codierung coding
COL = Computer Oriented Language
COL = Control Oriented Language
COM = Computer Output on Microfilm
Compiler compiler
Compunication = Compu(ter and Commu)nication
Computer computer
Computer-Sachversicherung computer property insurance
Computeranimation computer animation

19

Computerausgabe auf Mikrofilm
computer output on microfilm
Computerausgabe auf Papier hardcopy
Computerbetrug computer fraud
Computerbewertung computer evaluation
computergeführte Kommunikation computer directed communications
Computergeneration computer systems generation
computergesteuerter Dialog computer controlled dialog
Computergraphik computer graphics
Cumputerisierung computerization
Computerkompetenz computer literacy
Computerkriminalität computer criminality
Computerlinguistik computer linguistics
Computermanipulation computer manipulation
Computermaus computer mouse
Computermißbrauch computer abuse
Computermißbrauch-Versicherung insurance against computer abuse
Computersabotage computer sabotage
Computerschutz computer protection
Computersicherheit computer security
Computerspionage computer spying
Computerstreik computer strike
Computersystem-Architektur computer systems architecture
Computertomographie computerized tomography
computerunterstützte Druckvorlagenerstellung computer aided publishing
computerunterstützte Fertigung computer aided manufacturing
computerunterstützte Konstruktion computer aided design
computerunterstützte Montage computer aided assembling
computerunterstützte Planung computer aided planning
computerunterstützte Produktionsplanung und -steuerung computer aided production planning and scheduling
computerunterstützte Qualitätssicherung computer aided quality assurance
computerunterstützter Unterricht computer aided instruction
computerunterstütztes Büro computer aided office
computerunterstütztes Engineering computer aided engineering
computerunterstütztes Entwerfen und Zeichnen computer aided design and drafting

computerunterstütztes Konstruieren computer aided design
computerunterstütztes Lernen computer aided learning
computerunterstütztes Publizieren computer aided publishing, desktop publishing
computerunterstütztes Software Engineering computer aided software engineering
computerunterstütztes Testen computer aided testing
computerunterstütztes Training computer aided training
computerunterstütztes Übersetzen computer aided translation
Computerunterstützung computer aid
Computerverbrechen computer crime
Computerverbund computer grouping
Computerversicherung computer insurance
Computervirus computer virus
Computerwissenschaft Computer **Science**
Controller controller
Controlling controlling
Controllingmethode controlling technique
CORAL = Computer Online Realtime Applications Language
COS = Corporation for Open Systems
CPC = Card Programmed Calculator
CPF = Central Processing Facility
CPL = Characters Per Line
CP/M = Control Program for Microcomputers
cps = characters per second
cps = cycles per second
CPE = Computer Performance Evaluation
CPM = Critical Path Method
CPU = Central Processing Unit
CPU-Zeit CPU time
Cracker cracker, criminal hacker
CRAM = Card Random Access Memory
CRBE = Conversational Remote Batch Entry
CRC = Cyclic Redundancy Check
Cross-Impact-Analyse cross-impact analysis
CRT = Cathode Ray Tube
CSF = Critical Success Factor
CSI = Commercial System Integration
CSL = Computer Simulation Language
CSMA = Communication Systems Management Association
CSMA/CD = Carrier Sense Multiple Access/Collision Detection
CSP = Control Setting Panel

CUU = **Computerunterstützter Unterricht**

D

D/A-Wandler = Digital/Analog-Wandler
DAI = Distributed Artificial Intelligence
DAL = Design Analysis Language
DAM = Direct Access Method
DAP = Distributed Array Processor
Darstellung presentation, representation
Darstellungsmethode presentation method
Darstellungsschicht presentation layer
Darstellungstechnik presentation technique
DAT = Digital Audio Tape
Dataskop datascope
DATATEL = Datentelephon
Datei file, data set
Dateiänderung file change
Dateiaufbereiter file editor
Dateiende end of file
Dateientwurf file design
Dateigenerierung file generating
Dateikennsatz file label
Dateikomprimierung file compression
Dateiname file name
Dateiorganisation file organization
Dateiprofil file profile
Dateischutz file protection
Dateisegment file segment
Dateisicherung file assurance
Dateisperre file locking
Dateitransfer file transfer
Dateiübertragung file transmission
Dateiverarbeitung file processing
Dateivergleicher file comparator
Dateiverwaltung file management
Dateiverzeichnis file directory
Dateiwartung file maintenance
Dateiwiederherstellung file recovery
Dateizugriff file access
DATEL = Data Telecommunications
DATEL-Dienst DATEL service
Daten data
Daten-Direkteingabe immediate data entry
Daten-Sammelleitung data bus line
Datenabstraktion data abstraction
Datenadministrator data administrator
Datenanalyse data analysis
Datenaufbereitung data preparation
Datenausgabe data output
Datenbank data bank (external), data base (internal)
Datenbank-Abfragesprache data base query language
Datenbank-Administrator data base administrator
Datenbank-Architektur data base architecture
Datenbank-Auswahlkriterium data base selection criterion
Datenbank-Beschreibung data base description
Datenbank-Beschreibungssprache data base description language
Datenbank-Definition data base definition
Datenbank-Dienst data bank service
Datenbank-Entwurf data base design
Datenbank-Management data base management
Datenbank-Managementsystem data base management system
Datenbank-Maschine data base machine
Datenbank-Modell data base model
Datenbank-Rechner data base computer
Datenbank-Schema data base schema
Datenbank-Sprache data base language
Datenbank-Strukturdiagramm data base structure diagram
Datenbank-System data base system
Datenbank-Verwaltungssystem data base management system
Datenbank-Zugriff data base access
Datenbasis data base
Datenbauart data type
Datenbeschreibung data description
Datenbeschreibungssprache data description language
Datenbestand data set
Datenbeziehung data relationship
datenbezogenes Testen dataflow oriented testing
Datenblock data block
Datenbus data bus
datenchiffrierender Schlüssel data ciphering key
Datendefinitionssprache data definition language
Datendiebstahl data theft
Datendirekteingabe direct data entry
Datendurchsatz data throughput
Dateneingabe data input
Datenelement data element, elementary item
Datenendeinrichtung data terminal
Datenendgerät data terminal
Datenentwurf data design
Datenerfassung data collection, data capturing
Datenerfassungsbeleg data collection form, data collection sheet
Datenerfassungsmethode data collection method, data capturing method

Datenerfassungsstelle data collection platform, data entry location
Datenerfassungssystem data collection system, data capturing system
Datenfeld data item
Datenfernausgabe remote data output
Datenferneingabe remote data entry
Datenfernübertragung remote data transmission
Datenfernverarbeitung teleprocessing, remote data processing
Datenfluß data flow
Datenflußdiagramm data flow diagram, bubble chart
datenflußorientierte Feinstudie data-flow-oriented detailed analysis
Datenflußpfeil data flow arrow
Datenflußplan data flow chart
Datenflußrechner data flow computer
Datenflußsteuerung data flow control
Datenformat data format
Datenformatangabe data format specification
Datengeheimnis data secrecy
datengetriebene Vorwärtsverkettung data-driven forward chaining
Datengitter relations chart
Datengrenze data boundary
Datengröße data item
Datengruppe data group
Datenhaftpflicht-Versicherung data liability insurance
Datenintegration data integration
Datenintegrität data integrity
Datenkapsel data capsule
Datenkasse am Verkaufspunkt point of sale terminal
Datenkatalog data dictionary
Datenkatalog-System data dictionary system
Datenkeller data stack
Datenkommunikation data communications
Datenkomprimierung data compression
Datenkonsistenz data consistency
Datenkonversionsfehler data conversion error
Datenkonvertierung data conversion
Datenkonzentrator data concentrator
Datenkonzept data concept
Datenkorrektur data correction
Datenlexikon data lexicon
Datenmanagement data resource management
Datenmanipulation data manipulation
Datenmanipulationssprache data manipulation language

Datenmatrix data matrix
Datenmißbrauch-Versicherung data abuse insurance
Datenmodell data model
Datenmodellentwurf data model design
Datennetz data network
Datenobjekt entity
Datenorganisation data organization
datenorientierte Prüfung data-oriented auditing
datenorientierter Ansatz data-oriented approach, data-driven approach
Datenorientierung data orientation
Datenpaket data packet, datagram
Datenprüfung data check, data validation, data verification
Datenquelle data source
Datenrate data rate
Datenrechtsschutz-Versicherung data legal protection insurance
Datenreduktionsprogramm data reduction program
Datenredundanz data redundancy
Datenrekonstruktion data recovery
Datensatz data record
Datenschutz data privacy, data protection
Datenschutz-Versicherung insurance against data privacy violation
Datenschutzbeauftragter data protection officer
Datenschutzbericht data protection report
Datenschutzgesetz data privacy act, data protection act
Datenschutzkommission data privacy committee
Datenschutzmaßnahme data protection measure
Datenschutzrat data privacy council
Datenschutzrecht data protection right
Datensenke data sink
Datensicherheit data security
Datensicherung data assurance
Datensicherungsmaßnahme data assurance measure
Datensicht data view
Datensichtgerät display
Datensichtstation display station
Datenspeicher data memory
Datenspiegelung data mirroring
Datenspur data track
Datenstation data terminal
Datenstation bereit terminal ready
Datenstationsschutz terminal security
Datensteuerung data control
Datenstruktur data structure

Datenstrukturdiagramm

Datenstrukturdiagramm data structure diagram
Datenstrukturierung data structuring
Datensystem data system
Datentaste data key
datentechnische Vorbereitung data preparation
Datentelephon data telephone, dataphone
Datenträger data carrier, data medium, volume
Datenträger löschen volume cleanup
Datenträger-Archiv data medium archive
Datenträger-Austausch data medium exchange
Datenträger-Etikett volume label
Datenträger-Versicherung insurance against loss of data
Datenträger-Verwaltung data medium management
Datentyp data type
Datentypist data typist
Datenübermittlung data communications
Datenübermittlungsdienst data communications service
Datenübermittlungssteuerung data communications control
Datenübermittlungssystem data communications system
Datenübermittlungsverordnung data communications standards
Datenübertragung data transmission, data transfer
Datenübertragungseinrichtung data transmission equipment
Datenübertragungsgeschwindigkeit data transmission speed
Datenübertragungsleitung data transmission line
Datenübertragungsmedium data transmission medium
Datenübertragungsmodus data transmission mode
Datenübertragungsrate data transmission rate
Datenübertragungssteuerung data link control
Datenübertragungsweg data transmission line
Datenumfang data volume
Datenunabhängigkeit data independence
Datenverarbeitung data processing
Datenverarbeitung außer Haus external data processing
Datenverarbeitungsabteilung data processing department
Datenverarbeitungsanlage data processing equipment

Datenverarbeitungsberuf data processing profession
Datenverarbeitungsprozeß process of data processing
Datenverarbeitungsregister data processing register
Datenverarbeitungsregister-Nummer data processing registration number
Datenverarbeitungssystem data processing system
Datenverarbeitungszentrum data processing center
Datenverbund data sharing
Datenverdichtung data compression
Datenvereinbarung data declaration
Datenverlust data loss
Datenverschlüsselung data encoding, data encryption
Datenverschlüsselungsnorm data encryption standard
Datenverwalter data administrator
Datenverwaltung data administration, data management
Datenverwaltungssystem data base management system
Datenverwendungsanalyse data use analysis
Datenvolumen data volume
Datenweg data path
Datenwegleitung data routing
Datenwörterbuch data dictionary
Datenzugriff data access
Datenzugriffsdiagramm data access diagram
Datenzwischenträger temporary data medium
Datum date, data item
Dauerbeobachtung continuous observation
Dauerbetrieb continuous load, continuous processing, continuous operation
Dauerbuchung standing journal entry
Dauerfunktionstaste typamatic key
dauerhaftes Menü permanent menu
Dauertaste repeat key
Dauerton continuous tone
Dauerunterstreichung continuous underscore
Dauerversuch permanent test
dazwischenschreiben interperse (to)
db = Dezibel
DB/DC System = Data Base/Data Communications System
DBA = Data Base Administrator
DBMS = Data Base Management System
DCS = Distributed Computing System
DD = Data Dictionary
DD = Double Density

24

DDB = Distributed Data Base
DDL = Data Description Language
DDP = Decentralized Data Processing
DDP = Distributed Data Processing
DDS = Data Dictionary System
deaktivieren disable (to)
Debitoren accounts receivables
Debitorenbuchhaltung debit accounting
DEC = Data Exchange Control
dechiffrieren decode (to), decipher (to)
dediziert dedicated
dediziertes System dedicated system
Deduktion deduction
Deduktionssystem deductive system
DEE = Daten-Endeinrichtung
Defaultwert default value
defensive Strategie defensive strategy
definieren define (to)
DEKITZ = Deutsche Koordinationsstelle für IT-Normenkonformitätsprüfung und -zertifizierung
Deklaration declaration
deklarative Programmiersprache declarative programming language
deklarative Programmierung declarative programming
deklarative Wissensdarstellung declarative knowledge representation
dekodieren decode (to)
Dekodierung decoding
Dekomposition decomposition
Dekomprimierung decompression
Dekonzentration deconcentration
deliktische Handlung crime
Delphi-Methode Delphi method
Demodulation demodulation
demodulieren demodulate (to)
Demoskopie demoscopy, opinion research
Dependenzanalyse dependency analysis
DES = Data Encryption Standard
DES-Algorithmus DES algorithm
Designtest design test
Deskriptor descriptor
destruktive Strategie destructive strategy
DETAB = Decision Table
Detailentwurf detailed design
Determinismus determinism
Determinismus-Hypothese determinism hypothesis
deterministisch deterministic
deterministische Heuristik deterministic heuristics
Deutsches Forschungsnetz German Research Network
DEVO = Datenerfassungsverordnung
dezentrale Datenerfassung decentralized data collection

dezentrale Datenverarbeitung decentralized data processing
dezentrale Konzentration remote concentration
dezentrale Programmierung remote programming
Dezentralisation decentralization
Dezentralisierung decentralization
Dezibel decibel
Dezimalziffer decimal digit
DFD = Data Flow Diagram
DFN = Deutsches Forschungsnetz
DFN-Verein = Verein zur Förderung des Deutschen Forschungsnetzes
DFÜ = Datenfernübertragung
DGD = Deutsche Gesellschaft für Dokumentation
DIA = Distributed Intelligent Agent
Diagnose diagnosis
Diagnosefunktion diagnostic function
Diagnosemappe diagnostic map
Diagnosemodell diagnostic model
Diagnoseprogramm debugger
Diagnoseregel diagnostic rule
Diagnostikprogramm diagnostic program
diagnostizieren diagnose (to)
Diagramm diagram, chart
Diagrammtechnik diagramming technique, charting technique
Dialekt subset
Dialog dialog
Dialogauftrag dialog job, interactive job
Dialogbetrieb conversational mode, interactive mode
Dialogdatenerfassung interactive data collection
Dialogfähigkeit dialog ability
Dialogflexibilität dialog flexibility
Dialogführung dialog control
Dialoggenerator dialog generator
Dialoggestaltung dialog design
Dialoginhalt content of dialog
Dialogisierungsgrad degree of interaction
Dialogkellerung dialog stacking
Dialogmedium dialog medium
Dialogoberfläche dialog interface
Dialogpartnermodell dialog partner model
Dialogschnittstelle dialog interface
Dialogsprache dialog language
Dialogsteuerung dialog control
Dialogstruktur dialog structure
Dialogsystem dialog system
Dialogtechnik dialog technique, user interface technique
Dialogverarbeitung dialog processing, conversational processing

Dialogwechsel

Dialogwechsel dialog switching
DIANE = Direct Information Access Network for Europe
Dienstgüte service quality
Dienstintegration service integration
Dienstintegriertes Digitalnetz Integrated Services Digital Network
Dienstleister server
Dienstleistungsebene service level
Dienstleistungsebenen-Konzept service level concept
Dienstleistungsgrad service level
Dienstleistungsmarkt service market
Dienstleistungsprozessor server processor
Dienstleistungsrechenzentrum computer bureau
Dienstleistungsrechenzentrum computer service center, computing service center
Dienstleistungszentrum service center
Dienstprogramm utility program
Dienstübergang interworking
differenzierter Verrechnungspreis differentiated internal pricing
Differenzierung differentiation
diffuse Reflexion diffuse reflection
digital digital
Digital/Analog-Umsetzer digital/analog converter
digitale Darstellung digital representation
digitale Daten digital data
digitale Netzarchitektur digital network architecture
digitale Unterschrift digital signature
digitale Vermittlungstechnik circuit switching
digitaler optischer Computer digital optical computer
digitales Kassettenband digital audio tape
digitales Kommunikationssystem digital communications system
digitales Ortsnetz digital local area network
Digitalisierbrett digitizer board
digitalisieren digitize (to)
Digitalisierer digitizer
Digitalisiertablett digitizer board
Digitalrechner digital computer
DIGON = Digitales Ortsnetz
DIKOS = Digitales Kommunikationssystem
Diktiergerät dictation machine
DIN = Deutsche Industrienorm
DIN = Deutsches Institut für Normung
direkt direct, random
direkt verbunden on-line

direkt zurechenbare Kosten direct costs
Direktabfrage direct query
Direktanschluß direct line
Direktanschluß für Drucker local printer attachement
Direktdatenerfassung online data entry
Direktdatennetz direct data network
Direkteingabe direct input
direkte Manipulation direct manipulation
direkte Partizipation direct participation
direkte Verbindung direct connection
direkte Wissensdarstellung direct knowledge representation
direkter Blitzeinschlag direct lightning
direkter Zugriff direct access, random access
direktes Positionieren direct positioning
Direktruf speed call
Direktrufnetz speed call network
Direktspeicherzugriff direct memory access
Direktumstellung direct changeover
Direktwahl short dialling
Direktzugriffsspeicher direct access memory
Disjunktion disjunction
Diskette floppy disk
Diskettenlaufwerk flexible disk drive
Diskontinuität discontinuity
diskrete Optimierung discrete optimization
diskrete Simulation discrete simulation
Diskriminanzanalyse discriminant analysis
Diskussionsleiter moderator
Disposition disposition
Distribuierung distribution
Distribuierungsgrad degree of centralization/decentralization
divergierender Entscheidungsstil divergent decision making behavior
Division durch Null zero divide
Divisionsrest division remainder
Divisionsrest-Verfahren modulo method
DKS = Datenkatalog-System
DKZ = Datenkonzentrator
DL/1 = Data Language One
DLZ = Deutsche Leitzahl
DMA = Direct Memory Access
DML = Data Manipulation Language
DNA = Digital Network Architecture
DNC = Direct Numerical Control
DNIC = Data Network Identification Code
Dokument document
Dokumentation documentation

Dokumentationshandbuch documentation guide, documentation handbook
Dokumentationssprache documentation language
Dokumentationsstandard documentation standard
Dokumentationssystem documentation system
Dokumentdatum document date
Dokumenteanlierferung document delivery
Dokumenteauswertung document analysis
Dokumenteverarbeitung document processing
Dokumenteverteilung document dissemination, document distribution
Dokumenteverwaltung document management
Dokumentewiedergewinnung document retrieval
Dokumentieren documentation process
Dokumentprotokoll document log
Domäne domain
Doppeldruck double strike
doppelt gekettete Dateiorganisation double-linked data organization
doppelte Genauigkeit double precision
doppelte Schreibdichte double recording density
Doppelwort double word
DOS = Disk Operating System
DP = Data Processing
DP = Document Publishing
dpi = dots per inch
DQ = Draft Quality
drahtlose Übertragung radio transmission
drahtloses Telephon radio telephone
Drahtmodell line model
DRAM = Dynamic Random Access Memory
Drehfehler transposition error
Drehknopf paddle
3D-Modell = dreidimensionales Modell
Drei-Schema-Konzept three-level concept
dreidimensionales Modell three-dimensional model
dreidimensionales System three-dimensional system
3NF = dritte Normalform
dritte Normalform third normal form
DRM = Data Resource Management
druckaufbereitendes Datenfeld edited item
Druckausgabe print output
Druckband print ribbon
Druckbild print view

Druckbreite print span, print width
drucken print (to)
Drucken printing
Drucken von Kleinbuchstaben lower case printing
Drucken vorwärts und rückwärts bidirectional printing
Drucker printer
Druckerkapazität printer capacity
Druckerpuffer printer buffer
Druckersteuerzeichen printer control character
Druckerterminal printer terminal
Druckertreiber printer driver
Druckerverkleidung printer cover
Druckgeschwindigkeit printing rate
Druckkette print chain
Druckkopf print head
Druckmaske print mask
Druckmedium print medium
Druckqualität print quality
Druckrad print wheel
Drucksache printed matter
Druckserver print server
Drucktaste push button
Drucktype type, character, face
Druckwerk print device, print unit
DSE = Distributed System Environment
DSG = Datenschutzgesetz
DSS = Decision Support System
DTP = Desktop Publishing
DÜ = Datenübertragung, Datenübermittlung
Dualziffer binary digit
DÜE = Datenübertragungseinrichtung
Dünnfilmspeicher thin film memory
Duplexbetrieb duplex mode, duplex operation
Duplexsystem duplex system
Duplexverbindung duplex communications
Durchblättern browsing
durchdringen penetrate (to)
Durchdringung penetration
Durchdringungsgrad degree of penetration
Durchdringungsstrategie penetration strategy
durchführbar feasible
durchführbare Lösung feasible solution
Durchführbarkeit feasibility
Durchführbarkeitsstudie feasibility study
Durchführungsinformation execution information
Durchlaufzeit execution time
Durchmesser diameter
Durchsatz throughput

Durchsatzzeit throughput time
durchschalten connect (to)
Durchschaltevermittlung circuit switching
Durchschaubarkeit transparency, visibility
durchschnittliche Zugriffszeit average access time
Durchschnittskosten average costs
Durchschnittswert average value
Durchschreibpapier copying carbon paper
Durchschuß leading
durchsetzen enforce (to)
Durchsetzung enforcement
Durchsuchen der gesamten Datei full file search
DÜVO = Datenübermittlungsverordnung
DV = Datenverarbeitung
DV-Ausschuß DP committee
DV-Koordinator DP coordinator
DV-Manager DP manager
DV-Revisor DP auditor
DVD = Deutsche Vereinigung für Datenschutz
DVR = Datenverarbeitungsregister
DVR-Nummer = Datenverarbeitungsregister-Nummer

DVZ = Datenverarbeitungszentrum
dx = **duplex**
dynamisch dynamic
dynamische Autorisierung dynamic authorizing
dynamische Dateisicherung dynamic file backup
dynamische Datenstruktur dynamic data structure
dynamische Instrumentierung dynamic instrumentation
dynamische Programmanalyse dynamic program analysis
dynamische Speicherverwaltung dynamic memory management
dynamische Systemmittelzuordnung dynamic resource allocation
dynamische Topologie dynamic topology
dynamischer Lese-Schreibspeicher dynamic read-write memory
dynamischer Speicher dynamic memory
dynamisches Hilfesystem dynamic help system
dynamisches Qualitätsmaß dynamic quality measure
dynamisches Sitzen dynamic sitting
dynamisches System dynamic system
dynamisches Testen dynamic testing

E

E/A-Gerät I/O device
E/A-Prozessor = Eingabe/Ausgabe-Prozessor
EAN = Europaeinheitliche Artikelnummer
EAPROM = Electrically Alterable Programmable Read Only Memory
EARN = European Academic and Research Network
EAROM = Electrically Alterable Read Only Memory
Easiest-first-Strategie easiest-first strategy
EBCDIC = Extended Binary Coded Decimal Interchange Code
Ebene level
Ebenen-Konzept level concept
ECC = Error Correcting Code
ECCAI = European Committee for Artificial Intelligence
Echtheit authenticity
Echtzeit realtime
Echtzeit-Programmiersprache realtime programming language
Echtzeitbetrieb realtime mode
Echtzeituhr realtime clock
Echtzeitverarbeitung realtime processing
ECITIC = European Committee for Information Technology Certification
Eckstein cornerstone
ECMA = European Computer Manufacturers Association
ECMA-Symbolik ECMA symbolics
EDC = Error Detecting Code
EDFD = Entity Data Flow Diagram
EDI = Electronic Data Interchange
EDIF = Electronic Design Interchange Format
EDIFACT = Electronic Data Interchange for Administration, Commerce and Transport
EDP = Electronic Data Processing
EDS = Electronic Data Switching
EDV = Elektronische Datenverarbeitung
EDV-Abteilung EDP department
EDV-Berater EDP consultant
EDV-Funktion EDP function
EDV-Heimarbeit teleworking, telecommuting
EDV-orientierter Ansatz EDP-oriented approach
EDV-Rahmenplan EDP masterplan
EDV-Sachverständiger EDP expert
EDVA = Elektronische Datenverarbeitungsanlage
EEPROM = Electrically Erasable and Programmable Read Only Memory
EEROM = Electrically Erasable Read Only Memory
Effektivität effectivity
Effizienz efficiency
EFTS = Electronic Funds Transfer System
EHKP = Einheitliche Höhere Kommunikationsprotokolle
EIA = Electronic Industries Association
Eichung calibration
Eigenerstellung oder Fremdbezug make or buy
Eigenschaft attribute
Eigenschaften-Fenster property sheet
Eigenschaftswert attribute value
Eigner owner
Eigner/Zugehöriger-Beziehung owner/member relationship
Eignung acceptability, suitability, qualification, fitness
EIM = Enterprise Information Management
Ein-/Auslagern paging
einfach gekettete Dateiorganisation single-linked file organization
einfache Bedingung single condition
einfache Genauigkeit single precision
einfacher Entscheidungsstil single decision making behavior
einfaches Nutzungsrecht single right of use
Einfachfehler single error
Einfluß impact
Einfluß-Projektorganisation task force in staff function
Einflußgröße influence quantity
einfügen paste (to), insert (to), fit in (to)
Einfügeoperation push
Einfügung insertion
Einfügungsgrad degree of insertion
einführen implement (to)
Einführung implementation
Einführungskosten implementation costs
Einführungsplanung implementation scheduling
Einführungszeit implementation time
Eingabe input
Eingabe-/Abfragezeichen prompting character
Eingabe-/Ausgabe-Diagramm input/output diagram
Eingabe-/Ausgabeprozessor input/output processor
Eingabe-/Ausgabeschutz input/output protection

Eingabe-/Ausgabesteuerungssystem input/output control system
Eingabeaufforderung prompting
Eingabebeleg input document, source document
Eingabedaten input data
Eingabeeinheit input unit
Eingabefehler input error
Eingabegerät input device
Eingabegeschwindigkeit input rate
Eingabemedium input medium
Eingabeschutz input protection
Eingabetaste enter key
Eingabetechnik input technology
Eingabewarteschlange input job queue
Eingabewerk input unit
Eingangsstelle entry point
eingeben enter (to), input (to)
einheitliche Artikelnumerierung universal product code
einheitliche Benutzeroberfläche common user interface, standardized user interface
Einheitlichkeit uniformity
Einheitspreis standard price
Einkauf purchasing
einkaufen purchase (to)
Einkaufsdisposition purchase order disposition
Einkaufspreis purchase price
einleiten initialize (to)
einlesen read-in (to)
einmalige Verkaufsposition unic selling position
einmitten center (to)
Einplatinencomputer single board computer
Einplatzsystem single user system
Einprogrammverarbeitung single program processing
1:1-Beziehung one-to-one relationship
1:m-Beziehung one-to-many relationship
Einsatzattraktivität application attractiveness
einsatzfähig operational
Einsatzmittel resource
Einschub insert
einseitig single sided
einseitig gerichtete Leitung simplex line
einseitige Datenübertragung simplex data transmission
Eintrittsbarriere barrier to entry
Einwegverschlüsselung single way ciphering
Einzelarbeitsplatz individual workplace
Einzelblatteinzug document feed, sheet feeder
Einzelblattzuführung single sheet feeding
Einzelinterview individual interview
einzelner Benutzer individual user
Einzelplatzsystem single user system
Einzelworterkennung single word recognition
Einzelzeitmessung single time measurement
Einzelzuordnung assignment to one person
Einzweckcomputer single purpose computer
EIS = Executive Information System
EISA = Extended Industry Standard Architecture
Eisbergeffekt iceberg effect
ELAN = Elementary Language
Elastizität elasticity
elektrisch änderbarer Festwertspeicher electrically alterable read only memory
elektrisch änderbarer programmierbarer Festwertspeicher electrically alterable programmable read only memory
Elektro-Erosionsdrucker electro-engraving printer
elektro-optischer Wandler electro-optical transformer
elektrofotografischer Drucker electro-photographic printer
elektromagnetische Umweltverschmutzung electro-magnetic pollution
Elektronenstrahl cathode ray
Elektronenstrahlspeicher electron beam addressable memory
elektronische Datenverarbeitung electronic data processing
elektronische Datenverarbeitungsanlage electronic data processing equipment
elektronische Pinwand clipboard
elektronische Post electronic mail
elektronischer Briefkasten electronic mailbox
elektronischer Drucker electronic printer
elektronischer Kalender electronic calender
elektronischer Konferenzraum electronic conference room
elektronischer Kopierer electronic copier
elektronischer Malkasten electronic paint box
elektronischer Papierkorb electronic wastebasket, electronic garbage bin
elektronisches Bezahlen electronic cash payment
elektronisches Buch electronic book
elektronisches Handelspanel electronic commercial panel

elektronisches Postfach electronic post box
elektronisches Telephonbuch electronic telephone book
elektronisches Wörterbuch electronic dictionary
elektronisches Zahlungssystem electronic funds transfer system
elektrostatischer Plotter electrostatic plotter
elektrostatisches Druckwerk electrostatic print unit
Element element
Elementarblock basic block
elementarer Objekttyp basic entity type
elementarer Verteilungsschlüssel basic cost distribution key
Elementaroperation basic operation
emotionaler Prozeß emotional process
empfangen receive (to)
Empfangsaufruf addressing
empfangsbereit ready to receive
Empfangsbestätigung acknowledgement
Empfangsbetrieb receive mode
Empfangsschlüssel receiving key
Empfangsstation called station, receiving terminal
Empfangsunterbrechung receive interrupt
Empfindlichkeit sensitivity
Empfindlichkeitsanalyse sensitivity analysis
empirisch empirical
empirischer Befund empirical finding
empirisches Testen empirical testing
Empirismus empirism
Emulation emulation
Emulator emulator
Endanwender end-user
Endauslieferung final delivery
Endbedingung at end condition
Endbenutzer end-user
Endbenutzersprache end-user language
Endbenutzersystem end-user system
Endbenutzerwerkzeug end-user tool
Ende der Datei end of file
Ende der Nachricht end of message
Ende der Übertragung end of transmission
Ende des Bandes end of tape
Ende des Textes end of text
Ende des Übertragungsblocks end of transmission block
Ende-zu-Ende-Verschlüsselung end-to-end ciphering
Endgerät terminal
Endgeräte-Schnittstelle terminal interface
endliche Anzahl finite number

Endlosablage continuous form stacker
Endlosfehler continuous error, looping error
Endlosformular continuous form
Endlosformular mit Führungslochung continuous pin-feed form
Endlosformularführung continuous form feed device
Endlospapier fanfold paper
Endprodukt end product
Endsumme sum total
Engpaß bottleneck
Entbündelung unbundling
Entfaltung evolution
entfernt remote
entfernt stehende Datenstation remote station
Enthaltungspflicht obligation of abstention
Entität entity
Entitätsmenge entity set
Entitätsschlüssel entity key
entkoppeln decouple (to)
Entkopplung decoupling
Entnahmedatum date of movement
entscheiden decide (to)
Entscheidung decision
Entscheidungsanalyse decision analysis
Entscheidungsbaum decision tree
Entscheidungsbaumverfahren decision tree method
Entscheidungsbefugnis decision competence
Entscheidungsebene decision level
Entscheidungsfeld decision field
Entscheidungsfindung decision making
Entscheidungsinformation information for decision making
Entscheidungskonferenz decision making conference
Entscheidungskriterium decision criterion
Entscheidungsmatrix decision matrix
Entscheidungsmodell decision model
entscheidungsorientierter Ansatz decision making approach
Entscheidungsphase decision phase
Entscheidungsprinzip decision principle
Entscheidungsprozeß decision process
Entscheidungsregel decision rule
Entscheidungsschwelle decision threshold
Entscheidungsspielraum decision scope
Entscheidungsstil decision style
Entscheidungstabelle decision table
Entscheidungstabelle mit einfachen Eintragungen decision table with limited entries

Entscheidungstabelle

Entscheidungstabelle mit erweiterten Eintragungen decision table with extended entries
Entscheidungstabellentechnik decision table technique
Entscheidungstableau decision tableau
Entscheidungstechnik decision technique
Entscheidungstheorie decision theory
Entscheidungsträger decision maker
Entscheidungsunterstützungssystem decision support system
Entscheidungsunterstützungssystem für Gruppen group decision support system
Entscheidungsverhalten decision making behavior
Entscheidungswert decision value
entschlüsseln decode (to), decipher (to)
Entschlüsselung deciphering, decoding
Entstörung suppression
entwerfen design (to), project (to)
entwickeln develop (to)
Entwickler developer
Entwicklung development
Entwicklungsadministrator development administrator
Entwicklungsbibliothek development library
Entwicklungsdatenbank development data base
Entwicklungsfähigkeit evolvability
Entwicklungsmöglichkeit ease of development
Entwicklungsrechner development computer
Entwicklungsrückstau development backlog
Entwicklungsstrategie development strategy
Entwicklungstest development testing
Entwicklungsumgebung development environment
Entwicklungswerkzeug development tool
Entwicklungszyklus development cycle
entwürfeln descramble (to)
Entwürfler descrambler
Entwurfsbeschreibung design specification
Entwurfsdatenbank design data base
Entwurfsdimension design category
Entwurfsdokument design document
Entwurfsfunktion design function
Entwurfsinspektion design review
Entwurfsmatrix design matrix
Entwurfsmethode design technique
Entwurfsphase design phase
Entwurfsprinzip design principle
Entwurfsqualität draft quality

Entwurfsrichtlinie design guideline
Entwurfssprache design language
Entwurfstest design test
Entwurfswerkzeug design tool
Entwurfszuverlässigkeit inherent reliability
EOB = End of Block
EOF = End of File
EOJ = End of Job
EOM = End of Message
EOR = End of Reel
EOT = End of Tape
EOT = End of Text
EOT = End of Transmission
EOV = End of Volume
EP = Electronic Publishing
EPROM = Erasable Programmable Read Only Memory
ER = Externer Rechner
ER-Diagramm = Entity-Relationship-Diagramm
Ereignis event
Ereignisaufzeichnung logging
Ereigniskette event chain
Ereignisknoten-Netzplan event-node network plan
Ereignismessung event-driven monitoring
Ereignispuffer event buffer
Ereignistyp event type
Ereignisverfolgung trace
Erfahrung experience
Erfahrungskurve experience curve
Erfahrungskurvenkonzept experience curve concept
Erfahrungswissen know-how
erfaßbar tangible
erfaßbare Kosten tangible costs
erfaßbarer Nutzen tangible benefits
Erfassen des Istzustands survey of current system
Erfassungsbeleg collection form, collection sheet
Erfassungstechnik survey technique
Erfolg success
Erfolgsfaktor success factor
Erfolgsfaktoren-Analyse success factor analysis
Erfolgsfrühwarnung early success warning, critical event warning
Erfolgsposition success positioning
Erfolgspotential success potential
erforschendes Prototyping explorative prototyping
Ergänzung supplement
Ergänzungsprodukt add-on product, supplementary product
Ergänzungsspeicher amending memory

Ergebnis result, output
ergebnisorientiert output-driven, result-oriented
ergebnisorientierter Entwurf output-driven design, result-oriented design
Ergonomie ergonomics
Erhaltungsziel maintenance goal
Erheben der Anforderungen requirements survey
Erheben des Istzustands survey of current system
Erhebung survey, investigation
Erhebung durch Briefpost mail survey
Erhebungsbefund survey finding
Erhebungsmethode survey technique
Erkennen/Handeln-Zyklus recognize/act cycle
Erkennung recognition
Erkennungsexperiment identification experiment
Erklärung explanation
Erklärung mitten im Ablauf mid run explanation
Erklärungsmodell explanatory model
Erkundung exploration
Erkundungsexperiment exploratory experiment
Erlernbarkeit learnability
Erlös revenue
Erlössteigerung increase in revenue
ERM = Entity Relationship Model
ERMES = European Radio Message System
Ermüdungsfaktor fatigue factor
Erneuerung renewal
Erreichbarkeit accessibility
Ersatz-Rechenzentrum backup computing center
Ersatzgerät standby equipment
Ersatzspur alternate track
Ersatzteil spare part
Ersatztermin substitute due date
erschöpfende Suche exhaustive search
1NF = erste Normalform
erste Normalform first normal form
Ertragszentrum profit center
Erwartung expectation
Erweiterbarkeit expandability
erweitern expand (to), extend (to)
erweiterter Binärcode für Dezimalziffern extended binary-coded decimal interchange code
erweiterter Hauptspeicher extended main memory
erweitertes Menü extended menu
Erweiterungsplatine expansion board

Erwerb acquisition
Erwerb von Expertenwissen acquisition of expert knowledge
erwerben acquire (to)
erzwungenes Ende forced ending
ESC = Escape
ESPRIT = European Strategic Programme for Research in Information Technology
ESS = Executive Support System
ETB = Elektronisches Telephonbuch
ETB = End of Transmission Block
ETHICS = Effective Technical and Human Implementation of Computerbased Systems
Etikett label
Etikettendruck label printing
Etikettendrucker label printer
Etikettenleser label reader
EUC = End-User Computing
Euklidischer Abstand Euclidean distance
Europaeinheitliche Artikelnummer European Product Code
Eurosignal Euro signal
EUS = Entscheidungsunterstützungssystem
EVA = Eingabe-Verarbeitung-Ausgabe
EVA-Diagramm IPO chart
Evaluierung evaluation
Evolution evolution
evolutionäre Software-Entwicklung evolutionary software development
evolutionäres Prototyping evolutionary prototyping, versioning
Evolutionsmatrix evolution matrix
Evolutionstheorie evolution theory
EwIM = Enterprise-wide Information Management
EWS = Elektronisches Wählsystem
EX = Execute
EXAPT = Exact Automatic Programming of Tools
Experiment experiment
experimentelles Prototyping experimental prototyping
Expertenbefragung acquisition of expert knowledge, expert questioning
Expertenmodus expert mode
Expertensystem expert system
Expertenunterstützungssystem expert support system
Expertenwissen expert knowledge
explorative Datenanalyse exploratory data analysis
exploratives Prototyping exploratory prototyping

exponentielle Glättung exponential smoothing
externe Brücke external bridge
externe Daten external data
externe Datenbank external data bank
externe Priorität external priority
externe Revision external auditing
externe Unterbrechung external interrupt
externer Drucker external printer
externer Rechner external computer
externer Speicher external storage, external memory
externer Wiederanlauf external restart, restart on seperate system

externes Datenmodell user data model
externes Rechenzentrum computer bureau, computing service
externes Schema external model, external schema
extragenetische Information extragenetic information
Extraktmanagement extract management
extrasomatische Information extrasomatic information
Extremalkriterium unconstrained criterion
Extremalziel unconstrained goal

F

F & E = Forschung und Entwicklung
FAA = Fragebogen zur Arbeitsanalyse
Fabrik der Zukunft factory of the future
Fabrikautomation factory automation
Fachabteilung department, user area, user division
Fachabteilungskoordinator user liaison officier
Fachaufgabe specialist task
Fachsprache terminology
Fachzeitschrift specialised journal
Fähigkeit ability, capability, qualification, literacy
Faksimile facsimile
Faksimiledienst facsimile service
Faksimiletechnik facsimile technology
Faksimileübertragung facsimile transmission
Fakten-Datenbank facts data base
Faktorenanalyse factor analysis
Faktorentabelle table of factors
Faktum fact
Fakturierung invoicing
Falltür drap door
Falsifizierung falsification
FAM = Fast Access Memory
Farbband ribbon
Farbbandkassette ribbon cartridge
Farbbildschirm color screen
Farbpulver toner
Farbstrahldruckwerk color jet printer device
Faser fibre
Fax = Faksimile-Übertragung
Faxkarte fax card
FBA = Fehlerbaumanalyse
FCS = Frame Check Sequence
FDM = Frequency Division Multiplexing
FDMA = Frequency Division Multiplex Access
fdx = full duplex
FE-Methode = Finite-Elemente-Methode
Fehler error, fault
Fehlerabschätzung error estimation
Fehleranalyse fault analysis
Fehleranfälligkeit fault liability
Fehleranzeige fault indication
Fehleranzeiger fault indicator
Fehlerart kind of fault, fault type
Fehleraufzeichnung error recording
Fehlerbaum fault tree
Fehlerbaumanalyse fault tree analysis
Fehlerbehandlung error handling
Fehlerbericht error report, trouble report
Fehlerberichtigung error correction
Fehlerbeseitigung debugging
Fehlerdiagnose fault diagnosis
Fehlereingrenzung error isolation
Fehlererfassung error logging
fehlererkennender Code error detecting code
Fehlererkennung error detecting
Fehlererkennungscode error detection code
fehlerhaft faulty, defective
Fehlerhäufigkeit error frequency
Fehlerhäufung error burst
Fehlerklassifikation error classification
Fehlerkorrektur error correction
Fehlerkorrekturcode error correction code
Fehlerkorrektureinrichtung error correction feature
fehlerkorrigierender Code error correcting code
Fehlerliste error report
Fehlermeldung error message
Fehlernachricht error message
Fehlerprotokoll error log
Fehlerprüfcode error checking code
Fehlerrate error rate
Fehlerschutz error control
Fehlersuche und -beseitigung troubleshooting
Fehlersuchprogramm debugger, debugging program
fehlertolerant fault tolerant
fehlertolerantes System fault tolerant system
Fehlertoleranz fault tolerance
Fehlerüberwachung error control
Fehlerüberwachungseinheit error control unit
Fehlerumgebung error avoidance
Fehlerunempfindlichkeit error tolerance
Fehlerunterbrechungsprogramm fault interrupt routine
Fehlerunterdrückung fault suppression
Fehlerverwaltung problem management
Fehlerwahrscheinlichkeit error probability
Fehlfarbenverarbeitung offshade processing
Fehlfunktion malfunction
Fehlinvestition investment failure
Fehlverhalten malfunction
Fehlzeit absenteeism
Feinanalyse detailed analysis
Feinentwurf detailed design, fine design
Feinprojektierung detailed systems design
Feinschutz micro protection

Feinstudie detailed survey, detailed study
Feld array, field
feldabhängiger Entscheidungsstil subject-dependent decision making style
Feldbeschreibung field description
Feldexperiment field experiment
feldprogrammierbarer Festwertspeicher erasable programmable read only memory
Feldrechner array processor
feldunabhängiger Entscheidungsstil subject-independent decision making style
Fenster window
Fenstertechnik windowing
FEP = Front End Processor
fern remote
Fern-Stapelverarbeitung remote job entry
Fernabfrage remote query
Fernbetriebseinheit communications controller
Fernbrücke telebridge
Ferndiagnosesystem remote diagnosis system
Fernkopieren facsimile transmission
Fernkopierer facsimile machine, fax machine
Fernladen downline loading
Fernleitung trunk line
Fernlöschung remote cancellation
Fernmeldeanlagen-Gesetz telecommunications equipment regulation
Fernmeldedienst telecommunications service
Fernmeldehoheit telecommunications jurisdiction
Fernmeldetechnik telecommunications engineering
Fernmeldeweg telecommunications line
Fernmessen telemetering
Fernnetz long distance network
Fernrechnen remote computing
Fernschreibcode teletype code
Fernschreiben telemessage, telex
Fernschreiber teleprinter, teletyper, telewriter
Fernschreibverkehr teleprinter exchange, telex traffic
Fernsehtext teletext
Fernsprech-Nebenstellenanlage private automatic branch exchange
Fernsprechamt telephone exchange
Fernsprechanschluß telephone connection
Fernsprechapparat mit Nummernscheibe rotary dial telephone set
Fernsprechen telephony

Fernsprecher telephone
Fernsprechkanal telephone channel
Fernsprechkonferenz teleconference
Fernsprechnetz telephone network
Fernsprechteilnehmer telephone subscriber
Fernsprechvermittlung telephone exchange
Fernüberwachung remote monitoring, remote supervision
Fernverarbeitung teleprocessing
Fernwartung remote maintenance
Fernwirken remote control
Fernzeichner displayphone, scribophone, teleboard
Fertigerzeugnis finished goods
Fertigerzeugnisbestand finished goods inventory
Fertigkeit skill
Fertigmontage final assembly
Fertigstellungsdatum finish date
Fertigung manufacturing
Fertigungsautomation automation of manufacturing
Fertigungsautomatisierung manufacturing automation
Fertigungsbetrieb production plant
Fertigungsinformations- und -steuerungssystem manufacturing information and control system
Fertigungsinsel manufacturing unit
Fertigungskosten production costs
Fertigungslohn direct labor cost
Fertigungssteuerung manufacturing control
Fertigungsstraße assembly line
Fertigungsvorbereitung production scheduling
Fertigungszelle manufacturing cell
Fertigware finished product
fest verdrahtet hard wired
Festbildkommunikation picture communications
Festbildspeicher fixed picture storage
festgeschaltete Leitung leased line
Festkommadarstellung fixed point representation
Festplattenlaufwerk winchester disk drive
Festplattenspeicher fixed disk drive
festprogrammierter Computer fixed program computer
Festprogrammierung fixed programming
Festpunktdarstellung fixed point representation
Festspeicher read only memory
Festwertspeicher read only memory

FET = Feld-Effekt-Transistor
FET-Technologie FET technology
Fettdruck bold face
FF = Form Feed
FFS = Flexibles Fertigungssystem
FFZ = Flexible Fertigungszelle
Fibu = Finanzbuchhaltung
FIFO = First In First Out
Filter filter
Filterung filtering
Firmenverzeichnis trade directory
Firmenzeichen logo
Finanz- und Rechnungswesen finance and accounting
Finanzbuchhaltung general ledger
Finanzierung finance
Fingerspitzen-Tablett touch sensitive panel
Finite-Elemente-Methode finite element method
FIS = Fachinformationssystem
FIS = Fertigungsinformations- und -steuerungssystem
fixe Daten fixed data
fixe Kosten fixed costs
Fixpunkt checkpoint
FIZ = Fachinformationszentrum
Flachbettplotter beltbed plotter
flache Anzeige flat display
Flächen-Kreisdiagramm square-circle diagram
Flächendiagramm squaring diagram
Flächengraphik squaring graphic
Flächenmodell area model
flackern flicker (to)
FLAM = Frankenstein-Lidzba-Methode
Flattersatz unjustified text
flexibel flexible
Flexibilität flexibility
flexible Automation flexible automation
flexible Fertigungszelle flexible manufacturing cell
flexible Magnetplatte flexible disk, floppy disk
flexible Strategie flexible strategy
flexibles Fertigungssystem flexible manufacturing system
fliegender Druck flying print
Fließband production line, moving line
Fließbandfertigung line production
Fließbandverarbeitung pipelining
Fließsprache flow language
flimmern flicker (to)
FLOPS = Fließkommaoperationen pro Sekunde
Floyd's Methode Floyd's method
flüchtiger Speicher volatile memory

Flugsicherungssystem air traffic control system
Flußdiagramm flow diagram, flowchart
Flußplansymbol flowchart symbol
Flüssigkeitskristall-Anzeige liquid crystal display
FMS = Flexible Manufacturing System
FNI = Fachnormenausschuß Informationsverarbeitung
FO = Fiber Optic
Folgebedingung postcondition
Folgeprüfung sequence checking
Forderung accounts receivables
formale Anforderung formal requirement
formale Arbeitssituation formal job situation
formale Methode formal method
formale Notation formal notation
formale Organisation formal organization
formale Partizipation formal participation
formale Programminspektion structured walk-through
formale Spezifikation formal specification
formale Spezifikationsmethode formal specification method
formale Sprache formal language
Formalisierbarkeit ability of formalization
formalisieren formalize (to)
Formalisierung formalization
Formalproblem formalized problem
Formalziel quality goal
Format format
Formatfehler format error
Formatieren formatting
Formatierprogramm formatting program
formatierte Daten formatted data
Formular form, paper form
Formularentwurf form design
Formulargenerator form generator, table generator
Formularleser document reader, form reader
Formularsatz form set
Formularsteuerung form control
Formulartechnik input/output mapping
Formularvorschub form feed
Forschung research
Forschung und Entwicklung research and development
Forschungsbefund research finding
Forschungsmethodik research methodology
fortdauernd permanent
FORTRAN = FORmula TRANslator
fortschreiben update (to)

Fortschrittszahl

Fortschrittszahl accumulate figure
Fortschrittszahlen-System accumulate figure system
Fortschrittszeit-Messung elapsed time measurement
Fragebogen questionnaire
Fragebogenmethode questionnaire technique
Fragmentierung fragmentation
FRAM = Ferroelectronic Random Access Memory
frei wählbar fully optional
freie Abfrage open query
freie Daten public data
Freigabe release
Freihand-Symbolik customized command symbolics
Freihandzeichen freehand shape
Freiheitsspielraum scope of freedom
Freileitung open wire line
freischalten enable (to)
Fremdbezug buy
Fremdschlüssel foreign key
Fremdsoftware external software, purchased software
Frequenz frequency
Frequenzmultiplexing frequency division multiplexing
FROM = Factory Read Only Memory
FROM = Fusible Read Only Memory
frühester Anfangstermin earliest begin date
frühester Beginntermin earliest start date
frühester Endtermin earliest end date
frühester Starttermin earliest start date
Frühwarnfunktion early warning function
Frühwarnsystem early warning system
Frühwarnung early warning
FSS = Full Software Service
FSK = Frequency Shift Keying
FTAM = File Transfer Access Management
FTS = Fahrerloses Transportsystem
FTS = Fehlertolerantes System
FTZ = Fernmeldetechnisches Zentralamt
FTZ-Nummer = Fernmeldetechnische-Zentralamt-Nummer
Fühler sensor
führende Nullen leading zeros
führende Zeichen leading graphics
Führer leader
Führerschaft leadership
Führung management
Führungsaufgabe management task
Führungsebene managerial level

Führungsfunktion managerial function
Führungsgröße set point, reference variable
Führungsinformationssystem management information system
Führungskraft manager
Führungsloch im Papier feed hole
Führungsmethode managerial technique
Führungsspitze top management
Führungsstil leadership style
Führungsverhalten leadership attitude
Füllzeichen filler
Function-Point-Verfahren function point model
Funkentstörung interference suppression
Funkrufdienst radio telephone service
Funktion function
Funktion/Ereignis-Matrix function/event matrix
funktionale Abhängigkeit functional dependency
funktionale Programmierung functional programming
funktionaler Zusammenhang functional cohesion
Funktionalität functionality
funktioneller Entwurf functional design
Funktionsanalyse analysis of functions
Funktionsanforderung functional requirement
Funktionsausbreitung creaping functionality
Funktionsbereitschaft statement of functions
Funktionsbeschreibung functionability
funktionsbezogenes Testen functional testing
Funktionsdiagramm functional diagram
Funktionseinheit functional unit
Funktionsintegration integration of functions
Funktionsnetz nomogram
funktionsorientiertes System function-oriented system
Funktionspunkt function point
Funktionssicherung function assurance
Funktionstastatur keyboard with function keys
Funktionstaste function key, control key
Funktionstasten-Sicherung check keying, dual keying
Funktionstest function test
Funktionstrennung separation of functions
Funktionsumfang range of functions
Funktionsverbund function sharing
Funktionsweise functioning

Funkverbindung radio link   **Fußzeile** footer

G

G = Giga
Gamma-Veränderung gamma change
GAN = Global Area Network
Gantt-Diagramm Gantt chart
ganze Zahl integer
ganzheitlich holistic
ganzheitliches Denken holistic thinking
ganzheitliches Gestalten holistic design
Ganzheitsbild hologram
Ganzheitslehre holism
ganzzahlige Darstellung integer
Gastrechner host computer
Gastsprache host language
Gatter gate
GB = Gigabyte
Gbit = Gigabit
GCS = Generally Accepted Principles of Computer Security
GDD = Deutsche Gesellschaft für Datenschutz und Datensicherung
GDSS = Group Decision Support System
Geber sensor
Gebläse fan
Gebühr fee
gebührenfreie Telephonnummer toll-free number
Gebührenverzeichnis fee schedule
gebundene Strategie bundling
Gedächtnis memory
gedruckte Schaltung printed circuit
Gefahrenquelle safety hazard
Gefangenendilemma prisoner's dilemma
Gegenangebot counter offer
Gegenbetrieb duplex mode, duplex operation
Gegenmaßnahme countermeasure
gegenseitige Abhängigkeit interdependence
gegenseitige Blockierung deadlock
Gegensprechanlage duplex telephone system
Gehaltsabrechnung payroll
Gehaltskonto salary account
Gehäuse cover
Geheimbotschaft secret message
Geheimnisprinzip information hiding principle
geistig mental
gekettete Dateiorganisation linked file organization
Geldausgabe-Automat cash dispenser, autoteller terminal
gelegentlicher Benutzer casual user
gemäßigte Strategie moderate strategy
Gemeinkosten overhead, overhead costs
Gemeinkosten-System-Engineering overhead systems engineering
Gemeinkosten-Wertanalyse analysis of overheads, overhead value analysis
gemeinsam benutzen share (to)
gemeinsam benutzte Datei shared file
gemeinsame Betriebsmittelnutzung resource sharing
gemeinsamer Bereich common area
gemeinsamer Zugriff shared access
Gemeinschafts-Rechenzentrum group computing center
gemietete Leitung leased line
gemischte Hardware mixed hardware
gemischte Software mixed software
gemischte Systemauslegung mixed environment
Genauigkeit accuracy, precision
generalisieren generalize (to)
Generalisierung generalization
Generation generation
Generationsprinzip generation principle
Generator generator
geometrisches Modelliersystem geometric modelling system
geplante Menge planned quantity
geplante Stillstandzeit scheduled downtime
geplante Wartung scheduled maintenance
geplantes Fertigstellungsdatum target date
geradzahlig even
geradzahlige Parität even parity
Gerät device
Geräteausrüstung hardware
Gerätenummer device number
Geräteschein device certificate, device specification
Geräteschicht physical layer
gerätetechnische Vorbereitung hardware preparation
Geräteunabhängigkeit device independence
Geräuschpegel sound level
gerichtet directional
Gesamtbearbeitungszeit total processing time
Gesamtbildschirm full screen
Gesamtbildschirm-Editor full screen editor
Gesamtumstellung total changeover
Geschäftsbereich business area
Geschäftsgraphik business graphics
Geschäftsstrategie business strategy
Geschäftsvorgang business transaction
Geschäftszweig line of business
geschätzte Kosten estimated costs

geschätzter Nutzen estimated benefits
geschlossene Aufgabe closed task
geschlossene Benutzergruppe dedicated user group
geschlossene Entscheidungstabelle closed decision table
geschlossener Betrieb closed shop
geschlossener Schaltkreis closed circuit
geschlossener Schrifttyp fully formed character
geschlossenes System closed system
geschützte Datei protected file
Gesetz über den Amateurfunk Law on Radio Amateur Operations
gesicherte Datei secured file
Gesprächsbeginn beginning of conversation
Gesprächsende end of conversation
Gestaltpsychologie gestalt psychology
Gestaltungsalternative design alternative
Gestaltungsspielraum design scope
Gestaltungsziel creative goal
gestörte Leitung faulted line
gestreute Dateiorganisation random file organization
geteilter Bildschirm split screen
Gewährleistung warranty
Gewebefilter tissue filter
Gewerbe trade
Gewerkschaft labor union
gewerkschaftlicher Gegenmachtansatz union-controlled approach
gewichtete Quersumme weighted crossfoot
Gewichtung weighting
Gewichtungsmethode weighted ratio method
Gewinn profit
Gewinnschwelle break-even point
Gewinnschwellen-Analyse break-even analysis
Gewinnspanne profit margin
GFK = Glasfaserkabel
GGS = Gütegemeinschaft Software
GI = Gesellschaft für Informatik
GIGO = Garbage In - Garbage Out
GKS = Graphical Kernel System
Glasfaserkabel light wave cable, fiber optics, optical fiber
Glaubwürdigkeit credibility, plausibility
Gleichgewicht balance
Gleichheit parity
Gleichheitsbit parity bit
Gleichheitsfehler parity error
Gleichheitsprüfung parity check
Gleichheitszeichen equal sign
gleichlaufend synchronous
gleichrichten demodulate (to)
Gleichrichtung demudulation
Gleichstrom direct current
gleichzeitig simultaneous
gleichzeitige Mehrfachverarbeitung multitasking
Gleitkomma floating decimal
Gleitkommadarstellung floating decimal presentation
Gleitmenü slide menu
Gleitpunkt floating point
Gleitpunktdarstellung floating point presentation
Gleitzeit flexible working hours, flexitime
gliedern structure (to)
Gliederungszahl constructional figure
GoB = Grundsätze ordnungsmäßiger Buchführung
GoDS = Grundsätze ordnungsmäßigen Datenschutzes
GoDV = Grundsätze ordnungsmäßiger Datenverarbeitung
GoS = Grundsätze ordnungsmäßiger Speicherbuchführung
Gozinto-Graph Gozinto graph
GPIB = General Purpose Interface Bus
GPL = Graphical Programming Language
GPSS = General Purpose Systems Simulator
GRAF = Graphic Addition to FORTRAN
Grammatik grammar
Graph graph
Graphentheorie graph theory
Graphik graphics
Graphikdrucker graphics printer
Graphiktablett graphics tablet
graphische Beschreibung graphical description, graphical representation
graphische Darstellung graphical presentation, plot
graphische Datenverarbeitung graphical data processing, computer graphics
graphische Programmiersprache graphical programming language
graphischer Prozessor graphical processor
graphisches Kernsystem graphical kernel system
graphisches Modell graphical model
graphisches Tablett graphical tablet
Grenzkosten marginal costs
Grenzwert boundary value, limit
Griffel stylus
Grobanalyse preliminary analysis
Grobentwurf gross design, preliminary design
Grobprojektierung general design

Grobschutz macro protection
Großbuchstabe upper case character
Größe quantity
Größenreduzierung downsizing
Großrechner mainframe
Großschreibung capitalization
Großvater-Vater-Sohn-Prinzip grandfather-father-son principle
Grundausstattung basic equipment
Grundfunktion basic function, primitive function
Grundkonzeption basic concept, preliminary design
Grundlage base
Grundlage bildend basic
Grundsatz guideline, principle
Grundsätze ordnungsmäßigen Datenschutzes generally accepted data protection guidelines
Grundsätze ordnungsmäßiger Buchführung generally accepted accounting guidelines
Grundsätze ordnungsmäßiger Datenverarbeitung generally accepted data processing guidelines
Grundsätze ordnungsmäßiger Speicherbuchführung generally accepted storage accounting guidelines
Grundsatzkritik criticism of fundamentals
Grundstellung home position
Gruppe group
Gruppen-Entscheidungsunterstützungssystem group decision support system
Gruppenarbeit teamwork
Gruppenbegriff control break item
Gruppendynamik group dynamics
Gruppeninterview group interview
Gruppenstufe control level
Gruppentechnologie group technology
Gruppenwechsel group change
Gruppenzuordnung group assignment
GSE = **Gemeinkosten-System-Engineering**
gültig valid
Gültigkeit validity
Gummiband-Verfahren rubber banding
gut strukturiertes Problem well structured problem
Gutachten expert opinion
Gutachter expert
Güte quality
Gütekriterium quality criterion
GZS = **Gesellschaft für Zahlungssysteme**

H

Habenzeichen credit symbol
Hacker hacker
Haftpflicht liability
halbdirekte Verbindung semi-direct connection
halbduplex half duplex
Halbduplexbetrieb half-duplex mode
halbdynamische Instrumentierung semi-dynamic instrumentation
Halbgraphik semigraphics, low level graphics
Halbierungsmethode bisection method
Halbleiter semiconductor
Halbleiter-Schutzgesetz Semiconductor Chip Protection Act
Halbleiterkristall chip
Halbleiterspeicher semiconductor memory
halbstandardisiertes Interview semi-structured interview
Halbton half-tone
Haltepunkt breakpoint
Handauflage hand rest
Handbuch handbook, manual
Handcomputer hand held computer
Handel trade
Handhabbarkeit handiness
Handhabung handling
Handhabungssystem numeric control device
Handleser portable document reader
Handlungsalternative action alternative
Handlungsspielraum action scope
Handschriftenleser plain writing reader
Hantierbarkeit manageability, operability
Hardest-first-Strategie hardest-first strategy
Hardware-Ergonomie hardware ergonomics
Hardware-Kompatibilität hardware compatibility
Hardware-Konfiguration hardware configuration
Hardware-Schnittstelle hardware interface
Hardware-Schutz hardware protection
Hardware-Überwachung hardware monitoring
Hardware-Umgebung hardware environment
Hardware-Verträglichkeit hardware compatibility
Harmonisierung harmonization
Hartpostpapier bond paper
Häufigkeit frequency, rate
Häufigkeitsanalyse frequency analysis
Häufigkeitsverteilung frequency distribution
Hauptabteilung main department, central department
Hauptanforderung major requirement
Hauptanschluß master station
Hauptanschluß für Direktruf main station for speed call
Hauptband master tape
Hauptfunktion main function
Hauptmerkmal feature
Hauptprogramm main program, main routine
Hauptprozessor master processor
Hauptspeicher main memory, main storage
Hauptspeicherverwaltung memory management
Hauptsteuerprogramm master control program
Hauptziel main goal
Hauptzweck mission
HCI = Human Computer Interaction
HDLC = High Level Data Link Control
HDN = Hochgeschwindigkeitsdatennetz
HDR = Head Read
Headcrash head crash
Heimarbeit telecommuting
Heimarbeiter homeworker, teleworker
Heimarbeitsplatz teleworkplace
Heimcomputer home computer
Heimkauf teleshopping
heißes Rechenzentrum hot backup computing center
Helligkeit brightness
herabziehbares Menü pull down menu
Herrensystem master system
Hersteller manufacturer
Hersteller eines Originalsystems original equipment manufacturer
Herunterladen download
heterogene Modellierung heterogeneous modelling
Heuristik heuristics
heuristische Prognose heuristic forecasting
heuristische Programmierung heuristic programming
heuristischer Algorithmus heuristic algorithm
heuristisches Suchen heuristic search
hexadezimal hexadecimal
HfD = Hauptanschluß für Direktruf
HFS = Hierarchical File System
Hierarchie hierarchy
Hierarchiediagramm hierarchy diagram

hierarchisch strukturierte Prüfliste
hierarchically structured check list
hierarchische Struktur hierarchical structure
hierarchische Strukturierung hierarchical structuring
hierarchische Zerlegung hierarchical decomposition
hierarchisches Dateisystem hierarchical file system
hierarchisches Datenmodell hierarchical data model
hierarchisches Netz hierarchical network
Hilfefunktion help function
Hilfeinformation help information
Hilfesystem help system
Hilfsmittel means
Hilfsprogramm auxiliary program
Hilfsspeicher auxiliary storage
Hinaufladen upload
Hintergrund background
Hintergrundauftrag background job
Hintergrundnetz backbone network
Hintergrundprogramm background program
Hintergrundspeicher background memory
Hintergrundsystem backbone system, background system
Hintergrundverarbeitung background processing
HIPO = Hierarchy plus Input, Process and Output
Histogramm histogram
historische Mappe history map

HLL = High Level Language
Hochgeschwindigkeitscomputer high-speed computer
Hochleistungscomputer high-performance computer
Hochrechnung projection
Hochsprache high level language
Höchstbestand maximum stock
höhere Programmiersprache high level programming language
Holismus holism
Holografie holography
holografischer Speicher holographic memory
Hologramm hologram
Holsystem pull system
Homomorphismus homomorphism
Homonym homonym
hörbar auditive
horizontale Arbeitsstrukturierung job enlargement
Humanisierung der Arbeit quality of working life
Humanvermögen human asset
hx = halbduplex
hybride Dialogführung hybrid dialog control, semi-structured dialog control
hybride Modellierung hybrid modelling
Hybridrechner hybrid computer
Hypermedia-System hypermedia system
Hypertext hyper text
Hypothese hypothesis
Hypothesenprüfung test of hypothesis

I

IBC = Integrated Broadcast Communications
IBFN = Integriertes Breitband-Fernmeldenetz
IC = Information Center
IC = Integrated Circuit
ICAI = Intelligent Computer Assisted Instructions
ICAM = Integrated Computer Aided Manufacturing
ICASE = Integrated CASE
ICP = Intelligent Copier/Printer
ID = Identification
Ideenbildung ideation
Ideenfindung idea generating
Identifikationsexperiment identification experiment
Identifikationskarte identification card
Identifikationsprüfung identification check
Identifikationsschlüssel identification key
identifizieren identify (to)
Identifizierungsnummer identification number
Identnummer ident number
Identitätsüberprüfung identity verification
IDM = Information Display Matrix
IDMS = Integrated Database Management System
IDN = Integrated Digital Network
IDV = Individuelle Datenverarbeitung
IDV = Integrierte Datenverarbeitung
IE = Industrial Engineering
IE = Information Engineering
IEC = International Electronical Commission
IEEE = Institute of Electrical and Electronics Engineers
IFABO = Internationale Fachmesse für Büroorganisation
IFDN = Integriertes Fernschreib- und Datennetz
IFIP = International Federation for Information Processing
IGES = Initial Graphics Exchange Standard
ikonische Darstellung presentation with icons
ikonische Daten iconological data
Ikonogramm iconograph
IKS = Informations- und Kommunikationssystem
IKS-Abteilung I/S department
IM = Information Management

IMAIL-System = Intelligent Mail-System
IMIS = Integrated Management Information System
IMP = Interface Message Processor
imperative Programmierung imperative programming
implementieren implement (to)
Implementierung implementation
Implementierungsart type of implementation
Implementierungsmethode implementation method
Implementierungsplanung implementation scheduling
Implementierungsreihenfolge changeover sequence
Implementierungssprache implementation language
Implementierungstechnik implementation technique
Implementierungsvorbereitung preparation for implementation
Implementierungszeit implementation time
in Abschnitte zerlegen segment (to)
in Grundstellung bringen reset (to)
in Wartestellung bringen reset (to)
in Wettbewerb treten compete (to)
Indeterminismus indeterminism
Index index
Indexieren indexing
Indexliste subscript
indexsequentielle Dateiorganisation indexed-sequential file organization
indexsequentielle Zugriffsmethode indexed-sequential access method
Indextabelle index table
Indexzahl index figure
indifferente Zielbeziehung indifferent objective relation
Indifferenz indifference
Indikator indicator
indirekte Partizipation indirect participation
indirekte Wissensdarstellung indirect knowledge representation
indirekter Blitzeinschlag indirect lightning
indirektes Positionieren indirect positioning
Individualkommunikation one-to-one communications
Individualsoftware custom tailored software, single user software
Individualziel individual goal
individuelle Informationsverarbeitung personal computing

individuelles Rating individual rating
Individuum individual
indizierte Dateiorganisation indexed file organization
Induktion induction
Induktionssystem induction system
induktives Schlußfolgern inductive inferencing, learning from examples
Industrie industry
Industrieroboter industrial roboter
Inferenz inference
Inferenzmuster inference pattern
Inferenzregel inference rule
Inferenzsystem inference system
infizieren infect (to)
Inflexibilität inflexibility
informale Organisation informal organization
informale Partizipation informal participation
informale Spezifikation informal specification
Informatik Computer Science
Informatikabteilung I/S department
Informatikdienst I/S service
Information information
informationelle Selbstbestimmung information self-determination
Informations- und Kommunikationsfunktion information and communications function
Informations- und Kommunikationsprozeß process of information and communications
Informations- und Kommunikationssystem information and communications system
Informations- und Kommunikationstechnologie information and communications technology
Informationsanbieter information provider
Informationsarchitektur information architecture
Informationsart information type
Informationsaustausch communications, information exchange
Informationsaustauschprozeß information exchange process
Informationsbank information base
Informationsbedarf information requirement
Informationsbedarfsanalyse information requirements analysis
Informationsbedürfnis information need
Informationsberater information advisor
Informationsbeschaffung information procurement
Informationsbewertung information assessment
Informationsblock information cluster
Informationsdeformation information distortion
Informationsdienst information service
Informationseinheit unit of information
Informationserlös information profit
Informationsfluß information flow
Informationsflußdiagramm information flow diagram
Informationsflußmodell information flow model
Informationsfunktion information function
Informationshandel information retailing
Informationshändler information retailer
Informationsinfrastruktur information infrastructure
Informationsintensität information intensity
Informationskategorie information category
Informationskette information chain
Informationsklasse information class
Informationskosten information costs
Informationslogistik information logistics
Informationslücke information gap
Informationsmanagement information resource management
Informationsmanagement-Technik information engineering
Informationsmanager information manager
Informationsmenge amount of information
Informationsmodellierung information modelling
Informationsnachfrage information demand
informationsorientierte Unternehmensführung information-oriented business management
Informationsproduktion information production
Informationsprozeß information process
Informationsrecht information law
Informationsschleuse information gate
Informationsschock information shock
Informationsschutz information protection
Informationsselektion selection of information
Informationssicherheit information security
Informationssicherung information assurance
Informationsspur information trace

Informationsstrategie information strategy
Informationsstrategie-Planung information strategy planning
Informationssystem information system
Informationssystem-Analyse information system analysis
Informationssystem-Architektur information system architecture
Informationssystem-Einführung information system implementation
Informationssystem-Entwicklung information system development
Informationssystem-Entwurf information system design
Informationssystem-Studie information system study
Informationstafel information display matrix
Informationstechnik information technology
informationstechnik-gestützte Heimarbeit telecommuting
Informationstechnologie information technology
informationstechnologische Wirkungsforschung information technology assessment
Informationstheorie information theory
Informationstransfer information transfer
Informationsüberlastung information overload
Informationsübermittlung information transmission
Informationsverarbeiter information processor
Informationsverarbeitung information processing
Informationsverhalten information behavior
Informationsverlust loss of information
Informationsvermittler information broker
Informationsvermittlung information brokering
Informationsverteilung information distribution
Informationswert value of information
Informationswert-Analyse information value analysis
Informationswiedergewinnung information retrieval
Informationswirtschaft information economics
Informationswirtschaftlichkeit information efficiency
Informationswissenschaft Information Science
Informationszeitalter information age
Informationszentrum information center
informelles Berichtssystem grapevine
Infrarotdetektor infrared detector
Infrarotstrahlung infrared radiation
Infrarotübertragung infrared transmission
Infrastruktur infrastructure
Infrastruktur-Planung infrastructure planning
ingangsetzen dispatch (to), start (to)
Ingenieurwissenschaft technics
inhaltliche Validität validity of content
inhaltsadressierbarer Speicher content addressable memory
Inhaltsanalyse analysis of content
Inhaltsüberprüfung content verification
Inhaltsvalidität content validity
Inhaltsverzeichnis directory
initialisieren initialize (to)
inkonsistente Berichterstattung semiconfusion
Inkonsistenz inconsistency
Inkrement increment
inkrementeller Kompilierer incremental compiler
Inline-Dokumentation inline documentation
Inline-Kommentar inline comment
Innenkonflikt internal conflict
innerbetrieblich in-plant
innerbetriebliche Integration in-house integration
innerbetriebliches BTx inhouse BTx
innerbetriebliches System inhouse system
Innovation innovation
Innovationsstrategie innovation strategy
Innovationstechnik innovation technique
Inputmanipulation input manipulation
Input/Output-Analyse input/output analysis
Insellösung insular solution
Inside-Out-Ansatz inside-out approach
Inspektion inspection, preventive maintenance
Instabilität instability
Installation installation
Installationsanleitung installation instructions
Installationsanweisung setup instructions
installieren install (to)
Instandhaltung maintenance
Instruktion instruction
Instrumentierungstechnik instrumentation technique
Integration integration
Integrationsfähigkeit integration ability

Integrationsform

Integrationsform integration mode
Integrationsprinzip integration principle
Integrationstest integration test
Integrationswirkung effect of integration
integrieren integrate (to)
integrierte Datenverarbeitung integrated data processing
integrierte Dokumentation inline documentation
integrierte Schaltung integrated circuit
Integriertes Breitband-Fernmeldenetz Integrated Broadband Telecommunications Network
Integriertes Dienstnetz Integrated Services Network
integriertes Management-Informationssystem integrated management information system
integriertes System integrated system
integriertes Verschlüsselungssystem integrated ciphering system
Integrität integrity
Integritätsbedingung integrity constraint
integritätsbestimmte Dialogführung integrity-checked dialog control
Integritätsüberprüfung integrity verification
intelligent intelligent
intelligente Chipkarte supersmart card
intelligente Datenstation intelligent data terminal
intelligente Karte smart card
intelligenter Kopierer intelligent copier
intelligentes Lehrsystem intelligent courseware
intelligentes Unterstützungssystem intelligent support system
Intelligenz intelligence
Intelsat = International Telecommunications Satellite Organization
interagieren interact (to)
Interaktion interaction
Interaktionsdiagramm interaction diagram
Interaktionssprache interaction language
Interaktionswerkzeug interaction tool
interaktiv interactive
interaktive Programmiersprache interactive programming language
interaktive Programmierung interactive programming
interaktive Testhilfe interactive debugging tool
interaktiver Betrieb interactive mode
interaktives System interactive system
Interdependenz interdependence

interne Brücke internal bridge
interne Daten internal data
interne Operation internal operation
interne Revision internal auditing
interner Speicher internal storage, internal memory
interner Wiederanlauf internal restart
internes Schema internal model, internal schema
Interpretierer interpreter
Interviewmethode interviewing method
Interviewtechnik interviewing technique
Intransparenz intransparency
Intrusion intrusion
Intrusionsmeldeanlage intrusion signal facility
Intrusionsschutz intrusion protection
Intrusionstechnik intrusion technology
INVAS = Integriertes Verfahren zur Aufwandschätzung von Software-Entwicklungen
Inventur inventory, stock taking
invertieren invert (to)
invertierte Darstellung inverted presentation
invertierte Datei inverted file
Investition investment
Investitionskosten investment costs
IOCS = Input/Output Control System
Ionendrucker ion printer
IPL = Initial Program Load
IPO = Input/Processing/Output
IPO-Diagramm = Input/Processing/Output-Diagramm
IPSE = Integrated Project Support Environment
IRM = Information Resource Management
IRM-Committee = Information Resource Management Committee
IS = Informations System
IS = Integrierte Schaltung
IS-Architektur = Informationssystem-Architektur
I/S Management = Information Systems Management
ISAM = Indexed Sequential Access Method
ISDN = Integrated Services Digital Network
ISDOS = Information System Design and Optimization System
ISN = Integrated Services Network
ISO = International Organization for Standardization
ISO-Architekturmodell ISO architecture model

ISO-Referenzmodell ISO reference model
ISO-Schichtenmodell ISO layer model
ISO-7-Bit-Code ISO-7-bit code
Isomorphismus isomorphism
ISP = Information Strategy Planning
ISPBX = Integrated Services Private Branch Exchange
ISS = Information System Study
ISS = Intelligent Support System
Ist-Datenfluß current data flow
Istanalyse analysis of current system
Istaufnahme survey of current system
Istkosten actual costs
Istportfolio actual portfolio
Istsystem current system
Istwert actual value
Istzustand current system, existing system, status
Istzustandsanalyse analysis of current system
Istzustandserfassung survey of current system
Istzustandserhebung investigation of current system
Istzustandsoptimierung optimizing of current system
istzustandsorientierter Ansatz current system-based approach
Istzustandsuntersuchung study of current system
IT = Informationstechnik
IT = Intrusionstechnik
Iteration iteration
Iterationsschleife iteration loop
iterative Verfeinerung iterative refinement
ITG = Informationstechnische Gesellschaft
ITU = International Telecommunication Union
IuK = Information und Kommunikation

J

Jackson-Diagramm Jackson diagram
Jackson-Methode Jackson design methodology
JAD = **Joint Application Design**
Jahresplan annual plan
jährliche Betriebskosten annual operating costs
JCL = **Job Control Language**
JDS = **Job Diagnostic Survey**
JiT = **Just-in-Time**
Job-Control-Sprache job control language
Jobabrechnung job accounting
Jobauswahl job option
Jobkette job chain, series of jobs
Jobname job name
Jobwarteschlange job queue
JSD = **Jackson Structured Design**
JSP = **Jackson Structured Programming**
JURIS = **Juristisches Informationssystem**
juristische Integration legal integration
Just-in-Time-Produktion just-in-time production
justieren adjust (to)

K

K-Fall = Katastrophenfall
K-Schnittstelle K-interface
Kabel cable
Kabelanschluß cable connection
Kabelfernsehen cable television
Kabelkanal cable duct, conduit
Kabelnetz cable network
Kabeltext cable text
Kabelverlegung cable laying
Kalendermanagement calendering
Kalibrierung calibration
Kalkül calculus
Kalkulation calculation
Kalkülsprache calculus language
kalter Systemstart cold systems start
kalter Wiederanlauf cold restart
kaltes Ausweich-Rechenzentrum cold backup computing center
kaltes Ausweich-Rechenzentrum empty-shell backup computing center
Kaltstart cold start
Kanal channel
Kanalbefehl channel command
Kanalkapazität channel capacity
Kante edge
Kantenmodell edge model
Kapazität capacity
Kapazitätsauslastung capacity utilization
Kapazitätsengpaß capacity bottleneck
Kapazitätsmanagement capacity management
Kapazitätsplan capacity plan
Kapazitätsplanung capacity planning
Kapazitätsterminierung capacity scheduling
Kapazitätsüberwachung capacity monitoring, overflow indication
Kapsel capsule
kardinale Skala cardinal scale
Karriere career
Karriereplanung career planning
Karteikarte index card
Karteikasten card-index box
kartengesteuertes Zahlungssystem card-driven payment system
kartenprogrammierbarer Rechner card programmable calculator
kartographische Anwendung cartographic application
Kassenterminal point of sale terminal
Kassette cartridge
Kassettenlaufwerk cartridge drive
Katalogeintragung catalog entry
Katastrophe catastrophe, disaster
Katastrophenmanagement disaster management
Katastrophenplan contingency plan, disaster plan
Katastrophenschutz disaster protection
Kathodenstrahlröhre cathode ray tube
Kaufschein certificate of purchase
Kausaldiagramm causal diagram
Kausalität causality
KB = Kilobyte
Kbit = Kilobit
KBS = Knowledge-Based System
KDBS = Kompatible Datenbankschnittstelle
KDCS = Kompatible Datenkommunikationsschnittstelle
KEF = Kritischer Erfolgsfaktor
Keller stack
Kellerspeicher stack memory
Kellerzähler stack pointer
Kenndaten characteristics
Kennsatz header, label
Kenntnis awareness
Kennwort lock word, password
Kennwort für Lesen read password
Kennwortdatei security file
Kennzahl standard figure
Kennzahlenanalyse standard figure analysis
Kennzahlensystem standard figure system
Kennzeichen flag
Kennzeichenbit flag bit
Kennzeichner qualifier
Kennziffer standard digit
Kern core, kernel
Kernbereich core area
Kernprogramm nucleus
Kerntätigkeit core activity
Kette chain
Kettendrucker belt printer
Kettenspur pointer array
KI = Künstliche Intelligenz
KI-Programmierung AI programming
Kimball-Etikette Kimball tag
KIP = Knowledge Information Processing
KIPS = Kilo Instructions Per Second
Kiviath-Graph Kiviath graph
Klammer bracket, paranthesis
Klarheit clarity
Klarschriftbeleg OCR document
Klarschriftleser OCR document reader
Klarschriftzeichen optical character
Klartext plain text
klassifizieren classify (to)

klassifizierender Schlüssel classification key
Klassifizierung classification, taxonomy
Klassifizierungsnummer classification number
klassische Ergonomie classical ergonomics
Kleinbuchstabe lower case character
Klimaanlage air conditioning system
Klimatisierung air conditioning
Klone clone
Klumpen cluster
KMS = Knowledge Management System
KNA = Kosten/Nutzen-Analyse
Knoten node
Knotenrechner interface message processor
K.-o.-Kriterium k.o. criterion, mandadory feature
Koaxialkabel coaxial cable, coax
Koeffizient coefficient
Kognition cognition
Kognitionswissenschaft cognitive science
kognitiv cognitive
kognitive Benutzerschnittstelle cognitive user interface
kognitive Dissonanz cognitive dissonance
kognitive Ergonomie cognitive ergonomics
kognitive Modellierung cognitive modelling
kognitiver Entscheidungsstil cognitive decision style
kognitiver Prozeß cognitive process
kollektives Rating collective rating
Kollision collision
Kolumne column
kombinatorische Optimierung combinatorial optimization
kombinatorische Suche combinatorial search
kombinierte Verschlüsselungsmethode combined ciphering method
kombinierter Verteilungsschlüssel combined costs distribution key
Kommando command
Kommandodatei command file
Kommandomodus command mode
Kommandosprache command language, job control language
Kommandosteuerung command control
Kommentar comment
kommentieren comment (to)
kommerzielle Datenverarbeitung business data processing
Kommunikation communications

Kommunikationsanalyse communications analysis
Kommunikationsdiagramm communications diagram
Kommunikationseigenschaft communications attribute
Kommunikationseinheit communications device
Kommunikationsergonomie communications ergonomics
Kommunikationsforschung communications research
Kommunikationsintegration communications integration
Kommunikationslücke communications gap
Kommunikationsmatrix communications matrix
Kommunikationsnetz communications network
Kommunikationsprotokoll communications protocol
Kommunikationsprozeß communications process
Kommunikationsrechner front-end processor
Kommunikationsserver communications server
Kommunikationsspinne communications chart
Kommunikationssubsystem communications subsystem
Kommunikationssystem communications system
Kommunikationssystem-Studie communications system study
Kommunikationstabelle communications table
Kommunikationstechnik communications technology
Kommunikationsverbund communications group
Kommunikationsverhalten communications behavior
kommunizieren communicate (to)
Kompaktkassette compact cassette
Kompaktplatte compact disk
kompatibel compatible
Kompatibilität compatibility
Kompetenz competence
Kompilierer compiler
komplementäre Zielbeziehung complementary objective relation
komplexe Verschlüsselungsmethode complex ciphering method
komplexer Entscheidungsstil complex decision style

konzeptionelles Modellieren

komplexer Objekttyp complex entity type
Komplexität complexity
Kompliziertheit difficulty
Komponente component
Komponentenliste list of components
Komponententest module test
Komposition composition
komprimieren compress (to)
Komprimierung compression
Komprimierungsmethode compression method
Konferenz conference
Konferenz-Interview-Technik conference interview technique
Konferenzgespräch conference conversation
Konferenzschaltung conference call, conference switching
Konferenztechnik conferencing
Konfiguration configuration
Konfigurationsdiagramm configuration diagram
Konfigurationsmanagement configuration management
Konfigurationsmanager configuration manager
konfigurieren configurate (to)
Konflikt conflict
konfliktäre Zielbeziehung conflictary objective relation
Konfliktmanagement conflict management
Konfliktpotential conflict potential
Konformität conformity
Kongreß conference
Konjunktion conjunction
Konkurrent competitor
Konkurrenz competition
Konkurrenzfähigkeit competitiveness
Konkurrenzkraft competitive force
Konkurrenzposition competitive position
konkurrieren compete (to)
Konnektivität connectivity
konsensorientierter Ansatz socio-technical approach
Konsequenz consequence
Konsequenzanalyse analysis of consequences
Konsistenz consistency
Konsistenzfehler consistency fault
Konsistenzregel consistency rule
Konsole console
konsolidierte Entscheidungstabelle consolidated decision table
Konsolidierung consolidation
Konsoloperator console operator
Konstante constant
konstruiertes Gebilde construct

Konstrukt construct
Konstruktionszeichner draftsman
Konstruktvalidität construct validity
Kontaktbildschirm touch sensitive screen
Kontengliederung account classification
kontenorientierte Verarbeitung accounting-oriented processing
Kontenplan chart of accounts
Kontext context
Kontextdiagramm context diagram
Kontingenzanalyse contingency analysis
Konto account
Kontoauszug account statement
Kontoauszugsdrucker account statement printer
Kontokorrent account current
Kontomat automatic teller machine
Kontonummer account number
Kontostand account balance
Kontrast contrast
Kontrollbit check bit
Kontrolle checking
Kontrollebene level of control
Kontrollfluß flow of control
Kontrollfunktion control function
kontrollieren check (to), control (to)
kontrollierter Abbruch controlled cancellation
Kontrollinformation control information
Kontrollmodus control mode
Kontrollpfad control path
Kontrollspeicher control storage
Kontrollstruktur control structure
Kontrollsumme audit total, check sum
Kontrollsystem control system
Kontrolltaste CTRL key
Kontrollzahl check digit
konventioneller Ansatz conventional approach
konvergierender Entscheidungsstil convergent decision style
Konversationssystem conversational system
konvertieren convert (to)
Konvivialität conviviality
Konzentration concentration
Konzentrator concentrator
Konzentrierung concentration
konzeptionell conceptual
konzeptionelle Datenstruktur conceptual data structure
konzeptionelles Datenmodell conceptual data model
konzeptionelles Modell conceptual model
konzeptionelles Modellieren conceptual modelling

konzeptionelles Schema

konzeptionelles Schema conceptual schema
Konzeptqualität draft quality
konzeptuell conceptual
konzeptueller Entwurf conceptual design
konzeptuelles Wissen conceptual knowledge
Kooperation co-operation
Kooperationsunterstützung co-operation aid
kooperatives Dialogsystem co-operative dialog system
kooperatives Dialogverhalten co-operative dialog behavior
Koordinatenschreiber plotter
Koordination co-ordination
Koordinationsfähigkeit co-ordination ability
Koordinator co-ordinator
Koordinierungsgrad degree of co-ordination
Kopfsegement root segment
Kopfzeile header
Kopie copy
Kopie des Bildschirminhalts hard copy of screen
Kopienzähler copy counter
kopieren copy (to)
Kopierer copier
Kopiergerät copy equipment
Kopiermanagement copy management
Kopierprogramm copy program
Kopierschutz copy protection
Kopierstop copy stop
Koppler coupler
KOPS = Kilo Operations Per Second
Korrektheit correctness
Korrelationsanalyse correlation analysis
Korrelationsmatrix correlation matrix
Korrespondenzdrucker letter quality printer
korrigierende Arbeitsgestaltung corrective job design
korrigierende Wartung corrective maintenance
Kosten costs
Kosten- und Leistungsrechnung cost accounting
Kostenabbau cost reduction, cost cut
Kostenabschätzung cost assessment
Kostenanalyse cost analysis
Kostenanteil share of costs
Kostenart cost item
Kostenartenrechnung cost item accounting, cost item measurement
Kostenausgleich cost equalization
Kostenbeteiligung cost sharing

kostenbewußt cost-conscious
Kostenerhöhung increase in costs
Kostenerstattung refund of costs
Kostenfaktor cost factor
Kostenführerschaft cost leadership
Kostenfunktion cost function
Kostenhöhe amount of costs
Kosten/Kosten-Analyse cost/cost analysis
Kosten/Nutzen-Analyse cost/benefit analysis
Kosten/Nutzen-Technik cost/benefit technique
Kosten/Nutzen-Verhältnis cost/benefit ratio
Kosten/Wert-Analyse cost/value analysis
Kosten/Wirksamkeits-Analyse cost/effectiveness analysis
Kostenrechnung costing
Kostenschätzung estimation of costs, cost estimate
Kostenstellenrechnung cost center measurement
Kostenstruktur cost structure
Kostenteilung cost sharing
Kostenträgerrechnung cost accounting
Kostenüberwachung cost control
Kostenumlage cost allocation, cost distribution
Kostenvergleichsrechnung cost comparison measurement
Kostenverlagerung cost displacement
Kostenvermeidung cost avoidance
Kostenverrechnung cost chargeout, cost chargeback
Kostenverschiebung cost displacement
Kostenverteilung cost allocation
Kostenverteilungsschlüssel cost allocation key
Kostenvoranschlag estimate of costs, quotation
Kostenvorsprung cost lead
Kostenwirksamkeit cost effectiveness
Kostenwirtschaftlichkeit cost efficiency
KOZ = Kürzeste Operationszeit
KR = Knowledge Representation
kreativ creative
Kreativität creativity
Kreativitätstechnik creativity technique
Kreditoren accounts payables
Kreditorenbuchführung creditor accounting
Kreisdiagramm circle diagram
Kreiskausalität circular causality
Kreuz-Kompilierer cross compiler
Kreuz-Referenz-Liste cross reference list
Krisenmanagement crisis management

kriterienbezogene Validität criteria validity
Kriteriengewicht criteria weight
Kriterienkatalog criteria list
Kriterium criterion
Kritik criticism
kritischer Defekt critical defect
kritischer Erfolgsfaktor critical success factor
kritischer Fehler critical error
kritischer Vorgang critical event
kritischer Weg critical path
kritischer Wettbewerbsfaktor critical competition factor
Kryo-Computer kryo computer
Krypto-Hardware-Einheit crypto hardware device
Kryptoalgorithmus crypto algorithm
Kryptoanalyse crypto analysis
Kryptographie cryptography
kryptographische Verschlüsselungsmethode cryptographic ciphering technique
Kryptologie cryptology
KSR = Keyboard Send Receive
KSS = Kommunikationssubsystem
Kugelkopf spherical printhead
Kultur culture
Kunde customer
Kundenanpassung customization
Kundenauftrag customer order
Kundendienst customer service
Kundendienst-Informationssystem service information system
Kundenkonto customer account
kundenspezifisch customized
kundenspezifische integrierte Schaltung customer dependent integrated circuit
Kundenunterstützung customer support
Künstliche Intelligenz artificial intelligence
Kunstsprache artificial language
Kursivschrift italic
Kurvendiagramm curve diagram
Kurvenleser curve digitizer
Kurvenschreiber plotter
Kurzbeschreibung quick reference chart
Kurzdarstellung abstract
Kürze conciseness
kurzfristige Planung short-range planning
Kurzname short name
Kurzschluß short circuit
Kurzwahl compact dialing
Kurzwahltabelle abbreviation dialing list
Kurzzeitgedächtnis short time memory
Kybernetik cybernetics
kybernetisches Denken cybernetic thinking
kybernetisches Prinzip cybernetic principle

L

Labilität instability
Laborexperiment laboratory experiment
ladefähiges Programm loadable program
laden load (to), boot (to)
Lader loader
Ladeprogramm loader
Ladungstransport-Speicher charge coupled device
Lager warehouse
Lagerabgang inventory depletion
Lagerbestand stock
Lagerbewegung inventory activity
Lagerhaltung inventory management
Lagerhaltungskosten inventory holding costs
Lagersteuerung stock control
Lagerumschlag inventory turnover, stock turnover
Lagerzugang stock receipt
Laienmodus novice mode
LAN = Local Area Network
Landen headcrash
langfristige Planung long range planning
Langzeitgedächtnis long time memory
Lärmschutz noise protection
Laser = Light Amplification of Stimulated Emission of Radiation
Laserdrucker laser printer
Laserkarte laser card
Laserplatte laser disk
Laserstrahl laser beam
Lasertechnik laser technology
Lastprofil workload
Lastverbund load sharing
Latenzzeit latency time
laufende Betriebskosten ongoing running costs, ongoing operating costs
Lauf-Längen-Komprimierung run time compression
lauffähiges System runable system
Laufvariable control variable
Laufwerk drive
Laufzeit run time, running period
Laufzettel interoffice slip, routing slip
LCD = Liquid Crystal Display
LCD-Tastatur LCD keyboard
LCS = Liquid Crystal Shutter
LCS-Drucker LCS printer
LDV = Linguistische Datenverarbeitung
Lebensfähigkeit viability
Lebenszyklus life cycle
Lebenszyklus-Analyse life cycle analysis
Lebenszyklus-Management life cycle management

Lebenszyklus-Modell life cycle model
LED = Light Emitting Diode
Leerdiskette scratch floppy disk
Leerkapazität underload, spare capacity
Leerkosten dead costs
Leerschritt space
Leerspalte blank column
Leerstelle blank
Leertaste space bar
Leerzeichen blank character
Leerzeile blank line
Legalisireung authentication
Lehrprogramm tutorial program
leisten perform (to)
Leistung performance
Leistungsabfall decline of performance
Leistungsanalyse performance analysis
Leistungsanforderung performance requirement
Leistungsanreiz incentive
Leistungsbereitschaft performability
Leistungsbewertung performance evaluation
Leistungsbeurteilung performance appraisal
Leistungsdaten performance characteristics
Leistungserstellung production
Leistungsfähigkeit performance ability, productivity
Leistungsgrad performance level
Leistungskenngröße performance index
Leistungskennzahl performance measure
Leistungskriterium performance criterion
Leistungsmerkmal performance attribute
Leistungsmessung performance measurement
Leistungsmotivation achievement motivation
Leistungsnorm standard of performance
Leistungsprinzip performance principle
Leistungsprofil performance specification
Leistungsstandard performance standard
Leistungssteigerung increase in performance
Leistungssynthese performance synthesis
Leistungstest performance test
Leistungsverbund performance link, performance comparison
Leistungsvergleich benchmark
Leistungsvergleichstest benchmark test
Leistungsverlust drop in performance, loss of performance
Leistungsverstärker power amplifier
Leistungsziel performance objective
Leitbild model
Leiteinrichtung control equipment

leitender Angestellter executive
Leiterplatte board
Leitrechner control computer
Leitsatz pilot record, header record
Leitung line
Leitungsanschluß communications driver
Leitungsausnutzung line efficiency
Leitungsgebühr line charge
Leitungsunterbrechung disconnection
leitungsvermittelndes Netz circuit-switching network
Leitungsvermittlung line switching, circuit switching
Leitungsverschlüsselung line ciphering
Leitwerk control unit
LEMP = Lightning Explosion Magnetic Power
Lenkungsausschuß steering committee
Lernbarkeit learnability
Lernen learning
Lernprogramm courseware
lesbar legible
Lesbarkeit legibility, readability
Lese-/Schreibkopf read/write head
Lese-/Schreibspeicher read/write memory
Lesekopf read head
Lesepistole hand held scanner
Lesestift read pen
letztes Abgangsdatum last issue
Leuchtdichte luminescense
Leuchtdiode light emitting diode
Leuchtknopf lens
Leuchtstärke luminosity
Leuchtstift light pen
lexikographische Ordnung lexical order
LF = Line Feed
Licht emittierende Diode light emitting diode
Lichtempfindlichkeit light sensitivity
Lichtgriffel light stylus
Lichtstift light pen, electronic stylus
Lichtstifteingabe light pen detect
Lichtstrahl light beam
Lichtwelle light wave
Lichtwellenleiter fiber optics, optical fiber
Lieferangebot bid
Lieferant supplier, vendor
Lieferantenauswahl vendor selection
Lieferantenunterstützung vendor support
Lieferantenvorschlag vendor proposal
Lieferbereitschaft customer service level
Lieferbeschaffenheit delivery service quality
Lieferflexibilität delivery service flexibility
Lieferservice delivery service

Lieferung delivery
Lieferzeit delivery time
LIFO = Last In First Out
Limitierungskriterium limitational criterion
lineare Optimierung linear optimization
Linguistik linguistics
linguistische Datenverarbeitung linguistic data processing
Liniendiagramm line chart
Linienmanagement line management
Linienmodell line model
linksbündig left aligned, left justified
LIPS = Logical Inferences Per Second
Liquiditätsfrühwarnung liquidity early warning
LISP = List Processing Language
LISP-Maschine LISP machine
Liste list
Listenoperation list operation
Listenverarbeitung list processing
Literaturanalyse analysis of literature
Lizenz licence
Lizenzprogramm licence program
LMS = Logico Mathematical Structur
LoB = Line of Business
LoC = Line of Code
Lochstreifen punched tape
Log-Datei log file
Logbuch log
Logik logic
Logikdiagramm logic diagram
logisch logical
logische Beschreibung logical description
logische Bombe logical bomb
logische Datendefinitionssprache logical data definition language
logische Datensicherungsmaßnahme logical data security measure
logische Datensicht logical data view
logische Datenstruktur logical data structure
logische Datenstrukturierung logical data structuring
logische Datenunabhängigkeit logical data independence
logische Ebene logical level
logische Kette logical chain
logische Programmierung logical programming
logische Validität logical validity
logische Wissensdarstellung logical knowledge representation
logischer Entwurf logical design
logischer Informationssystem-Entwurf logical information systems design
logischer Satz logical record

logischer Speicher logical memory
logisches Datenflußdiagramm logical data flow diagram
logisches Datenmodell logical data model
logisches Löschen logical deletion
logisches Modell logical model
logisches Testen logical testing
Logistik logistics
Logistik-Informationssystem logistics information system
Logistikdenken logistics philosophy
Logistikkette logistics chain
Logistiksystem logistics system
Logogramm logogram
Lohn- und Gehaltsverrechnung payroll accounting
lokal local
Lokalbetrieb local mode
lokale Ausgabe local output
lokale Brücke local bridge
lokaler Bereich local area
lokales Netz local area network
Lokalisierung localization
Lokalität locality
löschbare Kompaktplatte compact disk erasable
löschbarer Festwertspeicher erasable programmable read only memory
löschbarer Speicher erasable storage
löschen delete (to)
löschendes Lesen destructive readout
Löschtaste back space key
Löschungsrecht deletion privilege
Losgröße lot quantity, batch size
Lösung solution
Lösungsansatz solution approach
Lösungsmethode solution method
Lösungsweg solution procedure
LOTOS = Language Of Temporal Ordering Specification
LOZ = Längste Operationszeit
LPC = Linear Predictive Coding
LPS = Lines Per Second
LQ = Letter Quality
LSI = Large Scale Integration
Lücke gap
Lückenanalyse gap analysis
LWL = Lichtwellenleiter

M

m:1-Beziehung many-to-one relationship
m:n-Beziehung many-to-many relationship
Machbarkeitsstudie feasibility study
Macht power
Mächtigkeit magnitude, power
Magnetband magnetic tape
Magnetband-Clearing-Verfahren magnetic tape clearing
Magnetbandkassette cartridge
Magnetbandlaufwerk magnetic tape deck
Magnetbandsicherung magnetic tape security
Magnetbandspeicher magnetic tape storage
Magnetbandverwaltung magnetic tape management
Magnetblasenspeicher magnetic bubble memory
Magnetdrucker magnetic printer
magnetische Aufzeichnung magnetic recording
magnetischer Konstanthalter line conditioner
magnetisches Aufzeichnungsverfahren magnetic recording technique
Magnetkarte magnetic card
Magnetkartenspeicher magnetic card memory
Magnetkonto magnetic ledger card feature
Magnetplatte magnetic disk
Magnetplattenspeicher magnetic disk memory
Magnetplattenstapel magnetic disk pack
Magnetplattenverwaltung magnetic disk management
Magnetschichtspeicher magnetic layer memory
Magnetschriftleser magnetic writing reader
Magnetstreifenkarte magnetic stripe card
Magnettinte magnetic ink
MAI = Marketing-Informationssystem
Makro macro
Makrobefehl macro instruction
Makrokommando macro command
MAN = Metropolitan Area Network
Management management
Management-Informationssystem management information system
Management-Potential-Analyse management potential analysis
Management-Unterstützungssystem management support system
Managementgraphik management graphics
Managementlehre management science
Managementprinzip management principle
Managementtechnik management technique
Mandantensystem mandant system
Mannjahr man year
manuelles Verfahren manual procedure
MAP = Manufacturing Automation Protocol
Marke label, token
Marketing-Informationssystem marketing information system
Markierer marker
Markierungsbeleg mark sensing document, mark sheet
Markierungsleser mark sensing reader
Marktanteil market share
Marktforschung market research
Masche mesh
Maschennetz mesh network
Maschentopologie mesh topology
Maschine machine
Maschine-Maschine-Kommunikation machine-machine-communications
maschinelles Lernen machine learning
Maschinenbefehl machine instruction
Maschinencode machine code
Maschinenfehler hardware malfunction
Maschinenlernen machine learning
maschinenlesbar machine-readable
Maschinennummer machine serial number
maschinenorientiert machine-oriented
maschinenorientierte Programmiersprache computer-oriented programming language
Maschinenprogramm machine language program
Maschinensprache machine language
Maschinenstundensatz machine hour rate
Maske mask
Maskengenerator mask generator
Maskengestaltung mask design
Maskenkennzeichnung mask identification
Maskenprogrammierung mask programming
Maskenprüfung picture check
Maskentechnik mask technique
maskieren mask (to)
Massendaten mass data
Massenkabel ground wire
Massenkommunikation mass communications

Massenspeicher mass memory, mass store
Maßnahme activity, measure
Maßsystem measure system
MAT-System = Mensch-Aufgabe-Technik-System
Material- und Warenfluß materials flow
Materialausgabe materials distribution, materials delivering
Materialbedarfsplanung material requirements planning
Materialbewirtschaftung materials management
Materialverbrauch consumption of material
mathematisches Modell mathematical model
Matrix matrix
Matrix-Projektorganisation matrix-project organization
Matrixanalyse matrix analysis
Matrixdrucker matrix printer
Matrixdruckwerk matrix printing device
Matrixorganisation matrix organization
Matrizendarstellung matrix representation
Matrizenkalkül matrix calculus
Matrizenschreibweise matrix notation
Maus mouse
Mauszeiger mouse pointer
MBA = Master of Business Administration
MBI = Master of Business Information
Mbit = Megabit
MBMS = Model Base Management System
MbO = Management by Objectives
MbS = Management by Strategies
Mbyte = Megabyte
MCBF = Mean Computation Before Failure
MCD = Master Clerical Data
MCI = Mensch-Computer-Interaktion
MCP = Master Control Program
MDE = Mobile Datenerfassung
mechanische Maus mechanical mouse
mechanischer Drucker impact printer
mechanistisches Modell mechanistic model
Medienbruch-Analyse media clash analysis
Medium medium
Mehraufwand overhead
Mehrbenutzerbetrieb multi-user mode
Mehrbenutzersystem multi-user system
Mehrebenenmodell multi-level model

mehrfach programmierbarer Festwertspeicher reprogrammable read only memory
Mehrfacharbeitsplatz multiple work station
Mehrfachaufforderung multiple requesting
Mehrfachauswahl multiple choice
Mehrfachbenutzung multiple usage
mehrfache Datenhaltung replicated data base
Mehrfachfehler multiple error
Mehrfachformularsatz multiple-part forms
Mehrfachkopien multiple copies
Mehrfachnutzung multiplexing
Mehrfachverbindung multiple connection
Mehrfachverwendung multiple usage
Mehrfachzugriff multiple access
Mehrfarbendrucker multi-color printer
mehrfunktional multifunctional
mehrfunktionaler Arbeitsplatz multifunctional workplace
Mehrhersteller multi-vendor
Mehrhersteller-Umgebung multi-vendor environment
Mehrkosten-Versicherung cost overrun insurance
mehrmediales Dokument multi-medial document
mehrorganisationales Anwendungssystem multi-organizational application system
Mehrplatzsystem multi-station system
Mehrprogrammbetrieb multi-programming mode
Mehrprogrammverarbeitung multi-programming
Mehrprozessorsystem multi-processor system
Mehrpunktverbindung multi-point connection
Mehrrechnersystem multi-computer system
Mehrschriftendrucker multifont printer
Mehrschriftenleser multifont reader
mehrsprachige Software multilingual software
Mehrstufenrating multi-stage rating
mehrstufiges Pop-up-Menü multistep pop-up menu
Mehrwegverschlüsselung multiple way ciphering
Mehrwert added value
Mehrwertdienst value added service
Mehrwertdienst-Netz value added network
Meilenstein milestone, cornerstone

Meinungsumfrage opinion poll
Melder warning device
Meldevermittlung message switching
Meldung message
Menge set
Mengengerüst quantity requirements
Mengenstaffel quantity discount
Mensch man, human
Mensch-Computer-Interaktion man computer interaction
Mensch-Computer-Schnittstelle man computer interface
Mensch-Maschine-Kommunikation man-machine communications
Mensch-Maschine-Schnittstelle man-machine interface
Menschenführung human resource management
mental mental
Mentale-Modelle-Forschung mental models research
mentales Modell mental model
mentales Ziel mental objective
Menü menu
Menüauswahl menu selection
menügesteuert menu-based, menu-controlled, menu-driven
Menümaske menu mask
Menüselektionstechnik menu selection technique
Menüsteuerung menu control
Menütyp menu type
Merkmal characteristic, feature
Merkmalanalyse feature analysis
Merkname mnemonic name
meßbar measurable
meßbare Kosten measurable costs
meßbarer Nutzen measurable benefits
Meßbedingung condition of measurement
Meßbereich effective range
Messe exhibition
messen measure (to)
Meßergebnis measuring result
Meßfehler measuring error
Meßfühler sensor
Meßgenauigkeit accuracy of measurement
Meßgerät measuring device
Meßgröße measuring figure
Meßinstrument measuring tool
Meßmethode measuring technique
Meßobjekt measuring entity
Meßort measuring point
Meßprogramm measuring program
Meßpunkt measuring point
Meßskala measuring scale, scale of measurement
Meßstation measuring platform
Meßtauglichkeit validity
Meßtheorie measuring theory
Messung measurement
Meßvorschrift measuring procedure
Meßwert measuring value
Meßziel measuring goal
meta meta
Metadaten meta data
Metakommunikation meta communications
Metapher metaphor
Metasoftware meta software
Metasprache meta language
Metasystem shell
Metawissen meta knowledge
Methode method, technique
Methode der Leistungsmessung performance measurement technique
Methode der parametrischen Schätzgleichungen method of parametric estimate equation
Methode des kritischen Wegs critical path method
methoden-orientiertes Programmieren method-oriented programming
Methodenadministrator methods administrator
Methodenanalyse methods analysis
Methodenbank methods base
Methodenbanksystem methods base system
Methodenbankverwaltungssystem methods base management system
Methodenbasis methods base
Methodenbeschreibungssprache methods description language
Methodenintegration methods integration
Methodenmangel methods deficiency
Methodenmodell methods model
Methodensystem methods system
Methodenverwaltungssystem methods management system
Methodik methodology
Methodik Systemplanung systems planning methodology
methodisches Verfahren methodism
Metra-Potential-Methode metra potential method
MFA = Mittlerer Fehlerabstand
MFLOPS = Million Floating Point Operations Per Second
MFM = Modified Frequency Modulation
MHS = Message Handling System
MIC = Microwave Integrated Circuit
MIDAS = Management Information Dataflow System

mieten lease (to), rent (to)
Mietgerät leased equipment
Mietschein lease certificate
Mietvertrag lease contract
mikro micro
Mikrobefehl micro instruction
Mikrochip microchip
Mikrochip-Schutzgesetz Semiconductor Chip Protection Act
Mikrocodeschutz microcode protection
Mikrocomputer microcomputer
Mikrofiche microfiche
Mikrofilm microfilm
Mikrofilmgerät microfilm device
Mikrofilmleser microfilm reader
Mikroprogramm microprogram
Mikroprogramm-Speicher microprogram memory
Mikroprogrammierung microprogramming
Mikroprozessor microprocessor
Mikroverfilmung microfilming
Mikrowellen-Identifikation microwave identification
mikrowellenintegrierte Schaltung microwave integrated circuit
milli milli
MIMD = Multiple Instruction/Multiple Data
Mindestbearbeitungszeit minimum run time
Mindestbestand minimum stock
MIPS = Million Instructions Per Second
MIS = Management Information System
Mischung mix
Mißbrauchversicherung insurance against abuse
Mitarbeit cooperation, collaboration
mitbestimmen codetermine (to)
Mitbestimmung codetermination
Mitbestimmungsgesetz Codetermination Act
Mitbestimmungsrecht right of codetermination
Mitbewerber competitor
Mitglied member
Mitteilung notification
Mitteilungsrating message rating
Mittel medium
Mittelwert mean value
mittlere Reparaturzeit meantime to repair
mittlere Zeitspanne zwischen Ausfällen meantime between failures
mittlere Zugriffszeit average access time, mean access time
mittlerer Fehler mean error

mittlerer Fehlerabstand average fault distance
mitwirken participate (to)
Mitwirkender participant
Mitwirkung participation
MMH = Multimoment-Häufigkeits-Zählverfahren
MMZ = Multimoment-Zeit-Meßverfahren
Mnemotechnik mnemonics
mnemotechnische Abkürzung mnemonic abbreviation
MNP = Microcom Networking Protocol
mobile Datenerfassung mobile data collection
mobile Kommunikation mobile communications
mobiler Speicher portable memory
Modell model, version
Modellanwendung application of model
modellbildender Ansatz modelling approach
Modellbildung modelling
Modelldarstellung model representation
Modellentwicklung model development
Modellentwurf model design
Modellexperiment model experiment
Modellgenerierungssystem model generating system
Modellieren modelling
modellierender Benutzer modelling end-user
Modellprinzip model principle
Modelltyp model type
Modellvertrag prototype contract
Modem = Modulator/Demodulator
Moderator moderator
Modifizierbarkeit modifiability
Modul module
modulare Programmierung modular programming
Modularisierung modularization
Modularisierungsprinzip module principle
Modularität modularity
Modularprogramm modular program
Modulation modulation
Modulentwurf module design
modulieren modulate (to)
Modulo-N-Kontrolle modulo n check
Modulo-Verfahren modulo method
Modultest module testing
Modus mode
Modusfehler mode error
Möglichkeit alternative
Momentum-Strategie momentum strategy
monochromer Bildschirm monochrome screen

monotones Schlußfolgern monotonic inferencing
Montageband assembly line
Monte-Carlo-Analyse Monte Carlo analysis
MOPS = Million Operations Per Second
morphologische Analyse morphological analysis
morphologischer Kasten morphological box
MOS = Metal Oxide Semiconductor
Mosaikdrucker mosaic printer
Mosaikgraphik mosaic graphics
MOSFET = Metal Oxide Semi-Conductor Field Effect Transistor
Motiv motive
Motivation motivation
motivational-konativer Prozeß motivational-conative process
motivieren motivate (to)
MPA = Management Potential Analysis
MPM = Metra Potential Method
mpx = multiplex
MRP = Materials Requirement Planning
MS-DOS = Microsoft Disk Operating System
MSI = Medium Scale Integration
MSS = Management Support System
MTBF = Mean Time Between Failures
MTBM = Meantime Between Malfunctions
MTM = Methods Time Measurement
MTTF = Mean Time To Failure
MTTR = Mean Time To Repair

Multimoment-Häufigkeits-Zählverfahren repeating frequency counting
Multimoment-Zeit-Meßverfahren repeating time measurement
Multimomentstudie work sampling
multiples Menü multiple menu
Multiplexbetrieb multiplex operation, multiplexing
Multiplexkanal multiplex channel
Multiplikatormethode multiplier technique
multivariable Prognose multivariable forecasting
MUMPS = Massachusetts General Hospital Utility Multiprogramming System
mündliche Befragung oral questioning
MUPID = Mehrzweck Universell Programmierbarer Intelligenter Decoder
Muß-Anforderung mandatory requirement
Muß-Kriterium kill criterion, mandatory criterion
Mußfeld mandatory field
Muster pattern, specimen
Mustererkennung pattern recognition
Musterimplementierung implementation of prototype
Mustervergleich pattern matching
Mustervertrag prototype contract, sample contract
Mutationsanomalie update anomaly
mutierender Virus mutating virus
MVS = Multiple Virtual Operating System

N

nachahmen emulate (to), simulate (to)
Nachahmer emulator, simulator
Nachahmung emulation, simulation
Nachbarschaftsbüro neighborhood work center
nachbestellen reorder (to)
Nachbildung facsimile
nachprüfen review (to)
Nachprüfung review
Nachrechner back-end processor
Nachricht message
Nachrichtenfluß message flow
Nachrichtenkanal message channel
Nachrichtenquelle message source
Nachrichtentechnik communications engineering
Nachrichtenüberlastung message overload
Nachrichtenübertragung message transmission
Nachrichtenvermittlung message switching
nachrüsten upgrade (to)
Nachrüstung upgrading
Nachsatz trailer
nächste auszuführende Anweisung next executable statement
nachträgliche Dokumentation post-completion documentation
nachträgliche Überprüfung postreview, postaudit
Nadeldrucker needle printer
Nadeldruckwerk needle printing device
Näherungswert approximate value
Nahtstelle interface
naiver Benutzer naive end-user
Nassi-Shneiderman-Diagramm Nassi-Shneiderman chart
natürlich-sprachlicher Dialog natural language dialog
natürliche Sprache natural language
NBS = National Bureau of Standards
NC = Numeric Control
NC-Maschine = numerisch gesteuerte Werkzeugmaschine
NCC = National Computing Centre
NCGA = National Computer Graphics Association
Nebenanschluß extension, shunt
Nebenbedingung constraint
Nebenfunktion side function
Nebenläufigkeit concurrency
Nebenstellenanlage private branch exchange
Nebenwirkung side effect

Negation negation
Negativdarstellung inverted representation
Negativschrift inversed type
NEMP = Nuclear Explosion Magnetic Power
Nettoabweichung net-change
Nettobedarfsermittlung material inventory planning
Nettolohn net pay
Netz net, network
Netz für Ballungsgebiete metropolitan area network
Netz-Zugangseinheit network interface unit
Netzanschluß current supply
Netzarchitektur network architecture
Netzausfall power breakdown
Netzbetriebssystem network operating system
Netzebene network level
Netzfilter net filter
Netzgeschwindigkeit network speed
Netzknoten network node, hub
Netzkonfiguration network configuration
Netzkonverter gateway
Netzlast network workload
Netzmanagement network management
Netzmodell network model
Netzoptimierung network optimization
Netzplan network plan
Netzplantechnik network planning technique
Netzschalter power switch
Netzschicht network layer
Netzsteuerung network control, network management program
Netzsteuerungsprogramm network control program
Netzstörung power supply interference
Netzstruktur network configuration, network structure
Netztechnik network technology
Netzteilnehmer network user
Netzteilnehmer-Adresse network user address
Netzteilnehmer-Erkennung network user identification
Netztopologie network topology
Netzüberlagerung network heterodyning
Netzunterbrechung power supply interruption
Netzunterspannung power supply undervoltage
Netzversorgung power supply
Neubewertung reevaluation
neue Medien new media

Nummernsystem

neue Technologie new technology
Neuerung innovation
neuronales Netz neural network
NI = Normenausschuß
Informationsverarbeitungssysteme
nicht aufteilbare Fixkosten joint fixed costs
nicht dauerhaftes Menü non-permanent menu
nicht direkt verbunden off-line
nicht direkt zurechenbare Kosten indirect costs
nicht durch Copyright geschützte Software public domain software
nicht flüchtiger Speicher non-volatile memory
nicht gemeinsam benutzbar non-sharable
nicht gleichlaufend asynchronous
nicht lineare Optimierung non-linear optimization
nicht mechanischer Drucker non-impact printer
nicht mechanisches Druckwerk non-impact printing device
nicht meßbarer Nutzen intangible benefits
nicht monotones Schlußfolgern non-monotonic inferencing
nicht nachprüfbares Erfahrungswissen soft facts
nicht numerisch non-numeric
nicht prozedurale Programmiersprache non-procedural programming language
nicht prozedurale Programmierung non-procedural programming
nicht quantifizierbar intangible
nicht standardisiertes Interview non-standardized interview
niedere Programmiersprache low-level programming language
NIP = Non Impact Printer
NKRO = N-Key-Roll-Over
NL = Natural Language
NLP = Natural Language Processing
NLQ = Near Letter Quality
nominale Skala nominal scale
NOP = Non Operation
Norm norm, standard
Norm-/Wertsystem norm/value system
normale Genauigkeit short form precision
Normalform normalized form
normalisieren normalize (to)
Normalisierung normalization
Normalisierungsprozeß normalization process
Normalschrift plain text
normen standardize (to)

Normenausschuß standardization committee
Normenfestsetzung standard setting
Normenkonflikt norm conflict
normieren scale (to), standardize (to)
normierte Programmierung standardized programming
Normung standardization
Normvorschrift standard specification
Notabschaltung emergency cutoff
Notation notation
Notbetrieb emergency operation
Notdienst emergency service
Notfall emergency
Notfall-Rechenzentrum backup computing center
Notfallplan contingency plan, emergency plan
Notfallplanung emergency planning
Notfallsystem emergency system
Notizblock scrapbook
Notizblockfunktion scrapbook function
notleidendes Projekt backlogged project
Notschalter emergency switch
Notsignal emergency signal
Notstromaggregat uninterruptable power supply system, standby power generator
Notstromgerät emergency power device
NPT = Netzplantechnik
NPV = Net Present Value
NRZ = Non Return to Zero
NS-Diagramm = Nassi-Shneidermann-Diagram
NTG = Nachrichtentechnische Gesellschaft
NUA = Network User Address
NUI = Network User Identification
Nullkontrolle crossfooting balance check, zero check
Nulloperation non operation
Nullunterdrückung zero suppression
numerieren number (to)
numerisch numeric
numerisch gesteuerte Werkzeugmaschine numeric-controlled machine tool
numerische Adresse numeric address
numerische Analyse numeric analysis
numerische Daten numeric data
numerische Datenbank numeric data base
numerische Steuerung numeric control
numerische Tastatur numeric keyboard
Nummer number
Nummernart number type
Nummernbereich range of numbers
Nummernschema numbering schema
Nummernsystem numbering system

Nummerung

Nummerung numbering
Nummerungsobjekt numbered entity
Nur-Lese-Speicher read only memory
Nutzanwendung application
Nutzen benefit
Nutzen/Kosten-Analyse benefit/cost analysis
Nutzenart type of benefit
Nutzenoptimierung optimization of benefit
Nutzenpotential potential of benefit
Nutzenpreis price of benefit
Nutzenprofil profile of benefit
Nutzenschätzung estimation of benefit
Nutzenstruktur benefit structure
Nutzer user
Nützlichkeit utility
Nutzung usage, utilization
Nutzungsbewilligung usage permission
Nutzungsdauer usage duration
Nutzungsform manner of usage
Nutzungsgrad utilization ratio
Nutzungskosten usage costs
Nutzungspotential potential of usage
Nutzungsrecht usufructuary right, right of usage
Nutzwert value of benefit
Nutzwertanalyse value benefit analysis

O

Objekt entity
Objekt/Beziehung-Diagramm entity realtionship diagram
Objekt/Beziehung-Prinzip entity relationship priciple
Objekt/Struktur-Diagramm entity structure diagram
Objekt-Verwendungsanalyse entity usage analysis
Objektbeziehung entity relationship
Objektcode object code
objektiv objective
objektive Arbeitssituation objective job situation
objektiver Informationsbedarf objective information requirement
objektiver Konflikt non-personal conflict
Objektivität objectivity
Objektmenge entity set
Objektmodell entity model
objektorientierte Programmierung object-oriented programming
Objektprogramm object program
Objektschlüssel entity key
Objektschutz intrusion protection
Objektsprache object language
Objektsystem object system
Objekttyp entity type
Objekttyp-Darstellung entity type representation
Objekttypen-Ansatz entity type approach
Objekttypen-Attribute-Tabelle table of entity type attributes
Objekttypen-Tabelle table of entity types
Objekttypen-Zusammenhangsgraph entity type graph
OCG = Österreichische Computergesellschaft
OCR = Optical Character Recognition
ODETTE = Organization for Data Exchange by Tele Transmission in Europe
ODIF = Office Document Interchange Format
ODP = On Demand Publishing
OEM = Original Equipment Manufacturer
offene Aufgabe open task
offene Beobachtung open observation
offene Kommunikation open communications
offene Schleife open loop
offener Betrieb open shop operation
offener Regelkreis open loop
offener Schrifttyp free formed character
offenes Kommunikationssystem open communications system
offenes Netz open network
offenes System open system
offenes Verschlüsselungssystem public key system
öffentliche Verwaltung public administration
öffentlicher Bereich public domain
öffentlicher Dienst public service
öffentlicher Rechtsbereich domain of common law
öffentlicher Zugriff public access
öffentliches Fernsprechnetz public switched network
öffentliches Netz public network
öffentliches Recht common law
ÖGI = Österreichische Gesellschaft für Informatik
OIS = Office Information System
Oktalziffer octal number
Online-Dokumentation online documentation
ONP = Open Network Provision
operational operational
operationalisieren make operational (to)
Operations Research operations research
operative Testplanung operative test planning
operatives Informationsmanagement operative information management
operatives Management operative management
operatives Ziel operative goal
Operator operator
Opportunitätskosten opportunity costs
OPT = Optimized Production Technology
Optimalplanung operations research
Optimalwert optimum value
optimieren optimize (to)
Optimieren des Istzustands optimization of current system
optimierender Compiler optimizing compiler
Optimierungsexperiment optimization experiment
Optimierungsmodell optimization model
Option option
optische Anzeigeeinheit visual display unit
optische Nachrichtenübertragung optical message transmission
optische Speicherplatte optical disk
optische Zeichenerkennung optical character recognition
optischer Computer optical computer
optischer Leser optical reader

Opto-Computer opto computer
opto-elektrischer Wandler opto-electrical transformer
Optronic = Op(tik und Elek)tronik
OR = Operations Research
ordinale Skala ordinal scale
Ordnung array, order
Ordnungsbegriff figure of order
Ordnungsdaten data of order
Ordnungskriterium criterion of order
Ordnungsmäßigkeit orderly
Ordnungsnummer number of order
Organigramm organization chart, organogram
Organisation organization
Organisationsabteilung organization and methods department
Organisationsanalyse organizational analysis
organisationsangepaßte Standardsoftware customized standard software
Organisationsberater management consultant
Organisationsdatenbank data base of organization
Organisationsdemoskopie organizational demoscopy
Organisationsentwicklung organizational development
Organisationsergonomie organizational ergonomics
Organisationsform organizational form
Organisationsform Programmierteam programmer team organization
Organisationsforschung organizational research
Organisationsfunktion organizational function
Organisationsgrundsatz organizational principle
Organisationskontrolle management control, organizational control
Organisationskultur organizational culture
Organisationslehre organizational theory
Organisationsmethodik methodology of organizing
Organisationsmittel organizational techniques
Organisationsmodell organizational model
Organisationsplan organizational plan
Organisationsplanung organizational planning
Organisationsprinzip organizational principle
Organisationsprogrammierer application programmer
Organisationspsychologie industrial psychology
Organisationsspielraum organizing scope
Organisationsstruktur organizational structure
Organisationssystem organizational system
Organisationstechnologie organizational technology
Organisationstheorie organizational theory
Organisationstyp organizational type
Organisationsziel organizational goal
Organisator organizer
organisatorische Gestaltungsalternative organizational design alternative
organisatorische Integration organizational integration
organisatorische Macht organizational power
organisatorische Schnittstelle organizational interface
organisatorische Vorbereitung organizational preparation
organisatorischer Lernprozeß organizational learning process
organisatorischer Wandel organizational change
organisieren organize (to)
Orientierung orientation
Orientierungshypothese orientation hypothesis
Originalbeleg source document, original document
OROM = Optical Read Only Memory
Orthogonalentwurf orthogonal design
örtlich local
örtliches Netz local network
Ortsbetrieb local mode
Ortsnetz local network
Ortsverbindung local connection
OS = Open Systems
OS = Operating System
Osborn-Verfremdung Osborn alienation
OSF = Open Software Foundation
OSI = Open Systems Interconnection
OSI-Modell OSI model
OTA = Office of Technology Assessment
Outputmanipulation output manipulation
Outside-in-Ansatz outside-in approach

P

PA = Public Access
Paarvergleich paired comparison
PABX = Private Automatic Branch Exchange
Packungsdichte packing density
PAD = Packet Assembler/Disassembler
Paket packet
Paketanordnung und -auflösung packet assembly/disassembly
Paketvermittlung packet switching
Paketvermittlungsnetz packet switching network
Panelbefragung panel questioning
PAP = Programmablaufplan
Papier paper
Papierbreite paper width
Papiereinzug paper feed
Papierformat paper size
papierlos paperless
papierloses Büro paperless office
Papiervorschub paper feed
Paradigma paradigm
Parallel-Nummernsystem parallel numbering system
Parallelbetrieb parallel mode, parallel operation
Parallelcomputer parallel computer
Paralleldrucker parallel printer
Paralleldruckwerk parallel printing device
parallele Programmierung parallel programming
parallele Verarbeitung parallel processing
parallele verteilte Verarbeitung parallel distributed processing
paralleler Dialog parallel dialog
Parallelschlüssel parallel key
Parallelsitzung parallel session
Paralleltest parallel test
Parallelumstellung parallel changeover
Parallelverarbeitung parallel processing
Parameter parameter
Parameterschätzung parameter estimation, parametric rating
parametrische Schätzgleichung parametric estimate equation
parametrisieren parameterize (to)
parametrisierender Benutzer parameterizing end-user
parametrisierte Abfrage parametric query
Parametrisierung parameterization
PARC = Palo Alto Research Center
Pareto-Analyse Pareto analysis

Parität parity
Paritätsbit parity bit
Paritätsfehler error parity
Partizipation participation
Partizipationsansatz participative approach
Partizipationsdimension degree of participation
Partizipationsforschung research on participation
Partizipationsziel participation objective
passive Beobachtung passive observation
passives Hilfesystem passive help system
Paßwort password
Paßwort-Algorithmus password algorithm
PATBX = Private Automatic Telex Branch Exchange
Patentanalyse analysis of patents
Patentschutz patent protection
PAX = Private Automatic Exchange
PAQ = Position Analysis Questionnaire
PBX = Private Branch Exchange
PC = Parity Check
PC = Personal Computer
PC = Personal Computing
PC = Plug Compatible
PC-DOS = Personal Computer Disk Operating System
PCM = Plug Compatible Manufacturer
PCM = Pulse Code Modulation
PD-Software = Public Domain Software
PDF = Program Development Facility
PDL = Page Description Language
PEARL = Process and Experiment Automation Realtime Language
penetrieren penetrate (to)
Penetrierung penetration
Perfektionskern hard core
Perfektionswartung perfective maintenance
Perimetersystem perimeter system
periphere Einheit peripheral unit
Peripherie peripheral equipment, peripherals
Peripherieanschluß peripheral connection
Peripheriegerät peripheral device
permanent permanent
permanente Fehlerunterdrückung failure stop
permanenter Speicher non-volatile memory
permanentes Menü permanent menu
Personal personnel
Personalabbau personnel reduction, staff reduction

Personalakte

Personalakte personnel record, personnel file
Personalausstattung staffing
Personalbedarf personnel requirements
Personalbedarfsplanung personnel requirements planning
Personalberichtswesen personnel reporting
Personalbeschaffung personnel procurement, personnel recruitment, staff hiring
Personalbestand personnel, staff
Personaleinsatz personnel deployment
Personalentwicklung personnel development
Personalführung human resource management
Personalinformationssystem personnel information system
personalintensiv personnel intensive
Personalkosten staff costs, personnel costs
Personalmanagement human resource management
Personalplanung staff planning, personnel planning
Personalqualifikation staff qualification
Personalschulung staff training
Personalumschichtung staff turnover, personnel turnover
Personalverwaltung personnel administration
Personalwesen personnel management, staffing
Personalzuordnung staff allocation, personnel allocation
personenbezogene Daten personal data
Personenkennzeichen personal identification number
persönlich personal
persönliche Arbeitstechnik personal time management
persönliche Identifikationsnummer personal identification number
persönlicher Computer personal computer
persönliches Informationsmanagement personal information management
persönliches Kennwort personal checkword
persönliches Paßwort personal password
PERT = Program Evaluation and Review Technique
Perzeption perception
Petri-Netz Petri net
Pfadverfolgung tracing
Pfeildiagramm arrow diagram
Pfeiltaste arrow key

Pfeilzeiger arrow pointer
Pflege maintenance, update
Pflegeschein maintenance certificate
Pflichtenheft requirements definition, specification
Pflichtfeld mandatory field
PH = Page Heading
Phasenansatz phased approach
Phasenkonzept life cycle concept
Phasenmodell life cycle model
Phasenschema life cycle schema
phasenweise Umstellung phased changeover
Photokopierpapier photocopying paper
Photosatz photo typesetting
physikalisches Modell physical model
physiologisches Bedürfnis physiological need
physische Datendefinitionssprache physical data definition language
physische Datensicherungsmaßnahme physical data assurance measurement
physische Datensicht physical data view
physische Datenstruktur physical data structure
physische Datenunabhängigkeit physical data independence
physisches Attribut physical attribute
physisches Datenflußdiagramm physical data flow diagram
physisches Löschen physical cancellation
physisches Modell physical model
PIA = Peripheral Interface Adapter
picken pick (to)
piko pico
Piktogramm pictograph
Pilotprojekt pilot project
PIM = Personal Information Management
PIM = Personal Information Manager
PIN = Personal Identification Number
Pipeline-Konzept pipeline concept
Pipeline-Verarbeitung pipelining
PIPO = Parallel in Parallel Out
PIS = Personal-Informationssystem
PISO = Parallel in Serial Out
Pixel pixel
PLA = Programmable Logic Array
Plan plan
planen plan (to), project (to)
Planentwurf plan design, blueprint
planmäßiger Abschluß orderly close down
PLANNET-Technik = PLANning-NETwork-Technique
Planung planning
Planungsansatz planning approach

Planungsgruppe task force
Planungsinformation planning information
Planungskosten planning costs
Planungsmethodik methodology of planning
Planungsprozeß planning process
Planungssprache planning modelling language
Planungszeitraum planning horizon
Planungsziel planning goal
Planzeichner plotter
Plasmabildschirm plasma display, plasma screen
Plastikkarte plastic card
Platine board
Platte disk, hard disk
Plattenbetriebssystem disk operating system
Platteneinheit disk unit
Plattenfehler disk error
Plattenspeicher disk storage
Plattenspeicherlaufwerk disk storage drive
Plattenspur disk track
Plattenstapel disk pack
Plattenzugriff disk access
Platzbedarf space requirement
Platzbuchung seat reservation
Platzhalter dummy
Plausibilität plausibility
Plausibilitätskontrolle plausibility check
PL/1 = Programming Language One
P.O. = Post Office
Polaritätsprofil polarity profile
Polarkoordinate polar coordinate
POM = Purchase Order Management
POP = Point Of Purchase
Portabilität portability
Portfolio portfolio
Portfolioanalyse portfolio analysis
Portierbarkeit portability
POS = Point Of Sale
POS-Banking = Point Of Sale Banking
POS-Terminal = Point Of Sale Terminal
Positionierung positioning
Positionsmarke cursor
Positionsparameter positional parameter
Postamt post office
Postausgang outgoing mail
Postdienst postal service
Posteingang incoming mail
Postfach post office box
Postleitzahl zip code
Postsendung mail
PPM = Pages Per Minute

PPS = Produktionsplanung und -steuerung
PPX = Private Packet Switching Exchange
Prädikatenkalkül predicate calculus
prädikative Programmierung predicative programming
Präferenz preference
Präferenzmatrix preference matrix
Präferenzordnung preference order
Prägeterminal embossing terminal
Pragmatik pragmatics
Praktikabilität practicability
Prämisse premise
Präprozessor preprocessor
Präsentationsgraphik presentation graphics
Präsentationstechnik presentation technique
Präzedenzanalyse precedence analysis
Preisabfrage price lookup
Preisangabe quotation
Preisbildung pricing
Preisbeurteilung price assessment
Preisbildung price determining
Prestel = Press button on telephone lines
Primärbedarfsplanung source requirements planning
Primärbibliothek source library
Primärdaten source data
Primärdatenträger source data medium
Primärprogramm source program
Primärschlüssel primary key, source key
Prinzip principle
Prinzip der Abstraktion principle of abstraction
Prinzip der Datenabstraktion principle of data abstraction
Prinzip der dezentralen Konzentration principle of remote concentration
Prinzip der hierarchischen Strukturierung principle of hierarchical structuring
Prinzip der integrierten Dokumentation principle of integrated documentation
Prinzip der Lokalität principle of locality
Prinzip der Mehrfachverwendung principle of multiple usage
Prinzip der Nettoabweichung net-change principle
Prinzip der schrittweisen Verfeinerung principle of stepwise refinement
Prinzip der strukturierten Programmierung principle of structured programming

Prinzip des funktionellen Entwurfs

Prinzip des funktionellen Entwurfs principle of functional design
Prinzip des Information Hiding information hiding principle
Prinzip des Schwarzen Kastens black box principle
Prinzip des Software-Lebenszyklus software life cycle principle
Prinzip des Weißen Kastens white box principle
Priorität priority
Prioritätensteuerung priority control
Prioritätsanalyse priority analysis
Prioritätsregel priority rule
private Nebenstellenanlage private branch exchange
private Verschlüsselung private ciphering
privater Rechtsbereich domain of private law
Privatrecht private law
Privatsphäre privacy
probabilistisch probabilistic
Probeinstallation trial installation
Probelauf test run
Problem problem
Problemanalyse problem analysis
Problembericht problem report
Problembeschreibung problem description
Problembeschreibungssprache problem description language, problem statement language
Problemdatenbank problem data base
Problemdefinition problem definition
Problemerfassung problem sensing
Problemerkennung problem definition
Problemformulierung problem formulation
Problemkoordinator problem co-ordinator
Problemlösen problem solving
Problemlösung problem solution
Problemlösungs-Datenbank problem solving data base
Problemmanagement problem management
problemorientierte Programmiersprache problem-oriented programming language
Problemtext problem text
Problemverarbeitungssystem problem solving system
Problemverfolgung problem tracking
PROCAL = Programmable Calculator
PROCOL = Process Control Oriented Language
Produktentwicklung product development
Produktentwicklungsprozeß product development process

Produkthaftung product liability
Produktion production
Produktionsbetrieb production operation
Produktionsgang phase of production, production step
Produktionskapazität production capacity, productive capacity
Produktionsleitung production management
Produktionsmanagement production management
Produktionsmenge production output
Produktionsmittel production resources
Produktionsplanung production planning
Produktionsplanung und -steuerung production planning and scheduling
Produktionsregel production rule
Produktionsstätte production plant
Produktionssteuerung production control
Produktionssystem production system
produktiv productive
produktives Anwendungssystem productive application system
Produktivität productivity
Produktivitätskennzahl productivity measure
Produktivitätssteigerung productivity improvement, increase in productivity
Produktlebenszyklus product life cycle
Produktverwaltungssystem product management system
Profildiagramm profile diagram
Prognose forecasting
Prognosemethode forecasting method
Prognoserechnung forecasting computation
Programm program
Programm-Instrumentierungstechnik program instrumentation technique
Programm-Manipulation program manipulation
Programmabbruch program crash, unusual end of program
Programmablauf program flow
Programmablaufplan program flow chart
Programmablaufsteuerung program flow control
Programmableitung program derivation
Programmadaption program adaption
Programmanalysator program analyzer
Programmaufbau structure of program
Programmausführung program execution
Programmbaustein program module
Programmbeschreibung program description, program specification
programmbezogenes Testen white box testing

Programmbibliothek program library
Programmcode program code
Programmcode-Generierung program code generating
Programmdaten program data
Programmdiebstahl program theft
Programmdokumentation program documentation
Programmentwurf program design
Programmfehler program error, bug
Programmfreigabe program release
Programmgenerator program generator
programmierbar programmable
programmierbare Entscheidung programmable decision
programmierbare Funktionstaste soft function key
programmierbare Rechenmaschine programmable calculator
programmierbarer Festwertspeicher programmable read only memory
Programmierbüro programming bureau
programmieren program (to)
Programmierer programmer
Programmierer-Arbeitsplatz programmer workbench
Programmiergerät programmer
Programmierhilfe programming aid
Programmiermethode programming method
Programmiersprache programming language
programmierter Unterricht programmed instruction
Programmierumgebung programming environment
Programmierung programming
Programmieruntrstützung programming support
Programmierverhalten programming behavior
Programmiervorgabe programming specification
Programmierwerkzeug programming tool
Programminnovation program innovation
Programminspektion program inspection
Programminstrumentierung program instrumentation
Programmkenndaten program flag data
Programmkonstruktion program construction
Programmkonvention program convention
Programmlader program loader
Programmlauf program run
Programmlaufzeit object time
Programmpaket program package
Programmpflege program maintenance

Programmprüfung program testing
Programmqualität program quality
Programmrevisor program auditor
Programmschutz program protection
Programmsegmentierung program segmentation
Programmsicherung program backup
Programmspeicher program storage
Programmsperre program barrier
Programmspezifikation program specification
Programmsteuerung program control
Programmstruktur program architecture
programmtechnische Vorbereitung program preparation
Programmtest program test, walk-through
Programmtesten program testing
Programmtyp program type
Programmüberprüfung program verification
Programmübersetzung program compiling
Programmumwandlung program conversion
Programmunterbrechung program interrupt
Programmunterstützung program support
Programmverwaltung program management
Programmzeile line of code
Projekt project
Projekt-Aufwandschätzung project estimating
Projektassistent project assistant
Projektaufforderung project call
Projektaufgabe project task
Projektauswahl project selection
Projektbeendigung project termination
projektbegleitende Dokumentation in-line documentation
Projektbibliothek project library
Projektdauer project duration
Projektdokumentation project documentation
Projektfortschritt project achievement, project progress
Projektführer project leader
Projektführerschaft project leadership
Projektgruppe project team, task force
Projekthandbuch project manual
projektieren project (to)
Projektkontrolle project controlling
Projektkoordinator project coordinator
Projektkosten project costs
Projektlebenszyklus project life cycle
Projektleiter project manager

Projektmanagement

Projektmanagement project management
Projektmanagement-Werkzeug project management tool
Projektordnung project ranking
Projektorganisation project organization
Projektplan project plan
Projektplanung project scheduling
Projektportfolio project portfolio
Projektrevision project audit
Projektsanierung project redevelopment
Projektsekretär project secretary
Projektsteuerung project controlling
Projekttagebuch project diary
Projektteam project team
Projektüberprüfung project review
Projektüberwachung project monitoring
Projektverfolgung project tracking
Projektverwaltung project administration
Projektvorschlag project proposal
Projektziel project goal
PROLOG = PROgramming in LOGic
PROM = Programmable Read Only Memory
Proportionalabstand proportional spacing
Proportionalschrift proportional writing
Prosodie prosody
Protokoll protocol
Protokollanpassung protocol adaption
Protokolldatei log, log file, logging file
Protokollkonverter protocol converter
Prototyp prototype
Prototyp-Entwurf prototype design
Prototyping prototyping
Prozedur procedure
prozedural procedural
prozedurale Programmiersprache procedural programming language
prozedurale Wissensdarstellung procedural knowledge representation
Prozedurteil procedure partition
Prozentsatzmethode percentage rate method
Prozeß process
prozeßabhängige Ablaufsteuerung process-oriented sequential control
Prozeßanalyse process analysis
Prozeßaufruf process call
Prozeßautomatisierung process automation
Prozeßbeschreibung description of process
Prozeßdatenverarbeitung process control computing
Prozeßmanagement process management, task management
Prozessor processor
Prozeßorganisation process organization
Prozeßorientierung process orientation
Prozeßrechner process control computer
Prozeßrechnersprache process computer language
Prozeßsteuerung process control
Prozeßüberwachung process monitoring
Prozeßumgebung process environment
Prozeßverantwortlicher process owner
Prozeßverwaltung task management
Prozeßvisualisierung visualization of process
Prüfbarkeit auditability
Prüfbericht audit report
Prüfbit check bit
Prüfcode check code
prüfen audit (to), check (to), test (to)
Prüfen durch Vergleich comparator check
Prüfgerät testing device
Prüfliste check list
Prüfpfad audit trail
Prüfprogramm audit program
Prüfpunkt checkpoint
Prüfsiegel seal of approval
Prüfsoftware audit software
Prüfsprache audit language
Prüfsumme hash total
Prüfung auditing, checking, testing
Prüfung auf Eingabefehler input error checking
Prüfung auf geradzahlige Parität even parity check
Prüfung auf ungeradzahlige Parität odd parity check
Prüfzahl check number
Prüfzahlverfahren check number mode
Prüfziffer check figure, check digit
Prüfziffernrechnung self-checking
Prüfziffernverfahren self-checking procedure
PSA = Problem Statement Analyzer
PSDA = Problem Statement and Design Analyzer
Pseudo-Code pseudo code
Pseudo-Graphik pseudo graphics
PSL = Problem Statement Language
Psychologie Psychology
Psychosomatik psychosomatics
psychosomatische Störung psychosomatic disturbance
psychosozialer Faktor psychosocial factor
PTT = Postes, Telegraphe et Telephone
PTZ = Posttechnisches Zentralamt
PU = Programmierter Unterricht
publizieren publish (to)
Publizieren auf Anforderung publishing on demand

Publizieren vom Schreibtisch desktop publishing
Puffer buffer
Pufferbatterie für Speicher backup battery unit
puffern buffer (to)
Pufferspeicher buffer memory
Pufferzeit slack
Punkt-zu-Punkt-Verbindung point-to-point connection

Punktbewertung scoring
Punktbewertungsverfahren scoring procedure
punktförmiges Zeichen point plotting
Punktmatrix dot matrix
Punktsteuerung coordinate setting
Punktzahl score
PWS = Personal Workstation

Q

QA = Quality Assurance
QBE = Query By Example
QL = Query Language
Quadrant quadrant
Qualifikation qualification
Qualifikationsbegriff qualifier
qualifizieren qualify (to)
Qualität quality
qualitative Bewertung qualitative evaluation
Qualitätskontrolle quality control
Qualitätskriterium quality criterion
Qualitätslenkung quality control
Qualitätsmaß quality measure
Qualitätssicherung quality assurance
Qualitätssicherungssystem quality assurance system
Qualitätssteigerung quality improvement
Qualitätssteuerung quality control
Qualitätsziel quality goal
Qualitätszirkel quality circle
quantifizierbar quantifiable, tangible
quantifizierbare Kosten tangible costs
quantifizierbarer Nutzen tangible benefits
quantifizieren quantify (to)
Quantifizierung quantification
quantitative Bewertung quantitative evaluation
quasi-paralleles Programm quasi-parallel program
Quellanweisung source statement
Quelle source
Quellprogramm source program
Quellprogramm-Hinterlegung deposit of source program
Quellsprache source language
Querkontrolle cross checking
Querparität vertical parity
Querrechnen crossfooting
Quersumme crossfoot
Quersummenkontrolle crossfooting
Querverbindung cross connection
Querverweis cross reference
Querwirkungsanalyse cross impact analysis
quittieren acknowledge (to)
Quittung acknowledgement
Quittungsbetrieb handshaking
QWERTY-Tastatur QWERTY keyboard
QWERTZ-Tastatur QWERTZ keyboard

R

R & D = Research and Development
Rabatt trade discount
Raddrucker wheel printer
Radius radius
Rahmen frame
Rahmenkonzept framework
Rahmenplan masterplan
Rahmenvorschlag outline proposal
Rahmenziel general goal
RAM = Random Access Memory
Randbedingung marginal condition
Rangordnung order of rank, hierarchy, ranking
Raster grid, matrix, raster
Rasterbildschirm raster display
Rasterbildverarbeitung raster image processing
Rastergraphik raster graphics
Rating-Methode rating technique
Rating-Skala rating scale
rationales Problemlösen rational problem solving
rationalisieren rationalize (to)
Rationalisierung rationalization
Rationalismus rationalism
Raubkopie pirated copy
Raumbedarf space requirement
Raumbedingung space condition
räumliche Datenverwaltung spatial data management
räumliche Vorbereitung site preparation
RBMS = Report Base Management System
Reaktion reaction
Reaktionszeit response time
real real, physical
reale Adresse physical address
realer Prozeß physical process
reales Betriebssystem physical operating system
Realexperiment reality experiment
Realisierungsphase implementation phase
Realproblem real problem
Realspeicher physical memory
Realzeitbetrieb realtime mode
Realzeitprogrammiersprache realtime programming language
Realzeitprogrammierung realtime programming
Realzeituhr realtime clock, timer
Realzeitverarbeitung realtime processing
Rechenanlage computer
Rechenergebnis computational result
Rechengenauigkeit computational precision
Rechenmaschine calculator
Rechensystem computer system, computing system
Rechenwerk arithmetic unit
Rechenzentrum computer center, computing center
rechnen compute (to)
Rechner computer
Rechnerarchitektur computer architecture
Rechnerauswahl computer selection
Rechnerfamilie computer family
Rechnernetz computer network
Rechnerschutz computer protection
Rechnerverbund computer network
Rechnung bill, invoice
Rechnungsbetrag invoice amount
Rechnungsdatei billing file
Rechnungserstellung billing, invoicing
Rechnungsprüfung auditing
Rechnungswesen accountancy, accounting
Recht law
Rechtfertigung justification
Rechtfertigung von Kosten cost justification
rechtliche Anforderung legal requirement
rechtsbündig right aligned, right justified
Rechtschreib-Prüfprogramm spell check program, spell checker
Rechtsinformatik law informatics
Rechtsschutz legal protection
Rechtsschutz-Versicherung legal protection insurance
Rechtzeitigkeit timeliness
Reduktionismus reductionism
redundant redundant
redundanter Code redundant code
Redundanz redundancy
Redundanz-Prüfung redundancy check
Redundanz-Reduzierung reducing redundancy
redundanzfreie Speicherung non-redundant storage
Referenz-Datenbank reference data base
Referenz-Monitor-Konzept reference monitor concept
Reflektormarke reflective mark
Reflexion reflection
Reflexionsgrad reflection factor
Regel rule
regelbasierte Sprache rule-based language
regelbasierte Wissensdarstellung rule-based knowledge representation
regelbasiertes Programm rule-based program
regelbasiertes System rule-based system

Regelinterpreter

Regelinterpreter rule interpreter
Regelkreis closed loop, control loop
regeln control (to)
regelorientierte Prüfung rule-oriented auditing
Regelstrecke control line
Regelsystem automatic control system, feedback control system
Regelung feedback control
Regelungstechnik control engineering
Registrierkasse cash register
Registrierungsgebühr registration fee
Regressionsanalyse regression analysis
Regressionstest regression test
Reihenfolge sequence
reihenförmige Anordnung array
Reihung sequence
reine Projektorganisation task force group
Rekonfiguration reconfiguration
Rekursion recursion
rekursive Beziehung recursive relationship, involuted relationship
rekursive Programmierung recursive programming
Relation relation
relationale Abfragesprache relational query language
relationale Datenbank relational data base
relationale Struktur relational structure
relationales Datenbanksystem relational data base system
relationales Modell relational model
Relationenmethode relation method
relative Autonomie relative autonomy
relative Häufigkeit relative frequency
relative Ressourcenstärke relative strength of resource
REM = Remark
Reorganisation reorganization, redesign
reorganisieren reorganize (to), redesign (to)
Reparaturzeit repair time
reparieren repair (to)
repräsentative Partizipation representative participation
Reproduzierbarkeit reproducibility
REPROM = Reprogrammable Read Only Memory
Reserve standby
reservieren reserve (to)
resident resident
Rest remainder
Restart restart
Restriktion constraint, restriction
Revision audit

Revisionsinformationssystem audit information system
Revisionsmethode audit technique
Revisionsverfahren audit procedure
Revisor auditor
REVS = Requirements Engineering and Validation System
RFI = Radio Frequency Interference
RFP = Request For Proposal
Richtfunk radio beam
Richtfunkübertragung radio beam transmission
Richtigkeit correctness
Richtigstellungsrecht correction privilege
Richtlinie guideline
Richtschnur norm
Ringleitung loop
Ringnetz ring network
Ringtopologie ring topology
RIP = Raster Image Processing
RISC = Reduced Instruction Set Computer
Risiko risk
Risikoanalyse risk analysis
Risikoeinschätzung risk assessment
Risikoerkennung identification of risk
Risikofaktor risk factor
Risikomanagement risk management
Risikomanagement-Modell risk management model
Risikotheorie risk theory
RIU = Ring Interface Unit
RJE = Remote Job Entry
RLL = Run Length Limited
RLS = Remote Link Service
ROA = Return On Asset
Roboter robot
Roboter-Arbeitsplatz robot workcell
Roboter-Programmiersprache robot programming language
Robotik robotics
Robustheit robustness
Rohmaterial raw material
Rohmaterialbestand raw material inventory
Rohrpost pneumatic postal system
ROI = Return On Investment
Rolle role
rollen scroll (to)
Rollenbeschreibung role description
Rollenerwartung role expectation
Rollenkonflikt role conflict
Rollkugel roller ball, tracker ball
Rollmodus scrolling
ROM = Read Only Memory
RPC = Remote Procedure Call
RPG = Report Program Generator

RSL = Requirements Statement Language
Rückantwort answer, reply
Rückfallsystem backup system
Rückfrage interrogation
Rückkopplung feedback
Rückkopplungsdiagramm feedback diagram
Rückmeldung feedback message
Rücksetzen backspacing
Rücksetztaste backspace key
Rücksprungtaste enter key
Rückstand backlog
Rückstau backlog

rückwärts reverse
rückwärts blättern page up (to)
rückwärtsgesteuertes Schlußfolgern backward-controlled inferencing
Rückwärtsverkettung backward chaining
Rückweisungsrate rejection rate
runden round (to)
Rundschreiben circular, circulation slip
Rundsenden multi-address message
Rundung rounding
Rundungsfehler rounding error, round-off error
Rüstzeit set-up time
RZ = Rechenzentrum

S

SA = Structured Analysis
Sabotageakt act of sabotage
Sachbearbeiter clerk, officier in charge
Sachbearbeitungsaufgabe clerical task
Sachgebiet subject area
Sachgebietsdatenbasis subject data base
Sachkontenbuchführung general ledger
Sachkonto general account, impersonal account
Sachmängelhaftung materials defect liability
Sachmittel aid
Sachregister index
Sachverständigengutachten expert opinion, expertise
Sachverständigenliste list of experts
Sachverständiger expert
Sachverzeichnis subject index
Sachwissen expert knowledge
Sachziel subject goal
Sachzwang inherent necessity
SADT = Structured Analysis and Design Technique
Saisonschwankung seasonal variation
Saldo balance
SAM = Sequential Access Method
Sammelleitungssystem bus line system
Sammelsystem bus system
Samplingverfahren sampling
sanieren redevelop (to)
Sanierung redevelopment
SAS = Statistical Analysis System
Satellitenbüro satellite work center
Satellitennetz satellite network
Satellitensystem satellite computer system
Satellitenübertragung satellite transmission
Satellitenverbindung satellite link
Satz record
Satz fester Länge fixed length record
Satz variabler Länge variable length record
Satzbau syntax
Satzlehre syntax
Satzsperre record locking
Satzverkettung record chaining, record linkage
Säulendiagramm bar chart
SBC = Single Board Computer
SBS = Satellite Business System
SBU = Strategic Business Unit
Scanner-Daten scanner data
Schablone template

Schablonen-Programmierung template programming
Schachtelung nesting
Schaden damage
Schadensausmaß extent of damage
Schale shell
Schalenmodell shell model
Schalldämpfung noise reduction
schallreflektierend sound reflecting
Schaltalgebra Boolean Algebra, switching algebra
schalten switch (to)
Schalter switch
Schaltung circuit
Schaltwerklogik logic device
schätzen estimate (to)
Schätzer estimator
Schätzfehler estimate error, error in estimating
Schätzfunktion estimate function
Schätzskala estimate scale
Schätzung estimate, estimation
Schätzverfahren estimate procedure
Schema schema, model
Schicht layer
Schichtbetrieb shift operation
Schichtenmodell Benutzerschnittstelle layer model user interface
Schlagwort catchword, descriptor, keyword
schlecht dokumentiert poorly documented
schlecht strukturiertes Problem ill-structured problem
Schleife loop
Schleifennetz ring network
Schlußbericht final report
Schlüssel key
Schlüsselangriff key attack
Schlüsselattribut key attribute
Schlüsselbegriff key term
schlüsselchiffrierender Schlüssel key-ciphering key
Schlüsselfaktor key factor
Schlüsselfaktoren-Analyse key factor analysis
schlüsselfertiges System turn-key system
Schlüsselgröße key variable
Schlüsselhierarchie hierarchy of keys
Schlüsselkarte smart card
Schlüsselrolle key role
Schlüsseltechnologie key technology
Schlüsseltext cypher text
Schlüsselwort keyword
Schlüsselwort-Technik keyword technique
Schlüsselzahl key number
schlußfolgern inference (to)
Schlußfolgern inferencing, reasoning

Schlußfolgerung inference
Schlußfolgerungsmuster inference pattern
Schlußfolgerungsregel inference rule
Schmalband baseband
Schmalbandnetz baseband network
Schneideeinrichtung guillotine
Schnelldrucker high-speed printer
schnelles Prototyping rapid prototyping
Schnellspeicher high-speed memory
Schnittstelle interface
Schnittstelle für Fabrik- und Büroautomatisierung technical and office protocol
Schnittstelle für Fabrikautomatisierung manufacturing automation protocol
Schnittstellenergonomie interface ergonomics
Schnittstellentechnik interface technology
Schönschreibdrucker letter-quality printer
schöpferisch creative
Schranksoftware cupboard software
Schreib-/Lese-Speicher write/read memory
Schreibdichte recording density
Schreibfehler typing error
Schreibkopf write head
Schreibmarke cursor
Schreibmarken-Taste cursor key
Schreibmaschine typewriter
Schreibrad daisy wheel
Schreibring write protection ring
Schreibschrift script
Schreibschutz write protection
Schreibtischtest desk test, logical test
Schreibweise notation
Schriftart font, kind of type
Schriftart A OCR A font
Schriftart B OCR B font
Schriftbild type face
Schriftgenerator font generator
Schriftgröße type size
schriftliche Befragung written questioning
Schriftstück document
Schriftzeichen character
Schriftzeichenerkennung character recognition
Schritt step
Schritt-für-Schritt-Methode single stepping
Schrittgeschwindigkeit clock speed
schritthaltende Verarbeitung realtime processing
Schrittmachertechnologie pacemaker technology
schrittweise Umstellung stepwise changeover

schrittweise Verfeinerung stepwise refinement
Schub batch
Schubladenplan drawer plan
Schubtraktor push tractor
Schuldner debitor
schulen train (to)
Schulung training
Schulungsanforderung training requirement
Schulungsplan training schedule
Schutzhüllenvertrag shrink-wrap licence
Schutzmaßnahme protective measure, safety measure
Schutztechnik protection technology
Schutzvorrichtung safeguard
Schwäche weakness
Schwächenkatalog list of systems weaknesses
Schwachstelle variance
Schwachstellenanalyse analysis of variances
Schwarzer Kasten black box
Schwarzer-Kasten-Test black box test
Schwelle threshold
Schwenken panning
Schwingspiegel-Bildschirm vibrating mirror display
Schwund inventory shrinkage
Scoring-Modell scoring model
SCT = Systems Construction Tool
SD = Structured Design
SDM = Spatial Data Management
SE = Software Engineering
SEE = Software Engineering Environment
SEES = Software Engineering Environment System
Segment segment
segmentieren segment (to)
Seite page
Seiten ein- und auslagern swapping
Seiten pro Minute pages per minute
Seitenaustausch page mapping, paging
Seitenaustauschverfahren paging algorithm
Seitenbeschreibungssprache page description language
Seitendrucker page printer
Seitenersetzung page replacement
Seitenlänge page length
Seitenleser page reader
Seitenrahmen page frame
Seitenrand Druckpapier margin
Seitenüberschrift page heading
Seitenumbruch pagination, page break, page makeup

Seitenvorschub page feed
Sekretariatsfunktion office function
Sekundärdaten alternate key, secondary data
Sekundärschlüssel secondary key
selbstadaptierende Benutzerschnittstelle self-adaptive user interface
Selbstanpassung self-adapting
Selbstaufschreibung self-recording
Selbstdokumentation in-line documentation
Selbstdurchschreibpapier carbonless paper, non-carbon required paper
selbsterfüllende Prophezeiung self-fulfilling prophecy
Selbsterklärungsfähigkeit ability of self-explanation
Selbstgestaltung self-design
Selbstkorrektur autocorrection
Selbstmanagement self-management
Selbstmotivation self-motivation
Selbstorganisation self-organization
selbstorganisierendes System self-organizing system
selbstprüfend self-checking
selbstprüfender Code error correcting code
Selbstprüfung automatic check, built-in check
Selbstreferenz self-reference
Selbstregelung self-controlling
Selbststart auto restart
selbststeuernde Gruppe self-controlling group
Selbststeuerung automatic control
Selbsttest self-test
Selbstverwirklichung self-realization
Selbstwähldienst automatic dial exchange
Selbstwissen self-knowledge
Selektion selection
Selektorkanal selector channel
Semantik semantics
semantische Datenintegrität semantic data integrity
semantisches Datenmodell semantic data model
semantisches Gedächtnis semantic memory
semantisches Netz semantic network
semi-formale Beschreibung semiformal description
semiotisches Dreieck semiotic triangle
Semiotik semiotics
Sendeaufruf polling
Sendebetrieb sending mode
Sendeschlüssel transmission key

Sendestation sending station
Senke sink
Sensibilität sensitivity
Sensibilitätsanalyse sensitivity analysis
sensitiver Schlüssel sensitive key
Sensitivitätsanalyse sensitivity analysis
Sensor sensor
Sensor-Bildschirm sensor screen
Sensorik sensorics
SEP = Strategische Erfolgsposition
sequentiell sequential
sequentielle Datei sequential file
sequentielle Dateiorganisation sequential file organization
sequentielle Suche sequential search
sequentielle Verarbeitung sequential processing
sequentielle Zugriffsmethode sequential access methode
sequentieller Speicher sequential memory
sequentieller Zugriff sequential access
sequentielles Programm sequential program
Sequenz sequence
Serialdrucker serial printer
seriell serial
serielle Datei serial file
serielle Schnittstelle serial interface
serielle Übertragung serial transmission
serieller Betrieb serial mode
serieller Zugriff serial access
serielles Druckwerk serial printing device
Serienbrief form letter
SEU = Software-Entwicklungsumgebung
SFuRD = Stadtfunk und Rufdienst
SI = Soziale Intelligenz
Sicherheit safety, security
Sicherheitsanforderung security requirement
Sicherheitsbeauftragter safety official, security officer
Sicherheitsbedürfnis security need
Sicherheitsbestand buffer stock, safety stock
Sicherheitsbestimmung safety regulation
Sicherheitseinrichtung safety facility
Sicherheitsfaktor safety factor
Sicherheitsingenieur safety engineer
Sicherheitskern security kernel
Sicherheitsmanagement security management
Sicherheitsrisiko security risk
Sicherheitsschloß security lock
Sicherheitsstandard security standard
Sicherheitstechnik security technology
Sicherheitsvorschrift safety regulation

sichern save (to), secure (to)
Sicherung assurance
Sicherungsanalyse assurance analysis
Sicherungsband streamer tape
Sicherungsdatei backup file
Sicherungsdiskette backup floppy disk
Sicherungsintegration integration of assurance measures
Sicherungskopie backup copy
Sicherungsmaßnahme assurance measure
Sicherungssoftware assurance software
Sicherungssystem assurance system
Sicherungsverfahren backup procedure
Sichtdaten view data
Sichtgerät visual display terminal
Sichtkartei visual file
Signal signal
Signalumsetzer signal converter
Silbentrennung hyphenation
SIMD = Single Instruction/Multiple Data
Simplexbetrieb simplex mode
SIMSCRIPT = Simulation Programming Language
SIMULA = Simulation Language
Simulation simulation
Simulationsexperiment simulation experiment
Simulationsmodell simulation model
Simulationsprogramm simulation program
Simulationssprache simulation language
Simulationsstudie simulation study
simulieren simulate (to)
Simulierer simulator
Simulmatik simulmatics
simultan simultaneous
Simultandokumentation simultaneous documentation
simultane Peripheriesteuerung simultaneous peripheral operations online
simultane Verarbeitung simultaneous processing
Sinnsystem sense system
sinnverwandtes Wort synonym
SIP = Strategische Informationssystem-Planung
SIPO = Serial in Parallel Out
SISO = Serial in Serial Out
situationsabhängig contingent
Situationsabhängigkeit contingency
Situationsanalyse situation analysis
situativ contingent
Sitzungsschicht session layer
Sitzungssteuerung session control
skalieren scale (to)
Sklavenprozessor slave processor

Sklavensystem slave system
Skonto cash discount
SLSI = Super Large Scale Integration
SLT = Solid Logic Technology
SMTP = Simple Mail Transfer Protocol
sofortige Umstellung instant changeover
sofortiger Abbruch immediate cancel
Sofortzugriff immediate access
Software-Angebot supply of software
Software-Anpassung software customizing, software tailoring
Software-Diebstahl software theft
Software-Entwickler software engineer, software developer
Software-Entwicklungssystem software development system
Software-Entwicklungsumgebung software development environment
Software-Entwurfsmethode software design methodology
Software-Entwurfsprinzip software design principle
Software-Ergonomie software ergonomics
Software-Fehlertoleranz software error tolerance
Software-Generator software generator
Software-Haftpflicht software liability
Software-Haus software house
Software-Ingenieur software engineer
Software-Inspektion software inspection
Software-Kompatibilität software compatibility
Software-Konfiguration software configuration
Software-Konfigurationsmanagement software configuration management
Software-Krise software crisis
Software-Lebenszyklus-Modell software life cycle model
Software-Lizenz software licence
Software-Mangel software deficiency
Software-Markt software market
Software-Paket software package
Software-Pflege software maintenance
Software-Pirat software pirate
Software-Produkt software product
Software-Projekt software project
Software-Prüfung software auditing
Software-Psychologie psychology of software development
Software-Qualität software quality
Software-Qualitätssicherung software quality assurance
Software-Schnittstelle software interface
Software-Schutz software protection
Software-Technik software engineering
Software-Technologie software technology

Software-Überwachung software monitoring
Software-Umgebung software environment
Software-Verschlüsselung software ciphering
Software-Verträglichkeit software compatibility
Software-Virus software virus
Software-Wartung software maintenance
Software-Werkzeug software tool
Software-Wiederverwendbarkeit software reusability
Software-Wiederverwendung software reuse
Software-Zuverlässigkeit software reliability
Soll-Ist-Vergleich actual vs. target comparison
Soll-Portfolio target portfolio
Sollkonzept target concept
Sollwert desired value, reference value
Sollzustand target system
sollzustandsorientierter Ansatz target system-based approach
Sonderzeichen special character
Sonst-Anweisung ELSE statement
Sortieralgorithmus sort algorithm
Sortierbegriff sort criterion
sortieren sort (to)
Sortierschlüssel sort key
soziale Auswirkung social impact
soziale Effizienz social efficiency
soziale Innovation social innovation
soziale Intelligenz social maturity
soziales Bedürfnis social need
soziales System social system
Sozialverhalten social behavior
Sozialwissenschaft Social Science
Soziobiologie Sociobiology
Soziologie Sociology
soziotechnisch sociotechnical
soziotechnischer Ansatz sociotechnical approach
soziotechnisches System sociotechnical system
SPAG = Standards Promotion and Application Group
Spaghetti-Programm spaghetti program, unstructured program
Spalte column
SPARC = Standards Planning and Requirements Comittee
spätester Beginntermin latest start date
Speicher memory, storage
Speicher mit schnellem Zugriff fast access memory

Speicher mit seriellem Zugriff serial access memory
Speicher mit wahlfreiem Zugriff random access memory
Speicherauslegung memory configuration
Speicherauszug dump
Speicherbereich storage partition
Speicherbildschirm memory screen
Speicherform storage mode
Speicherfunktion hash function, storage function
Speichergerät storage device
Speicherhierarchie storage hierarchy
Speicherkapazität storage capacity
Speicherkarte memory card, micro circuit card
Speicherkontrolle storage check
Speichermedium storage medium
speichern store (to)
speichernde Stelle storing authority
Speicherorganisation storage organization
Speicherschreibmaschine memory typewriter
Speicherschutz memory protection
Speichertechnik storage technology
Speichervermittlung store and forward switching
Speicherverwaltung memory management, storage management
Speicherwerk storage unit
Speicherzugriff memory access
Sperrecht confidentiality right
sperren block (to), lock (to)
Sperrfrist blocking period
Spezialaufgabe special task
Spezialisierung specialization
Spezifikation specification
Spezifikationsschein specification certificate
Spezifikationssprache specification language
spezifizieren specify (to)
Spiegelplatten-Konzept mirror-disk concept
Spiegelung mirroring
Spieltheorie game theory
Spinnennetz-Diagramm cobweb diagram, spiderweb diagram
Spitzenbelastung peak load
Spool = Simultanuous Peripheral Operations Online
Spooldatei spool file
Sprachanalyse speech analysis
Sprachannotationssystem speech annotation system
Sprachausgabe speech output

Sprachausgabesystem speech output system
Sprachbox voice box
Sprachcodierer speech encoder, voice coder, vocoder
Sprache speech, voice, language
Sprache der vierten Generation fourth generation language
Spracheingabe speech input
Sprachen-Kompatibilität language compatibility
Spracherkennung voice recognition
Sprachgeneration programming language generation
Sprachkommunikation speech communications
Sprachkompression speech compression
Sprachmächtigkeit power of language
Sprachnachrichtensystem voice message exchange system
Sprachsignal speech signal
Sprachspeicherdienst voice message service
Sprachspeichersystem speech filing system
Sprachsynthese speech synthesis
Sprachteil language subset
Sprachübersetzer programming language translator
Sprachübersetzung language translation
Sprachübertragung voice communications
Sprachumfang power of language
Sprachverarbeitung speech processing
Sprachwiedergabe speech retrieval
Sprecheridentifikation identification of speaker
Sprecherverifikation verification of speaker
Sprinkleranlage automated sprinklers set
SPSS = Statistical Package for the Social Science
Spur track
Spurbreite track width
Spurdichte track density
SQL = Structured Query Language
SSADM = Structured Systems Analysis and Design Methodology
SSI = Small Scale Integration
SSW = Systemsoftware
Stabdiagramm bar chart, rod diagram
Stabilität stability
Stabilitätsanalyse stability analysis
Stabs-Projektorganisation staff-project organization
Stadtfunk- und Rufdienst city radio call service
Stammdatei master file
Stammdaten permanent data, master data
Stammdatenpflege updating
Standard standard
Standardanwendungsprogramm standard application program
Standardauswertung standard report
Standardbericht standard report
Standarddatenformat standard data format
standardisiertes Interview standardized interview
Standardisierung standardization
Standardprogramm standard program
Standardsoftware standard software
Standardsoftware-Paket application package
Standardtext standard text
Standardwert default value
ständig anwesend resident
Standleitung dedicated connection, dedicated line
Standort location
Stapel batch
Stapelauftrag batch job
Stapelbetrieb batch mode
Stapelfernverarbeitung remote batch processing
Stapelverarbeitung batch processing
Stärke strength
Stärken/Schwächen-Analyse strengths/weaknesses analysis
Stärken/Schwächen-Katalog list of systems strengths/weaknesses
Stärken/Schwächen-Profil strengths/weaknesses profile
Stärkenkatalog list of systems strengths
starre Magnetplatte rigid magnetic disk
Starrheit inflexibility
Start/Stop-Betrieb start/stop operation
stationärer Belegleser fixed document reader
statisch static
statische Autorisierung static authorizing
statische Datei static file
statische Dateisicherung static file backup
statische Instrumentierung static instrumentation
statische Programmanalyse static program analysis
statische Topologie static topology
statischer Speicher static memory
statisches Hilfesystem static help system
statisches Qualitätsmaß static quality measure
statisches Sitzen fixed sitting

statisches System static system
statisches Testen static testing
Statistik statistics
Statistikinterpreter statistics interpreter
statistische Analyse statistical analysis
Status-quo-Portfolio status quo portfolio
Statusanzeiger status indicator
Statusinformation status information
Stecker plug
Stecker-Kompatibilität plug compatibility
Steckerbuchse port
steckerkompatibel plug compatible
Steckkarte board
Steckplatz slot
Steckrahmen backplane
Stelle position
Stellenbeschreibung job description
Stellenbesetzungsplan staffing table, employee roster
Stellenbildung Informationsfunktion information function structuring
Stelleninhaber incumbent, jobholder
Stellenplan appointment schema
Stellglied controlling element
Stellgröße independent variable
Stereo-Bildbetrachter 3D terminal
Sternnetz star network, wheel network
Sternring-Topologie loop topology
Sterntopologie star topology, wheel topology
Steuerbarkeit controllability
Steuerbefehl control command
Steuereinheit control unit
Steuerfluß flow of control
Steuerhebel control lever, joy stick
Steuerknüppel joy stick
Steuerkonsole control console
steuern control (to)
Steuerprogramm control program
Steuerrechner control computer
Steuerregel control rule
Steuersprache control language
Steuerung control
Steuerungsdaten control characters, control record
Steuerungsfunktion control function
Steuerungsgröße control quantity
Steuerungsinformation control information
Steuerungsprogramm controller program
Steuerungstechnik control engineering
Steuerwerk control unit
Steuerzeichen control character
Stichprobe sample
Stichprobenprüfung sampling inspection
Stichprobenverfahren sampling
Stichtag deadline

Stichtagsumstellung fixed day changeover, one-for-one changeover
Stiftplotter pen plotter
Stillstand deadlock
Stillstandzeit downtime
stochastisch stochastic
stochastische Heuristik stochastic heuristics
Störgröße disturbance, interference factor, disturbance variable
stornieren cancel (to)
Störquelle noise source
Störsignal drop-in signal
Störspitze noise peak
Störung interference, disturbance
störungsfreier Betrieb fault-free operation
Strahlenschutz radiation protection
Strategie strategy
Strategie der Unternehmung corporate strategy
Strategieplanung strategy planning
Strategietyp type of strategy
strategische Erfolgsposition strategic success position
strategische Frühaufklärung strategic early warning
strategische Geschäftseinheit strategic business unit
strategische Informationssystem-Einheit strategic information system component
strategische Informationssystem-Planung strategic information system planning
strategische Lücke strategic gap
strategische Planung strategic planning
startegische Stoßrichtung strategic thrust
strategische Testplanung strategic test planning
strategischer Schlüsselfaktor strategic key factor
strategisches Informationsmanagement strategic information management
strategisches Informationssystem strategic information system
strategisches Management strategic management
strategisches Ziel strategic goal
Streß stress
Streßfaktor stressor
Streßprogramm program for stress testing
Strichcode bar code
String-Verarbeitung string processing
Strom power
Stromausfall power failure
Stromkreis power circuit
Stromverbrauch power consumption

Stromversorgung power supply
Stromversorgungsgerät power supply unit
Struktogramm structured box chart, Nassi-Shneiderman chart, Chapin chart
Struktur structure
Struktur-Modellierungswerkzeug structure modelling tool
Strukturähnlichkeit similarity of structure
Strukturblock structure block
Strukturdiagramm structure diagram
Struktureinheit organizational unit
strukturerhaltend structure preserving
Strukturgleichheit equality of structure
Strukturierbarkeit ability of structuring
strukturieren structure (to)
strukturierte Analyse structured analysis
strukturierte Programmbeschreibung structured program specification
strukturierte Programmierung structured programming
strukturierte Systemanalyse structured systems analysis
strukturierter Datentyp structured data type
strukturierter Entwurf structured design
strukturierter Systementwurf structured systems design
strukturiertes Gruppengespräch team-oriented inspection
strukturiertes Programm structured program
strukturiertes Programmieren structured programming
strukturiertes Testen structured walk-through
Strukturiertheit structuredness
Strukturierung structuring
Strukturierungsgrad degree of structuring
Strukturierungsmethode structuring method
Strukturkonzept structuring concept
Strukturorganisation organizational structure
Strukturtest interior test, test of structure
Stück-Perioden-Ausgleich part-period balancing
Stückkosten unit costs
Stückliste bill of materials, parts list
Stücklistenauflösung bill explosion
Stücklistenprozessor bill of materials processor
Stufenkonzept stage hypothesis
Stufenmodell stage model

stufenweise Umstellung stagewise changeover
stufenweise Verfeinerung stagewise refinement
subjektiv subjective
subjektive Arbeitssituation subjective job situation
subjektiver Informationsbedarf subjective information requirement
subjektiver Konflikt personal conflict
substantielles Organisieren substantial organizing
Substitution substitution
Suchabfrage search query
Suchbaum search tree
suchen search (to)
Suchen mit Mehrfachbegriffen multiattribute search
Suchschlüssel search key
Suchstrategie search strategy
Suchverfahren search procedure
summarische Arbeitsplatzbewertung global job evaluation
summarischer Verrechnungspreis overall internal price
Summenkontrolle summation check
Summenkreuzprüfung crossfooting, crossfoot check
summieren sum (to), add (to)
Supercomputer super computer
SUS = Software Update Service
SV = Sachverständiger
SVA = Strategic Value Analysis
SVD = Schweizerische Vereinigung für Datenverarbeitung
SWIFT = Society for Worldwide Interbank Financial Telecommunications
sx = simplex
symbolische Adresse symbolic address
symbolische Informationsverarbeitung symbolic information processing
symbolische Logik symbolic logic
symbolisches Organisieren symbolic organizing
symbolisches Rechnen symbolic computing
symbolisches Testen symbolic testing
symmetrische Störung periodic interference
Symptom symptom
synchron synchronous
Synchronbetrieb synchronous mode
synchrone Datenübertragung synchronous data transmission
Synchronisiereinheit synchronization device
Synchronisierung synchronization

Synektik

Synektik synectics
Synergetik synergetics
Synergie synergy
Synonym synonym
Synonymerkennung identification of synonyms
Syntax syntax
Syntaxdiagramm syntax diagram
Synthese synthesis
synthetischer Job synthetic job
synthetisches Denken synthetic thinking
synthetisches Schlußfolgern synthetic inferencing
System vorbestimmter Zeiten time and motion measurement
Systemabbruch unusual end, systems crash
Systemabmeldung systems log-off, systems sign-off
Systemabnahme systems sign-off
Systemanalyse systems analysis
Systemanmeldung systems log-on, systems sign-on
Systemansatz systems approach
Systemarchitektur systems architecture
Systematisierung systematization
Systemaufruf systems call
Systemaufzeichnung systems logging
Systemausfall systems crash, systems failure, systems outage
Systemausgang systems exit
Systemauslegung systems layout
Systemauswahl systems selection
Systembediener systems operator
Systembefehl systems command
Systembelastung systems load
Systembetrieb systems operational mode
Systemdatum systems date
Systemdenken systems thinking
Systemdokumentation systems documentation
Systemeinführung systems implementation
Systemeinheit systems unit
Systementwicklung systems development
Systementwurf systems design

Systemfehlermeldung systems error report
Systemforschung systems research
Systemgenerierung systems generating
Systemgestalter systems designer
Systemgrenze systems boundary
Systemhaus systems house
Systemimplementierung systems implementation
Systemintegration systems integration
systemisches Denken systemic thinking
Systemkomponente systems component
Systemkonfiguration systems configuration
Systemlehre systems teachings
Systemnutzung systems usage
Systemparameter systems parameter
Systempflege systems maintenance
Systemplaner systems analyst
Systemplanung systems planning
Systemplanungsprojekt application systems project
Systemprogramm systems program
Systemprogrammierer systems programmer
Systemprogrammiersprache systems programming language
Systemprüfung systems auditing, systems check
Systemrevisor systems auditor
Systemschein systems certificate
Systemsoftware systems software
Systemstandard systems default
Systemstruktur systems structure
Systemtechnik systems engineering
Systemtest systems test
Systemtheorie systems theory
Systemuhr realtime clock
Systemumgebung systems environment
Systemverfügbarkeit systems availability
Systemverhalten systems behavior
Systemwiederherstellung systems recovery
Systemzusammenbruch systems crash
Szenario scenario
Szenario-Technik scenario technique

T

TA = Technology Assessment
TA = Terminal Adapter
Tabelle table
Tabellenkalkulation spreadsheet
Tabellenkalkulationssystem spreadsheet system
Tabellenkopf table header
tabellenorientierte Planungssprache table-oriented planning modelling language
Tabellensteuerung table control
Tablett digitizer
TAE = Telekommunikations-Anschluß-Einheit
Tagesdurchschnitt average per day
täglicher Sicherungsdatenträger daily backup volume
Taktfrequenz clock frequency
Taktgeber clock generator, internal clock
taktil tactile
taktile Rückmeldung tactile feedback
taktile Schnittstellentechnik tactile man-machine interface technology
taktisches Management tactical management
TAN = Transaktionsnummer
Taschentelephon pocket telephone
Tastatur keyboard, keypad
Tastaturauswahl keyboard selection
Tastaturschablone keyboard template
Tastaturverschlüsseler keyboard encoder
tastbar tactile
Taste button, key
Tastenanschlag key touch
Tastendruck keystroke
Tastenfolge key sequence
Tastenrückmeldung key feedback
Tätigkeit work element
Tätigkeitenkatalog list of work elements
Tätigkeitsbericht time estimate report
Tätigkeitsbeschreibung job description
Tätigkeitsspielraum job scope
Tätigkeitswechsel job rotation
Tatsache fact
tauschen barter (to)
Tauschgeschäft bartering
TBF = Time Between Failures
TBT = Technology Based Training
TBx = Telebox
TCAM = Telecommunications Access Method
TCP = Transport Control Protocol
TCS = Telecommunications System
TDM = Time Division Multiplexing
TDMA = Time Division Multiplexing Access
Technik technics, technology
Technikanalyse performance engineering
Technikbedarf equipment requirements
Techniksystem technological system
Techniktyp equipment type
technische Beschränkung technological constraint
technische Datenverarbeitung non-administrative data processing
technische Eigenschaft physical characteristic
technische Grenze technological constraint
technische Innovation technological innovation
technische Integration technological integration
technische Nutzungsdauer physical life
technische Spezifikation technological specification
technische Unterstützung technical support
technische Vorschrift technical regulation
technischer Datenschutz technical data protection
technischer Entwurf technical design
technischer Kundendienst technical service
technischer Mangel physical deficiency
Technologie technology
Technologiefolgen-Abschätzung technology assessment
Technologiemanagement technology management
Technologiestrategie technology strategy
Technologietransfer technology transfer
Technologietrend-Analyse analysis of technological trend
Technologievorhersage technology forecasting
Technologiewirkungsanalyse technology impact analysis
technologischer Determinismus technological determinism
technologischer Wandel technological change
Technometrie technometry
Technovation = techno(logy and inno)vation
technozentrischer Ansatz technocentric approach
Teil part
Teilaufgabe subtask
teilautonome Gruppe semi-autonomous group

Teilerhebung

Teilerhebung partial survey
Teilfunktion subfunction
Teilhaberbetrieb transaction-driven mode
Teilhabersystem transaction-driven system
Teilkostenrechnung direct costing
Teilmenge subset
Teilnahme participation
Teilnehmer participant, subscriber
Teilnehmerbetrieb time sharing mode
Teilnehmerendgerät customer terminal
Teilnehmerklasse class of subscribers
Teilnehmerstation subscriber station
Teilnehmersystem timesharing system
Teilphase subphase
Teilproblem subproblem
Teilprojekt subproject
Teilschema subschema
Teilstrategie partial strategy
Teilsystem subsystem
Teilsystembildung partitioning system
Teilumstellung partial changeover, stagewise changeover
Telearbeit teleworking, telecommuting
Telearbeitsplatz workplace for telecommuting
Telebox-Dienst telebox service
Telebrief-Dienst teleletter service
Teledienst teleservice
Telefax = Teleprinter Facsimile Exchange
Telefax-Dienst telefax service
Teleheimarbeit telehome working
Telekauf teleshopping
Telekommunikation telecommunications
Telekommunikationsdienst telecommunications service
Telekommunikationsnetz telecommunications network
Telekommunikationsordnung telecommunications order
Telekommunikationssystem telecommunications system
Telekonferenz teleconference
Telematik telematics
Telematik = Tele(kommunikation und Infor)matik
Telemetrie telemetry, telemetering
Telephon telephone
Telephon-Kreditkarte telecredit card
Telephon-Nebenstellenanlage private automatic branch exchange
Telephonanschluß telephone connection
Telephonie telephony
Telephonnetz telephone network
Telephonüberwachung telephone monitoring

Telephonvermittlung telephone exchange
Telepost telepost
Teleprogramm teleprogram
Teleprogrammierung teleprogramming
Telesoftware telesoftware
Teletex = Teleprinter Text Exchange
Teletex-Dienst teletex service
Teletext teletext
Telex = Teleprinter Exchange
Telex-Dienst telex service
Telexnetz telex network
TEMEX = Telemetry Exchange
Temex-Dienst temex service
TEMPEST = Temporary Emanation and Spurious Transmission
Tempest-Gerät tempest device
Tendenz tendency, trend
Terminierung scheduling
Terminkalender-Management calendar management
Terminologie terminology
Test-Abdeckungsgrad ratio of test coverage
Testabdeckung test coverage
Testbarkeit testability
Testbericht test report
Testdaten test data
Testdaten des Benutzers user test data
Testdaten-Generator test data generator
Testdatenerstellung preparing test data
Testdokumentation test documentation
Testen testing
testen test (to)
Testergebnis test result
Testfall testcase
Testfallmatrix testcase matrix
Testhilfe debugging aid
Testinstallation test installation
Testlauf test run
Testling object of testing
Testmethode testing method
Testmuster test pattern
Testobjekt testling
Testplan testing plan
Testproduktivität testing productivity
Testprogramm test program
Testrate testing rate
Testresistenz testing resistance
Teststrategie testing strategy
Testsystem testing system
Testtreiber test driver
Testumgebung testing environment
Testunterstützung debugging support
Testwerkzeug debugging tool
Text-Reduktionsmechanismus text reducing mechanism

Textautomat word processing equipment, word processor
Textbearbeitung word editing
Textende end of text
Textfax textfax
Textfax = Text und Faksimile
Textkommunikation text communications
Textprozessor text processor
Textseite text page
Textverarbeitung text processing, word processing
Textverarbeitungssystem word processing system, word processor
Textvergleich comparison of text
TFA = Technologiefolgen-Abschätzung
Theorie der kognitiven Komplexität cognitive complexity theory
Theorie des Verhandelns theory of bargaining
Thermo-Transfer-Drucker thermo transfer printer
Thermodrucker thermo printer
Thesaurus thesaurus
Tiefensuche depth-first search
Tieftemperatur-Computer cryo computer
Time-Sharing time sharing
Time-Sharing-Rechenzentrum time sharing computer center
Tintenspritzplotter ink jet plotter
Tintenstrahldrucker ink jet printer
Tippfehler typing error
Tischplotter table plotter
Tischrechner calculator
TKD = Technischer Kundendienst
TKO = Telekommunikationsordnung
TMU = Time Measurement Unit
TMO-Technology = Thermo-Magnetic-Optic Technology
Token-Passing-Verfahren token passing procedure
Tongenerierung sound generating
TOP = Technical and Office Protocols
Top-down-Entwurf top-down design
Top-down-Strategie top-down strategy
Top-down-Test top-down test
Top-Ereignis top event, root event
Topographie topography
Topologie topology
Torkeln tumbling
Tortendiagramm pie chart
Totalausfall black failure, total breakdown
Totalerhebung complete survey
Totalumstellung total changeover
TP = Teleprocessing
TP-Monitor = Teleprocessing Monitor

tpi = tracks per inch
Tracingverfahren tracing
tragbar portable
tragbarer PC laptop, portable
Tragbarkeit portability
Trägerdienst bearer service
Trägerprogramm bearer program
Traktor tractor
Trainingsprogramm trainee program
Transaktion transaction
Transaktionsanalyse transaction analysis
Transaktionsbetrieb transaction mode
Transaktionsdiagramm transaction diagram
Transaktionsnummer transaction number
transaktionsorientierte Kostenverrechnung transaction pricing
Transaktionsrate transaction rate
Transaktionssystem transaction system
Transaktionswegleitung transaction routing
transienter Störer power transient
transitiv transitive
transitive Abhängigkeit transitive dependency
Transparenz transparency
Transportdienst communications service
transportieren transport (to)
Transportschicht transport layer
Transportsicherung shipping cardboard
Transporttechnik communications technology
Treiber driver
Trendanalyse trend analysis
Trendermittlung trend identification
Trennsymbol separate clause
Trieb motive
Trockentest dry running, dry testing
Trommeldrucker drum printer
Trommelplotter drum plotter
TSS = Telephone Software Service
TSS = Time-Sharing System
TTC = Teletype Code
TTU = Teletex-Telex-Umsetzer
Ttx = Teletex
TTY = Teletype Terminal
Tupel tupel
Tutorialprogramm tutorial program
Typ type
Typenbanddrucker type band printer
Typendrucker type printer
Typenrad type wheel, print wheel
Typenraddrucker daisy wheel printer
Typenvereinbarung type declaration

U

überarbeiten edit (to)
Überblick overview
überbrücken bridge (to)
Überbrückungsprogramm bridge program
Übereinstimmung conformity
Übergangszeit inter-operation time
übergehen skip (to)
übergeordnetes System master system
Überkapazität overcapacity
überlagern overlay (to)
Überlagerung overlay
Überlappung overlap
Überlappungsfehler capture error
Überlassungsschein cession certificate
Überlastbarkeit overload capacity
überlasten overload (to)
Überlastung congestion, overload
Überlauf overflow
übermitteln transmit (to)
Übermittlung transmission
Übermittlungsabschnitt data link
Übermittlungsvorschrift link protocol, link procedure
überprüfen review (to), verify (to)
Überprüfung check, review, verification
Übersetzer translator
Übersetzungsrate compilation rate
Übersichtsdiagramm general diagram
Überspannung overvoltage
Überspannung durch Blitzentladung lightning explosion magnetic power
Überspannung durch Nuklearexplosion nuclear explosion magnetic power
Überspannungsschutz overvoltage protection
Überspannungsschutz-Element overvoltage protection device
Überstunden overtime
übertragbar portable
Übertragbarkeit portability
Übertragung portation, transmission
Übertragungseigenschaft transmission property
Übertragungsfehler line transmission error
Übertragungsgeschwindigkeit transmission speed
Übertragungskanal transmission channel
Übertragungskapazität transmission capacity
Übertragungsleitung transmission line
Übertragungsmedium transmission medium
Übertragungsmodus transmission mode
Übertragungsrate transmission rate
Übertragungstechnik transmission technology
überwachen monitor (to)
Überwacher monitor
Überwachung monitoring
Überwachungseinrichtung monitoring device
Überwachungsverfahren monitoring procedure
UCD = Universal Decimal Classification
UFAB = Unterlagen für Ausschreibung und Bewertung von DV-Leistungen
UHSIC = Ultra High Speed Integrated Circuit
UL = User Language
Ultracomputer ultra computer
umbenennen rename (to)
Umdrehung turn
umfassend global
umfassender Entwurf global design
Umgebung environment
Umgebungsanforderung environmental requirement
Umgebungsbedingung environmental condition
umkehren invert (to)
Umprogrammierung reprogramming
Umrißplan outline guide
Umsatz gross income, turnover
Umsatzfrühwarnung early sales warning
umschalten shift (to)
Umschalter alteration switch
Umschalttaste shift key
Umschichtung turnover
Umschlag turnover
Umschlagshäufigkeit turnover rate
Umschulung retraining, reeducation
Umstellung changeover, cutover
Umstellungseinrichtung changeover device
Umstellungsplan changeover plan
Umstrukturierung restructuring
Umwandlung conversion
Umwandlungszeit assembly time
Umweltanforderung environmental requirement
Umweltbedingung environmental condition
Umweltinformationssystem ecological information system
Umweltverschmutzung pollution
unabhängig independent
unabhängig arbeitend stand alone
unabhängige Variable independent variable
unangemessen inadequate

unbefugte Entschlüsselung unauthorized deciphering
unbefugter Zugriff unauthorized access
Unempfindlichkeit robustness
Unfähigkeit inability
unformatierte Daten unformatted data
ungeblockter Satz unblocked record
ungeplant unscheduled
ungeplante Stillstandzeit unscheduled downtime
ungeplante Wartung unscheduled maintenance
ungeradzahlig odd
ungeradzahlige Parität odd parity
ungeübter Benutzer novice user
Ungewißheit uncertainty
Ungleichheit odd parity
ungültig invalid
ungültige Adresse invalid address
ungültige Zeichenkombination invalid combination of characters
unipolarer Transistor unipolar transistor
univariable Prognose univariable forecasting
Universalcomputer all purpose computer, general purpose computer, mainframe
Universelle Dezimalklassifikation Universal Decimal Classification
universelle Programmiersprache universal programming language
universelles Ersatzzeichen wild card
unlauterer Wettbewerb unfair competition
unstrukturierte Aufgabe unstructured task
unterbrechen interrupt (to)
unterbrechen durch Operatoreingriff flush (to)
Unterbrechung interrupt
unterbrechungsfreie Stromversorgung uninterruptable power supply
unterbrechungsfreier Computer non-stop computer
unterbrechungsloser Betrieb non-stop processing
unterbrochene Beobachtung intermittent observation
Untergebener subordinate
untergeordnetes System slave system
Untermenü submenu
unternehmen enterprise (to)
Unternehmen enterprise
Unternehmensberater management consultant
Unternehmensberatung management consulting
Unternehmensbereich enterprise area
Unternehmensebene corporate level

Unternehmenserfolg corporate success
Unternehmensforschung operations research
Unternehmenskultur corporate culture
Unternehmensmodell corporate model
Unternehmenspersönlichkeit corporate identity
Unternehmensplan corporate plan
Unternehmenspolitik corporate politics
Unternehmensstrategie corporate strategy
unternehmensweite Datenbasis corporate data base
unternehmensweites Informationsmanagement enterprise-wide information management
Unternehmensziel corporate objective, corporate goal
Unterprogramm subprogram, subroutine
Unterricht mit Computergraphik animated computer education
Unterschriftenleser signature reader
unterstützen aid (to), assist (to), support (to)
Unterstützung assistance, support
Unterstützungsaufgabe support task
Unterstützungsdienstleistung support service
Unterstützungsfunktion support function
Unterstützungsmaßnahme support activity
untersuchen investigate (to)
Untersuchen des Istzustands study of current system
Untersuchungsbefund survey finding
Untersystem subsystem
unvereinbar incompatible
Unvereinbarkeit incompatibility
unverschlüsselte Daten unciphered data
unvollständig incomplete
unvollständiger Prototyp incomplete prototype
Unvollständigkeit incompleteness
unwirksam ineffective
unwirtschaftlich inefficient
Unwirtschaftlichkeit inefficiency
Unzufriedenheit dissatisfaction
UPC = Universal Product Code
UPL = Universal Programming Language
UPS = Uninterruptable Power Supply
Urbeleg original document, source document
Urheberrecht copyright
UrhG = Urheberrechtsschutz-Gesetz
Urlader bootstrap
Ursache cause
Ursachenanalyse analysis of causes

Ursache/Wirkung-Analyse
cause/effectivity analysis
Ursache/Wirkung-Beziehung
cause/effectivity relation
Ursprungsbereich source area
Ursprungsprogramm source program

USP = Unic Selling Position
USV = Unterbrechungsfreie Stromversorgung
UWG = Gesetz gegen den unlauteren Wettbewerb

V

Validität validity
Validitätstest validity test
VAN = Value Added Network
VANS = Value Added Network Services
VAR = Value Added Reseller
Variable variable
variable Daten variable data
variable Kosten variable costs
Varianz variance
Varianzanalyse analysis of variances
Varianzmatrix matrix of variances
VAS = Value Added Service
VDE = Verband Deutscher Elektrotechniker
VDF = Verband der Datenverarbeitungs-Fachleute
VDRZ = Verband Deutscher Rechenzentren
VDT = Visual Display Terminal
VDU = Visual Display Unit
Vektor vector
Vektorgraphik vector graphics
Vektorprozessor vector processor
Vektorrechner vector computer
Venn-Diagramm Venn diagram
Verallgemeinerung generalization
Veränderliche variable
verändern modify (to), change (to)
Veränderung modification, change
Veränderungsalternative change alternative
Veränderungsanalyse change analysis
Veränderungsprozeß change process
Veränderungswiderstand resistance to change
veranlassen order (to)
Verantwortlichkeit accountability
Verantwortung responsibility
Verantwortungsbereich area of responsibility
verarbeiten process (to)
Verarbeiter processor
Verarbeitung processing
Verarbeitung natürlicher Sprache natural language processing
Verarbeitungsfehler processing error
Verarbeitungsleistung processing performance
Verarbeitungsrechner host
Verarbeitungsregel processing rule
Verarbeitungstechnik processing technology
verbale Beschreibung verbal description, narrative (in DFD)
Verband association

verbessern improve (to), upgrade (to)
Verbesserung upgrade
Verbesserungsfähigkeit upgradability
Verbindbarkeit connectivity
verbinden connect (to), link (to)
Verbindlichkeit accounts payables, liability
Verbindung connection, link
Verbindungsabbruch break
Verbindungsglied link
Verbindungsgeräte interface hardware
Verbindungsgrad degree of interconnectivity
Verbindungsleitung link line
Verbindungsschicht data link layer
Verbindungszeit link time
Verbund grouping
Verbund-Nummernsystem compound numbering system
Verbundnetz linked network
Verbundschlüssel compound key
verdeckte Beobachtung hidden observation
Verdrahtung cabling
vereinbar compatible
Vereinbarkeit compatibility
Vereinbarung agreement, declaration
Vereinbarungsteil declaration partition
Vereinfachung rationalization, simplification
Vereinigung association
Vererbung inheritance
Verfahren procedure, technique
Verfahrensbeschreibung procedure specification
Verfahrensentwurf procedure design
Verfahrenshandbuch procedure manual
Verfahrenskritik process analysis
Verfallsdatum expiration date
Verfeinerung refinement
verfügbarer Bestand free stock balance
verfügbarer Lagerbestand stock on hand
Verfügbarkeit availability
Verfügbarkeitsgrad availability ratio
Verfügbarkeitstermin des Materials material availability date
Vergleich comparison
vergleichen compare (to)
Vergleicher comparator
Vergleichsoperation comparative operation
vergrößern magnify (to)
Verhalten behavior
Verhaltenshypothese behavior hypothesis
Verhaltensmuster behavioral pattern
Verhaltenswissenschaft behavioral science

Verhältnisskala

Verhältnisskala proportional scale
Verhältniszahl proportional figure, ratio figure
Verifikation verification
verifizieren verify (to)
Verkauf sales, selling
Verkäufer salesperson
Verkäuferprofil salespeople profile
Verkaufsdatenerfassung sales data capturing
Verkaufsgebiet sales territory
Verkaufsinformationssystem sales information system
Verkaufspreis sales price, retail price
Verkaufspunkt point of sale
Verkehrsanalyse traffic analysis
Verkehrsgüte traffic quality
verkettete Dateiorganisation chained file organization
Verkettung chaining, linkage
Verklemmung deadlock
Verlängerung renewal
Verlust loss
Verlustrate loss rate
Vermittlung exchange
Vermittlungsart exchange mode
Vermittlungsstelle switchboard, switching center
Vermittlungstechnik switching technology
Vermögenswert asset
Verneinung negation
Vernetzungsgrad connectivity
verpflichtend mandatory, obligatory
Verpflichtung commitment
Verrechnungspreis internal price
Verrechnungsverkehr clearing
Versalsatz capital letters
Versand shipping
verschiebbar relocatable
Verschluß fastener
verschlüsseln cipher (to), encode (to)
verschlüsselte Daten ciphered data, encoded data
verschlüsselter Text ciphertext, cryptogram
Verschlüsselung ciphering, encryption, encoding
Verschlüsselungsmethode ciphering method, encoding method
Verschlüsselungssystem ciphering system
Verschränkung interleaving
Versicherung insurance
Version release
Versionsplanung version planning
Versorgungskette supply chain
Verständlichkeit understandability
Verstärker amplifier

verstümmeln mutilate (to)
Versuch experiment, test
Versuch und Irrtum trial and error
Versuchsbetrieb trial mode
Vertauschung commutation, transposition
Vertauschungsfehler transposition error
verteilen distribute (to)
Verteiler dispatcher
Verteilerliste distribution list
verteilte Datenbank distributed data base
verteilte Datenbasis distributed data base
verteilte Datenverarbeitung distributed data processing
verteilte Intelligenz distributed intelligence
verteilte künstliche Intelligenz distributed artificial intelligence
verteilte Wissensbasis distributed knowledge base
verteiltes Computersystem distributed computer system
verteiltes Programm distributed program
Verteilung allocation, distribution
vertikale Arbeitsstrukturierung job enrichment
Vertrag contract
vertraglich by contract, contractual
Verträglichkeit compatibility
Verträglichkeitseinrichtung compatibility device
Vertragsdauer life of contract
Vertragsentwurf contract design, draft contract
Vertragsgegenstand object of contract
Vertragspartner contracting party
Vertragsrecht contract law
Vertragsstrafe contractual penalty
Vertragsverhältnis contractual relationship
Vertragsverhandlung contract negotiation
Vertragsverpflichtung contractual obligation
Vertrauensschaden-Versicherung insurance against damage of confidence
vertraulich confidential
Vertraulichkeit confidentiality
Vertriebsbeauftragter sales representative
Vertriebsinformationssystem sales information system
Vertriebslogistik distribution logistics
vervielfältigen duplicate (to), copy (to)
Vervielfältigen von Software duplication of software
Verwalter administrator

Verwaltung administration, stewardship
Verwaltungsarbeit administrative work
Verwaltungsautomation automation of public administration
Verwaltungsinformatik public administration informatics
Verweilzeit job around time
Verwendbarkeit usability
verwenden use (to)
Verwendungsnachweis implosion
Verwertung utilization
Verwertungsziel utilization goal
Verwundbarkeit vulnerability
Verwundbarkeitsanalyse vulnerability analysis
verwürfeln scramble (to)
Verwürfler scrambler
verzahnt ablaufende Verarbeitung concurrent processing
Verzeichnis index
verzögerter Wiederanlauf deferred restart
Verzögerung delay
verzweigen branch (to)
Verzweigung branch
VHLL = Very High Level Language
VHSIC = Very High Speed Integrated Circuit
Vielfachzugriff multiplexing access
4GL = fourth generation language
virtuell virtual
virtuelle Adresse virtual address
virtuelle Kommunikation virtual communications
virtuelle Leitung virtual line
virtuelle Mappe virtual map
virtuelle Maschine virtual machine
virtuelle Peripherie virtual periphery
virtuelle Verbindung virtual connection
virtueller Speicher virtual storage
virtuelles Betriebssystem virtual operating system
virtuelles Endgerät virtual terminal
Virus virus
Virus-Programm virus program
Visualisierung visualization
Visualisierungstechnik visualization technique
VLAN = Very Local Area Network
VLSI = Very Large Scale Integration
Vocoder = vo(ice and)coder
voll gekennzeichneter Name fully qualified name
vollduplex full duplex
Vollduplexbetrieb all duplex mode
Vollkosten total costs
vollständig complete

vollständiger Prototyp complete prototype
vollständiges Testen exhaustive testing
Vollständigkeit completeness
Vollständigkeitsüberprüfung check of completeness
Volltext-Datenbank full text data base
Volumenmodell volume model
vom Bediener eingeleiteter Abbruch operator initiated termination
vorausschauende Arbeitsgestaltung prospective job design
Voraussetzung premise
voraussichtliche Lebensdauer life expectancy
Vorbedingung prerequisite
Vorbereiten der Implementierung preparation for implementation
vorbeugende Arbeitsgestaltung preventive job design
vorbeugende Wartung preventive maintenance
Vordergrund foreground
Vordergrundauftrag foreground job
Vordergrundprogramm foreground program
Vordruck printed form
Vorentwurf preliminary design
Vorfeldrechner front-end processor
Vorgabezeit-Einheit time measurement unit
Vorgang activity, transaction
Vorgänger predecessor
Vorgangsanalyse activity analysis
Vorgangsintegration integration of activities
Vorgangskette activity chain, trigger chain
Vorgangsknotennetz activity-node network
Vorgangskonzept trigger concept
vorgangsorientiertes System activity-oriented system, trigger-oriented system
Vorgangspfeilnetz activity-arrow network
Vorgangstyp activity type
Vorgehensmodell action model
Vorgesetzter superior, supervisor
vorherige Anweisung previous statement
Vorhersage forecasting
Vorhersagefehler forecast error
Vorhersagemethode forecasting method
Vorkehrung disposition
Vorkopplung feed-forward
Vorlage original
Vorlaufprogramm preprocessor
vorprogrammierte Abfrage programmed query

Vorprozessor preprocessor
Vorrang priority
Vorrechner front-end processor
Vorschaltrechner front-end processor
Vorschau outlook
Vorschlag proposal, proposition
Vorschrift regulation
Vorschub feed
Vorstudie initial study, preliminary study
Vortragstechnik presentation technique
Vorübersetzer precompiler

vorwärts blättern page down (to)
Vorwärtsdokumentation forward documentation
vorwärtsgesteuertes Schlußfolgern forward-controlled inferencing
Vorwärtsverkettung forward chaining
Vorzeichen leading sign
Vorziehenswürdigkeit preference
Vorzug priority
VTAM = **Virtual Teleprocessing Access Method**
VTOC = **Volume Table of Contents**

W

W-Technik = **Warum Technik**
Wachhund watchdog
Wachstum growth
Wachstumsrate growth rate, rate of growth
Wahl option
wählbar optional
Wähldatennetz dialup network
wahlfrei random
wahlfreier Zugriff random access
Wählleitung dialup connection
Wählverbindung switched connection
wahlweise optional
Wahlwort optional word
Wahrnehmung perception
Wahrscheinlichkeit likelihood, probability
Wahrscheinlichkeitsrechnung probability calculus
Wahrscheinlichkeitstheorie probability theory
Währungs- und Devisenmanagement cash management
Währungszeichen currency sign
WAN = **Wide Area Network**
Wanze bug
Wareneingang goods received
Wareneingangsprüfung goods inwards inspection
Warenfluß materials flow
Warenwirtschaftssystem stock inventory management system
Warenzeichenschutz trademark protection
warmer Wiederanlauf warm restart
warmes Ausweich-Rechenzentrum warm backup computing center
Warmstart warm systems restart
Warnanzeige warning indicator
Warnmeldung warning message
Warnsystem warning system
Wartbarkeit maintainability, serviceability
warten maintain (to), serve (to)
Warteschlange queue
Warteschlangenname queue name
Wartezeit queue time
Wartung maintenance
Wartung durch Flickarbeit maintenance by patching
Wartungsanforderung maintenance request
Wartungsbereich service area
Wartungsdokumentation maintenance documentation
Wartungsgebühren maintenance charges
Wartungskonsole maintenance console
Wartungskosten maintenance costs
Wartungsplan maintenance schedule
Wartungsprozessor maintenance processor
Wartungsschein maintenance certificate
Wartungstest maintenance test
Wartungsvereinbarung maintenance agreement
Wartungsvertrag maintenance contract
Wartungszeit maintenance period
Wartungszeitraum maintenance rate
Warum-Technik why-technique
Was/Wenn-Analyse what/if analysis
Wasserfallmodell waterfall model
WBS = **Wissensbasiertes System**
Wechsel-Winchester-Plattenspeicher removable winchester disk storage
Wechselbetrieb asynchronous communications
Wechselbeziehung interaction, interrelation
Wechselplattenspeicher removable disk memory
Wegwahl routing
Wegwerf-Prototyp throw-away prototype
Weißer Kasten white box
Weißer-Kasten-Test white box test
Weiterleitung routing
Weitverkehrsnetz wide area network
Werkbank workbench
Werknutzungsbewilligung permission of usage
Werknutzungsrecht usufructuary right, usage right
Werkschutz industrial police
Werkstattprogrammierung shop-floor programming
Werkstattsteuerung shop-floor control
Werkzeug tool
Werkzeugkasten tool kit
Werkzeugmaschine machine tool
Werkzeugmaschinen-Steuerung machine tool control
Werkzeugschnittstelle tool interface
Wert value
Wertaktivität value activity
Wertanalyse value analysis
Wertanalyse-Arbeitsplan value analysis job plan
Wertbereich domain
Wertdaten value data
Wertgeber valuator
Wertgestaltung value assurance, value engineering
Wertkette value chain
Wertketten-Analyse value chain analysis

Wertsystem value system
Wertverbesserung value improvement
wesentliche Ziffer significant digit
Wettbewerb competition
Wettbewerbsanalyse competition analysis
Wettbewerbsantrieb competitive dynamic
Wettbewerbsbedrohung competitive threat
Wettbewerbsfähigkeit competitiveness
Wettbewerbsfaktor competitive factor
Wettbewerbskraft competitive force
Wettbewerbsposition competitive position
Wettbewerbsreaktion competitive response
Wettbewerbsrecht competition law
Wettbewerbsstrategie competitive strategy
Wettbewerbsvorsprung competitive advantage
Wettbewerbsvorteil competitive advantage
Wettbewerbswaffe competitive weapon
Wettbewerbswirkung competitive impact
Widerruf undo
widersprüchlich inconsistent
Widersprüchlichkeit inconsistency
widerspruchsfrei consistent
Widerspruchsfreiheit consistency
Widerstand resistance
Wiederanlauf restart
Wiederanlaufpunkt checkpoint
Wiederanlaufverfahren restart procedure
wiederauffinden retrieve (to)
Wiederauffüllung des Lagers stock replenishment
Wiederbeschaffungskosten replacement costs
Wiederherstellung recovery
Wiederherstellungsblock recovery block
wiederholbar repetitive
Wiederholbarkeit reproducibility
Wiederholtaste repeat action key
Wiederholung iteration
Wiederholungsschleife iteration loop
Wiederholungstest iterative test
wiederverwendbar reusable
wiederverwendbare Software reusable software
wiederverwendbarer Prototyp reusable prototype
Wiederverwendbarkeit reusability
wiederverwenden reuse (to)
Wildwuchs wild growth
Winchester-Plattenspeicher winchester disk
wirklich real
Wirklichkeit reality
wirksam effective
Wirksamkeit effectiveness

Wirksamkeitsanalyse effectiveness analysis
Wirkung effect
Wirkungsanalyse impact analysis
Wirkungsbereich sphere of actions, scope of activities
Wirkungsbeziehung effectiveness relation
Wirkungsebene effectiveness level
Wirkungsforschung assessment research
Wirkungskette effectivity chain
Wirkungsnetzwerk effectivity network
wirkungsvoll effective
wirtschaftlich efficient
wirtschaftliche Auswirkung economic impact
wirtschaftlicher Nutzen economic benefits
wirtschaftlicher Wert economic value
Wirtschaftlichkeit efficiency
Wirtschaftlichkeitsanalyse efficiency analysis
Wirtschaftlichkeitskennzahl efficiency measure
Wirtschaftlichkeitsrechnung efficiency calculus
Wirtschaftsinformatik economic informatics
Wirtschaftsprüfer chartered accountant
Wirtsprogramm host program
Wirtsrechner host computer
Wirtssprache host language
Wissen knowledge
Wissensakquisition knowledge acquisition
wissensbasierte Arbeit knowledge work
wissensbasierte Benutzerschnittstelle knowledge-based man-machine interface
wissensbasierter Entwurf knowledge-based design
wissensbasiertes System knowledge-based system
Wissensbasis knowledge base
Wissenschaft science
wissenschaftliche Methode scientific method
wissenschaftliche Tagung symposion, symposium
wissenschaftliches Problem scientific problem
Wissensdarstellung knowledge representation
Wissensdatenbank know-how data base, knowledge data base
Wissenseditor knowledge editor
Wissenserwerb knowledge acquisition
Wissensingenieur knowledge engineer
Wissenskoordinator knowledge coordinator
Wissenstransfer knowledge transfer

Wissensverarbeitung knowledge processing
Wissensverwaltungssystem knowledge management system
wohlstrukturiertes Problem well structured problem
WORM = Write Once Read Mostly
Wort word

Wörterbuch dictionary
Wortstammanalyse word stem analysis
Wortzeichen logogram
WS = **Work Station**
WSI = **Wafer Scale Integration**
WYSIWYG = **What You See Is What You Get**

X

XPS = Expertensystem

XTEN = Xerox Telecommunications Network

Z

Z/s = Zeichen pro Sekunde
Zahlendarstellung number representation
Zahlendreher swapper
Zahlenmeer mass of numbers
Zahlensystem number system
Zählnummer sequence code, sequence number
Zahlung payment
Zahlungsverkehr payments system
Zählwerk counter
Zch = Zeichen
Zehnerblock numeric keypad
Zehnertastatur ten keypad
Zeichen character
Zeichen pro Zeile characters per line
Zeichenabfühlung mark scanning, mark sensing
Zeichenauflösung character resolution
Zeichenbildschirm character display
Zeichendichte density of characters
Zeichendrucker character printer
Zeichendruckwerk character printing device
Zeichenerkennung character recognition
Zeichenfehler-Wahrscheinlichkeit character error probability
Zeichenfolge string
Zeichenfolgeverarbeitung string processing
Zeichengerät plotter
Zeichenmaschine plotter
Zeichensatz character set
Zeichentablett digitizer
Zeichenverschlüsselungstabelle character code chart
Zeichenvorrat character set
Zeichnung drawing
Zeichnungsleser drawing reader
Zeigeinstrument pointing device
Zeiger pointer
Zeilenabstand line space, spacing
Zeilendisplay line display
Zeilendrucker line printer
Zeilenlineal ruler
Zeilentransport carriage space
Zeilenvorschub line feed
Zeilenvorschub rückwärts reverse line feed
Zeit zwischen Fehlern time between failures
Zeit- und Bewegungsstudie time and motion study
Zeit/Kosten/Fortschrittsdiagramm time-costs-progress diagram
Zeitanalyse time analysis
Zeitanforderung time requirement
Zeitaufnahme time study
Zeitaufnahmebogen time study sheet
Zeitaufteilung time sharing
Zeitbedarf time need, time requirement
Zeitbegrenzung time out
Zeitdiebstahl time theft
Zeiterfassung time determination
Zeiterfassungsstation time and attendance terminal
Zeitgeber interval timer
zeitgeführte Ablaufsteuerung time-oriented sequential control
zeitgerechte Produktion just in time production
Zeithorizont time horizon
zeitkritischer Arbeitsgang time critical operation
zeitlich planen schedule (to)
zeitliche Planung scheduling
zeitlicher Testplan testing schedule
Zeitmessung time measurement
Zeitmultiplex-Verfahren time multiplexing
Zeitmultiplexing time division multiplexing
Zeitplan schedule
Zeitplanung scheduling
Zeitraum time span
Zeitschätzung time estimate
Zeitscheibe time slice
Zeitstudie time study
Zeitteilung time slicing
Zeitvergleich time comparison
Zelle cell
zentrale Abrechnungsstelle accounting center
zentrale Datenerfassung centralized data collection
zentrale Netzinformation network information center
Zentraleinheit central processing unit
zentraler Arbeitsrechner host computer
zentrales Computersystem centralized computer system
zentrales Unterstützungssystem backbone system
Zentralisation centralization
zentralisieren centralize (to)
zentralisierte Speicherhierarchie centralized memory hierarchy
Zentralisierung centralization
Zentralprozessor central processor
Zentralspeicher central memory, central storage
zentrieren center (to), justify (to)
zerlegen decompose (to)

103

Zerlegung decomposition
Zerlegungsdiagramm decomposition diagram
Zerlegungsgrad degree of decomposition
zerstörendes Lesen destructive readout
zerstörungsfreies Lesen non-destructive readout
Zerstückelung fragmentation
zickzackgefaltet fanfolded
zickzack gefaltetes Papier fanfold paper
Ziel goal, objective, target
Ziel-Portfolio target portfolio
Zielanalyse target analysis
Zielanweisung target statement
Zielausmaß domain of goal
Zielbeziehung goal relationship
Zielcomputer object computer
Zieldatenverarbeitung target data processing
Zielerreichung goal achievement
Zielertrag goal production
Zielfindung goal identification
zielgerichtete Beobachtung goal-oriented observation
zielgetriebene Rückwärtsverkettung goal-driven backward chaining
Zielinhalt content of goal
Zielkonflikt goal conflict
Zielkriterium goal criterion
Ziellücke goal gap
Zielmaßstab goal standard
Zielplanung goal setting planning
Zielpriorität festlegen prioritizing goals
Zielprogramm goal program
Zielsetzung goal-setting
Zielsetzungsanalyse goal-setting analysis
Zielsprache object code, object language
Zielsystem goal system
Zielwert scaled goal production
Ziffer digit
Ziffernblock digit block
Zifferntaste digit key
ZSI = Zentralstelle für Sicherheit in der Informationstechnik
Zufallsfehler accidental error, random error
Zufallsgenerator random generator
Zufallszahlen-Generator random number generator
Zufriedenheit satisfaction
Zufriedenheitsniveau satisfaction level
Zugänglichkeit accessibility
Zugangskontrolle admission check
Zugangsüberwachung admission control
Zugangsüberwachungssystem admission control system
Zugehöriger member

Zugehörigkeit membership
zugeordneter Prozessor attached processor
Zugriff access
Zugriffsanforderung access requirement
Zugriffsart access mode
Zugriffsberechtigung access authority
Zugriffsfunktion access function, hashing
Zugriffskontrolle access check
Zugriffsmethode access method
Zugriffsoperation access operation
Zugriffspfad access path
Zugriffspfad-Analyse access path analysis
Zugriffsprotokoll access protocol
Zugriffsrecht access right
Zugriffsschlüssel access key
Zugriffsschutz access protection
Zugriffssteuerung access control
Zugriffstrategie access strategy
Zugriffszeit access time
Zugtraktor pull tractor
Zukunftsanalyse future analysis
Zukunftsforschung future research
Zukunftstechnologie future technology
Zulässigkeit acceptability, admissibility
zuordnen allocate (to)
Zuordnung allocation
Zuordnungstabelle cross reference table
Zurücksetzen backout
Zusammenbruch crash
Zusammenfassen von Geldbeträgen pooling
Zusammenhang context, interrelation
zusammenschließen integrate (to)
Zusammenschluß integration
Zusammenwirken synergy
Zusatzfunktion miscellaneous function
zusätzlich additional, optional
Zustand state
Zustand 'Hörer abgehoben' offhook condition
Zustand 'Hörer aufgelegt' onhook condition
zuständig competent
Zuständigkeit competency
Zustandsanalyse state analysis
Zustandsanzeiger state key
Zustandsdiagramm state diagram
Zuteilung von Betriebsmitteln resource allocation
Zuverlässigkeit credibility, reliability
Zuverlässigkeitsangabe reliability date
Zuverlässigkeitsgrad degree of reliability
Zuverlässigkeitsuntersuchung reliability study

Zuwachs increment
Zuwachsrate growth rate
zuweisen assign (to), allocate (to)
Zuweisung allocation, assignment
zweckbestimmt dedicated
zweckbestimmtes System dedicated system
Zweckbezogenheit purpose orientation
Zweckhaftigkeit purposefulness
Zweckmäßigkeit purposiveness
zweidimensionales Modell two-dimensional model
zweidimensionales System two-dimensional system
Zweifachbelegung double covering
zweifach gerichtet bidirectional
Zweipunktverbindung point-to-point connection
zweiseitig double sided
2NF = zweite Normalform
zweite Normalform second normal form
Zwiebelmodell onion model

Zwillingsdrucker double-sided printer, twin printer
zwingend mandatory
zwingender Verbindungsabbruch mandatory disconnection
Zwischenablage clipboard
zwischenbetriebliche Integration interorganizational integration
zwischenbetriebliche Zusammenarbeit interorganizational collaboration
Zwischenraum space
Zwischenschicht intermediate layer
Zwischenspeicher intermediate storage
Zwischensprache intermediate language
Zwischensumme subtotal
Zwischenträgerpapier intermediate transfer paper
zyklisches Ablaufdiagramm cyclic flowchart, loop flowchart
Zykluszeit cycle time
Zylinder cylinder

Englisch - Deutsch
English - German

A

AAE = Automatic Answering Equipment
abbreviation dialing list
Kurzwahltabelle
ABC classification ABC Analyse
ability Fähigkeit, Leistungsfähigkeit
ability of formalization
Formalisierbarkeit
ability of self-explanation
Selbsterklärungsfähigkeit
ability of structuring Strukturierbarkeit
ability of user involvement
Beteiligungsfähigkeit
abnormal condition abnormale
Bedingung
abnormal end Abbruch, abnormales Ende
absenteeism Fehlzeit
absolute frequency absolute Häufigkeit
absolute programming absolute
Programmierung
absolute right absolutes Recht
absolute value Absolutwert
abstract Kurzdarstellung
abstract data type abstrakter Datentyp
abstract machine abstrakte Maschine
abstract model abstraktes Modell
abstract program abstraktes Programm
abstraction Abstraktion
abstraction system Abstraktionssystem
abuse Betrug
abuse of automatic device
Automatenmißbrauch
accept (to) abnehmen, annehmen
acceptability Eignung, Zulässigkeit
acceptance Abnahme, Akzeptanz
acceptance analysis Akzeptanzanalyse
acceptance protocol Abnahmeprotokoll
acceptance research Akzeptanzforschung
acceptance test Abnahmetest,
Akzeptanztest
accepted system akzeptiertes System
access Zugriff
access authority Zugriffsberechtigung
access check Zugriffskontrolle
access control Zugriffssteuerung
access function Zugriffsfunktion
access key Zugriffsschlüssel
access method Zugriffsmethode
access mode Zugriffsart
access operation Zugriffsoperation
access path Zugriffspfad
access path analysis
Zugriffspfad-Analyse
access protection Zugriffsschutz
access protocol Zugriffsprotokoll
access requirement Zugriffsanforderung

access right Zugriffsrecht
access strategy Zugriffsstrategie
access time Zugriffszeit
accessibility Erreichbarkeit,
Zugänglichkeit
accidental error Zufallsfehler
account Abrechnung, Konto
accountability Verantwortlichkeit
account balance Kontostand
account classification Kontengliederung
account current Kontokorrent
account number Kontonummer
account statement Kontoauszug
account statement printer
Kontoauszugsdrucker
accountancy Rechnungswesen
accounting Rechnungswesen
accounting center zentrale
Abrechnungsstelle
accounting data Buchungsdaten
accounting deadline Buchungsschnitt
accounting oriented processing
kontenorientierte Verarbeitung
accounting program
Buchhaltungsprogramm
accounting routine Abrechnungsroutine
accounting system Abrechnungssystem
accounting unit Abrechnungseinheit
accounting voucher Buchungsbeleg
accounts payables Kreditoren,
Verbindlichkeit
accounts receivables Debitoren,
Forderung
accumulate figure Fortschrittszahl
accumulate figure system
Fortschrittszahlen-System
accumulator Akkumulator,
Arbeitsregister
accuracy Genauigkeit
accuracy of measurement
Meßgenauigkeit
ACE = Animated Computer Education
ACE = Automatic Calling Equipment
ACE = Automatic Circuit Exchange
achievement motivation
Leistungsmotivation
ACIA = Asynchronous Communications
Interface Adapter
Acknowledge = Acquisition of Knowledge
acknowledge (to) quittieren
acknowledgement Bestätigung,
Empfangsbestätigung, Quittung
ACL = Application Control Language
ACL = Association for Computational
Linguistics
ACM = Association for Computing
Machinery

acoustic alarm device akustischer Alarmgeber
acoustic coupler akustischer Koppler
acoustic cursor Akustik-Cursor
acoustic muff Akustikmuff
acquire (to) erwerben
acquisition Erwerb
acquisition of expert knowledge Erwerb von Expertenwissen
ACS = Advanced Communications Services
ACS = Australian Computer Society
ACS = Auxiliary Core Storage
act of sabotage Sabotageakt
action Aktion
action alternative Handlungsalternative
action code technique Aktionscode-Technik
action diagram Aktionsdiagramm
action entry Aktionsanzeiger
action message Aktionsnachricht
action model Vorgehensmodell
action plan Aktionsplan
action scope Aktionsspielraum, Handlungsspielraum
action stub Aktionsbezeichner
activate (to) aktivieren
activation error Aktivationsfehler
active fault aktiver Fehler
active file aktive Datei
active help system aktives Hilfesystem
active line aktive Zeile
active observation aktive Beobachtung
active state aktiver Status
activity Maßnahme, Vorgang
activity analysis Vorgangsanalyse
activity arrow network Vorgangspfeilnetz
activity chain Vorgangskette
activity node network Vorgangsknotennetz
activity oriented system vorgangsorientiertes System
activity rate Bewegungshäufigkeit
activity type Vorgangstyp
ACTS = Automatic Computer Telex Services
actual argument Aktualparameter
actual costs Istkosten
actual portfolio Istportfolio
actual value Istwert
actual vs. target comparison Soll-Ist-Vergleich
adapt (to) anpassen
adaptability Anpassungsfähigkeit
adaptation Anpassung
adaptible user interface adaptierbare Benutzerschnittstelle

adapting device Anpassungseinrichtung
adapting protocol Anpassungsprotokoll
adaptive maintenance Anpassungswartung
adaptive user interface adaptive Benutzerschnittstelle
adaptor Anpassungseinrichtung
ADC = Analog/Digital Converter
add (to) summieren
add-on product Ergänzungsprodukt
add-on strategy Add-on-Strategie
added value Mehrwert
adding machine Addiermaschine
additional zusätzlich
address Adresse
address (to) adressieren
address bus Adreßbus
address chaining Adreßverkettung
address counter Befehlszähler
address field Anschriftfeld
addressable memory adressierbarer Speicher
addressing Empfangsaufruf
addressing machine Adressiermaschine
addressing mode Adressierungsart
adequacy Angemessenheit
adhoc query Ad-hoc-Abfrage
adjacent matrix Adjazenzmatrix
adjust (to) justieren
administration Verwaltung
administrative data processing administrative Datenverarbeitung
administrative goal administratives Ziel
administrative information management administratives Informationsmanagement
administrative work Verwaltungsarbeit
administrator Verwalter
admissibility Zulässigkeit
admission check Zugangskontrolle
admission control Zugangsüberwachung
admission control system Zugangsüberwachungssystem
ADP = Automatic Data Processing
advise (to) beraten
advisor Berater
advisory system Beratungssystem
affected individual Betroffener
AGC = Automatic Gain Control
aggregation Aggregierung
agreement Vereinbarung
agressive strategy agressive Strategie
AHP = Analytic Hierarchy Process
AI = Artificial Intelligence
AI programming KI-Programmierung
AID = Automatic Interaction Detector
aid Sachmittel
aid (to) unterstützen

air conditioning Klimatisierung
air conditioning system Klimaanlage
air traffic control system Flugsicherungssystem
alarm device Alarmgeber
alarm guide Alarmplan
alarm system Alarmeinrichtung
ALGOL = Algorithmic Language
algorithm Algorithmus
algorithmic programming algorithmische Programmierung
algorithmic programming language algorithmische Programmiersprache
algorithmics Algorithmik
alias name Aliasname
align (to) ausrichten
alignment Ausrichtung
all duplex mode Vollduplexbetrieb
all purpose computer Universalcomputer
allocate (to) aufschlüsseln, verteilen, zuordnen, zuweisen
allocating the order Auftragsvergabe
allocation Aufschlüsselung, Verteilung, Zuordnung, Zuweisung
alpha change Alpha-Veränderung
alphabet Alphabet
alphabetic character alphabetisches Zeichen
alphabetic data alphabetische Daten
alphanumeric alphanumerisch
alphanumeric character alphanumerisches Zeichen
alphanumeric data alphanumerische Daten
alphanumeric keyboard alphanumerische Tastatur
alteration switch Umschalter
alternate key Sekundärschlüssel
alternate track Ersatzspur
alternative Alternative, Möglichkeit
alternative solution Alternativlösung
amending memory Ergänzungsspeicher
amendment data Bewegungsdaten
amount Betrag
amount of costs Kostenhöhe
amount of information Informationsmenge
amplifier Verstärker
analog analog
analog computer Analogrechner
analog control analoge Steuerung
analog data analoge Daten
analog/digital converter Analog/Digital-Umsetzer
analog quantity Analogwert
analog recording Analogaufzeichnung
analog representation analoge Darstellung
analog signal Analogsignal
analogism Analogieschluß
analogy Analogie
analogy reasoning Analogieschließen
analysis Analyse
analysis by inspection Besichtigungsanalyse
analysis cycle Analysezyklus
analysis method Analysemethode
analysis of causes Ursachenanalyse
analysis of consequences Konsequenzanalyse
analysis of content Inhaltsanalyse
analysis of current system Istanalyse, Istzustandsanalyse
analysis of functions Funktionsanalyse
analysis of literature Literaturanalyse
analysis of overheads Gemeinkosten-Wertanalyse
analysis of patents Patentanalyse
analysis of tasks Aufgabenanalyse
analysis of technological trend Technologietrend-Analyse
analysis of variances Schwachstellenanalyse, Varianzanalyse
analysis of work environment Arbeitsumgebungsanalyse
analysis of work organization Analyse der Arbeitsorganisation
analysis tool Analysewerkzeug
analyst Analytiker
analytic inferencing analytisches Schlußfolgern
analytic job evaluation analytische Arbeitsplatzbewertung
analytic model analytisches Modell
analytic thinking analytisches Denken
analyze (to) analysieren
analyzer Analysator
analyzing Auswertung
animated computer education Unterricht mit Computergraphik
animation Bewegung
annual plan Jahresplan
anomaly Anomalie
ANSI = American National Standards Institute
answer Rückantwort
answering machine Anrufbeantworter
answerphone Anrufbeantworter
anthropocentric anthropozentrisch
anthropocentric approach anthropozentrischer Ansatz
APL = A Programming Language
APLG = A Programming Language for Graphics
appendix Anhang

assign (to)

appetence conflict Appetenzkonflikt
applicability Anwendbarkeit
application Anwendung, Nutzanwendung
application analysis Anwendungsanalyse
application attractiveness
Einsatzattraktivität
application dependent integrated circuit
anwendungsspezifische integrierte
Schaltung
application backlog Anwendungsrückstau
application design Anwendungsentwurf
application development
Anwendungsentwicklung
application factory Anwenderbetrieb
application informatics
Anwendungsinformatik
application layer Anwendungsschicht
application of model Modellanwendung
application package
Standardsoftware-Paket
application password
Anwendungskennwort
application program
Anwendungsprogramm
application programmer
Anwendungsprogrammierer,
Organisationsprogrammierer
application software Anwendersoftware,
Anwendungssoftware
application software package
Anwendungssoftware-Paket
application software system
Anwendungssoftware-System
application system Anwendungssystem
application systems administrator
Anwendungssystem-Administrator
application systems generation
Anwendungsgeneration
application systems life-cycle
Anwendungssystem-Lebenszyklus
application systems management
Anwendungssystem-Management
application systems planning
Anwendungssystem-Planung
application systems portfolio
Anwendungssystem-Portfolio
application systems projekt
Systemplanungsprojekt
application task Anwendungsaufgabe
applied informatics Angewandte
Informatik
apply (to) anwenden
appointment schema Stellenplan
approach Ansatz
appropriateness Angemessenheit
approximate value Näherungswert

APSE = ADA Programming Support Environment
APT = Automatic Programming for Tools
architecture Architektur
archival medium Archivierungsmedium
archive Archiv
archiving Archivierung
area Bereich
area model Flächenmodell
area of responsibility
Verantwortungsbereich
arithmetic operation arithmetische
Operation
arithmetic operator arithmetischer
Operator
arithmetic processor Arithmetikprozessor
arithmetic unit Rechenwerk
ARPANET = Advanced Research Project Agency Network
array Feld, Ordnung, reihenförmige
Anordnung
array processor Feldrechner
arrow diagram Pfeildiagramm
arrow key Pfeiltaste
arrow pointer Pfeilzeiger
artificial intelligence Künstliche
Intelligenz
artificial language Kunstsprache
ASA = American Standards Association
ASA = Austrian Smart Card Association
ascending key aufsteigender
Sortierbegriff
ascending order aufsteigende Folge,
aufsteigende Reihenfolge
ASCII = American Standard Code for Information Interchange
ASIC = Application Specific Integrated Circuit
ASLT = Advanced Solid Logic Technology
ASME = American Society of Mechanical Engineers
ASME symbolics ASME-Symbolik
ASR = Automatic Send Receive
assemble (to) assemblieren
assembler Assembler, Assemblierer
assembler language Assemblersprache
assembly Baugruppe
assembly line Fertigungsstraße,
Montageband
assembly time Umwandlungszeit
assess (to) abschätzen, beurteilen
assessment Abschätzung, Beurteilung
assessment research Wirkungsforschung
asset Vermögenswert
assign (to) zuweisen

assignment

assignment Zuweisung
assignment of tasks Arbeitszuordnung
assignment to one person Einzelzuordnung
assist (to) unterstützen
assistance Unterstützung
association Verband, Vereinigung
association type Assoziationstyp
associative memory Assoziativspeicher
assume (to) annehmen
assumed decimal point angenommenes Dezimalkomma
assumption Annahme
assurance Sicherung
assurance analysis Sicherungsanalyse
assurance measure Sicherungsmaßnahme
asynchronous asynchron, nicht gleichlaufend
asynchronous communications Wechselbetrieb
asynchronous mode Asynchronbetrieb
asynchronous transmission asynchrone Übertragung
at end condition Endbedingung
ATM = Automated Teller Machine
attached processor zugeordneter Prozessor
attendence reporting Anwesenheitserfassung
attendence time Anwesenheitszeit
attribute Attribut, Eigenschaft
attribute list Attribute-Spezifikationstabelle
attribute type Attributtyp
attribute usage Attributverwendung
attribute usage matrix Attribute-Verwendungsmatrix
attribute value Attributwert, Eigenschaftswert
audible alarm akustische Anzeige, akustisches Warnsignal
audiovisual communications audiovisuelle Kommunikation
audit Rechnungsprüfung, Revision
audit (to) prüfen
audit information system Revisionsinformationssystem
audit language Prüfsprache
audit procedure Revisionsverfahren
audit program Prüfprogramm
audit report Prüfbericht
audit software Prüfsoftware
audit technique Revisionsmethode
audit total Kontrollsumme
audit trail Prüfpfad
auditability Prüfbarkeit
auditing Prüfung

auditive auditiv, hörbar, den Hörsinn betreffend
auditive feedback auditive Rückmeldung
auditor Revisor
authentication Beglaubigung, Legalisierung
authenticity Authentizität, Echtheit
author Autor
author support system Autorenunterstützungssystem
author-instructor principle Autor-Lektor-Prinzip
author-reviewer cycle Autor-Kritiker-Zyklus
author's programming language Autorensprache
author's right Autorenrecht
author's software Autorensoftware
authority Befugnis, Berechtigung
authority number Berechtigungsnummer
authorization Berechtigung
authorize (to) autorisieren, berechtigen
authorized user autorisierter Benutzer
authorizing Autorisieren, Berechtigen
auto answer automatische Antwort
auto answer equipment automatische Rufbeantwortungseinrichtung
auto carriage return automatischer Wagenrücklauf
auto correction Selbstkorrektur
auto correlation Selbstkorrelation
auto dialing automatische Telephonnummernwahl
auto line feed automatischer Zeilenvorschub
auto restart Selbststart
automat Automat
automatable automatisierbar
automated bank machine Bankautomat, Kontomat
automated banking Bankautomation
automated sprinklers set Sprinkleranlage
automated teller machine Bankomat
automatic answering equipment automatische Rufbeantwortungseinrichtung
automatic answering set automatischer Anrufbeantworter
automatic answerphone automatischer Anrufbeantworter
automatic calling equipment automatische Wähleinrichtung
automatic character recognition automatische Schrifterkennung
automatic check Selbstprüfung
automatic circuit exchange automatische Wählvermittlung

automatic computer telex services automatischer Fernschreibdienst
automatic control Selbststeuerung
automatic control system Regelsystem, Selbststeuerungssystem
automatic data capturing automatische Datenerfassung
automatic data processing automatische Datenverarbeitung
automatic data processing system automatisches Datenverarbeitungssystem
automatic dial exchange Selbstwähldienst
automatic gain control automatische Optimierungssteuerung
automatic manufacturing automatische Fertigung
automatic mode automatische Betriebsart
automatic programming automatisches Programmieren
automatic speech recognition automatische Spracherkennung
automation Automation, Automatisierung
automation of manufacturing Automatisierung der Fertigung
automation of public administration Verwaltungsautomation
autonomy Autonomie
autoteller terminal Geldausgabe-Automat
auxiliary program Hilfsprogramm
auxiliary storage Hilfsspeicher
AV = Audiovision
availability Verfügbarkeit
availability ratio Verfügbarkeitsgrad
average access time durchschnittliche Zugriffszeit, mittlere Zugriffszeit
average costs Durchschnittskosten
average fault distance mittlerer Fehlerabstand
average per day Tagesdurchschnitt
average value Durchschnittswert
aversion conflict Aversionskonflikt
awareness Kenntnis
axiom Axiom

B

Bachmann diagram Bachmann-Diagramm
back tracking Backtracking-Verfahren
backbone network Hintergrundnetz
backbone system Hintergrundsystem, zentrales Unterstützungssystem
backend processor Nachrechner
background Hintergrund
background job Hintergrundauftrag
background memory Hintergrundspeicher
background processing Hintergrundverarbeitung
background program Hintergrundprogramm
background system Hintergrundsystem
backlog Rückstau
backlogged project notleidendes Projekt
backout Zurücksetzen
backplane Steckrahmen
backspace key Löschtaste, Rücksetztaste
backspacing Rücksetzen
backtracking Ablaufrückverfolgung
backup Ausweichbetrieb
backup battery unit Pufferbatterie für Speicher
backup computer Ausweichcomputer
backup computing center Ausweich-Rechenzentrum, Ersatz-Rechenzentrum, Notfall-Rechenzentrum
backup copy Sicherungskopie
backup file Sicherungsdatei
backup floppy disk Sicherungsdiskette
backup procedure Ausweichverfahren, Sicherungsverfahren
backup system Rückfallsystem
backward chaining Rückwärtsverkettung
backward-controlled inferencing rückwärtsgesteuertes Schlußfolgern
bactericide paper bakterizides Papier
badge Ausweis
badge reader Ausweisleser
balance Gleichgewicht, Saldo
BAM = Block Availability Map
bandwidth Bandbreite
bank counter terminal Bankschalter-Terminal
bar Balken
bar chart Balkendiagramm, Säulendiagramm, Stabdiagramm
bar code Barcode, Strichcode
bar code scanner Barcode-Leser
bar code scanning Barcode-Abtastung
barrier Barriere
barrier to entry Eintrittsbarriere
barrier to exit Austrittsbarriere
barter (to) tauschen
bartering Tauschgeschäft
base Basis, Grundlage
baseband Basisband, Schmalband
baseband network Basisbandnetz, Schmalbandnetz
baseband transmission Basisbandübertragung
BASIC = Beginners All Purpose Symbolic Instruction Code
basic Basis bildend, Grundlage bildend
basic application Basisanwendung
basic block Elementarblock
basic concept Grundkonzeption
basic cost distribution key elementarer Verteilungsschlüssel
basic entity type elementarer Objekttyp
basic equipment Grundausstattung
basic event Basis-Ereignis
basic function Grundfunktion
basic operation Elementaroperation
basic software Basissoftware
basic system Basissystem
basic technology Basistechnologie
batch Stapel, Schub
batch job Stapelauftrag
batch mode Batchbetrieb, Stapelbetrieb
batch processing Stapelverarbeitung
batch size Losgröße
baud Baud
BBA = Bachelor of Business Administration
BCD = Binary Coded Decimal
BCS = British Computer Society
Bd = Baud
bearer of tasks Aufgabenträger
bearer program Trägerprogramm
bearer service Trägerdienst
begin (to) beginnen
beginning of conversation Gesprächsbeginn
behavior Verhalten
behavior hypothesis Verhaltenshypothese
behavioral pattern Verhaltensmuster
behavioral science Verhaltenswissenschaft
belt printer Kettendrucker
beltbed plotter Flachbettplotter
benchmark Benchmark, Leistungsvergleich
benchmark test Benchmarktest, Leistungsvergleichstest
benchmarking Benchmarking
benefit Nutzen
benefit/cost analysis Nutzen/Kosten-Analyse

benefit structure Nutzenstruktur
beta change Beta-Veränderung
BIAIT = Business Information Analysis and Integration Technique
bibliometry Bibliometrie
BICS = Business Information Control Study
bid Lieferangebot
bid analysis Angebotsanalyse
bid evaluation Angebotsbewertung
bidder Anbieter
bidding Angebotseinholung
bidirectional bidirektional, zweifach gerichtet
bidirectional printer bidirektionaler Drucker
bidirectional printing Drucken vorwärts und rückwärts
bill Rechnung
bill explosion Stücklistenauflösung
bill of materials Stückliste
bill of materials processor Stücklistenprozessor
billing Rechnungserstellung
billing file Rechnungsdatei
bin card Behälterkarte
binary binär
binary character Binärzeichen
binary digit Dualziffer
binary menu binäres Menü
binary search binäres Suchen
binary synchronous communications binäre synchrone Datenübertragung
bio computer Bio-Computer
biometric data biometrische Daten
bionics Bionik
BIP = Business Information Planning
bipolar transistor bipolarer Transistor
bisection method Halbierungsmethode
Bit = binary digit
bit parallel bitparallel
bit pattern Binärmuster, Bitmuster
bit rate Bitrate
bit serial bitseriell
bit transmission error probability Bit-Fehlerwahrscheinlichkeit
bit transmission error rate Bit-Fehlerrate
bit width Bitbreite
BIU = Bus Interface Unit
black box Schwarzer Kasten
black box principle Black-Box-Prinzip, Prinzip des Schwarzen Kastens
black box test Schwarzer-Kasten-Test
black box testing aufgabenorientiertes Testen
black failure Totalausfall

blank Leerstelle
blank character Leerzeichen
blank column Leerspalte
blank line Leerzeile
blind copy Blindkopie
blink (to) blinken
blinking output option Blinkfunktion
block Block
block availability map Blockverfügbarkeitsliste
block check Blockprüfung
block check character Blockprüfzeichen
block chiffre Blockchiffre
block concept Blockkonzept
block diagram Blockdiagramm, Blockschaltbild
block error rate Block-Fehlerrate
block graphic Blockgraphik
blocking factor Blockungsfaktor
blocking period Sperrfrist
blueprint Planentwurf
board Leiterplatte, Platine, Steckkarte
bold face Fettdruck
bond paper Hartpostpapier
Boolean Algebra Boole'sche Algebra, Schaltalgebra
Boolean function Boole'sche Funktion
boot (to) laden
bootstrap Urlader
BOSP = Business Office Systems Planning
bottleneck Engpaß
bottom-up strategy Bottom-up-Strategie
bottom-up test Bottom-up-Test
boundary value Grenzwert
Box-Jenkins method Box-Jenkins-Methode
bpi = bits per inch
bps = bits per second
bps Bit/s
BPU = Basic Processing Unit
bracket Klammer
braille Blindenschrift
Braille terminal Braille-Terminal
branch Abzweigung, Verzweigung
branch (to) verzweigen
branch and bound procedure Branch-and-Bound-Verfahren
breadth-first search Breitensuche
break Verbindungsabbruch
break-even analysis Gewinnschwellen-Analyse
break-even point Gewinnschwelle
breakdown Ausfall, Betriebsunterbrechung
breakdown insurance Betriebsunterbrechungs-Versicherung
breakpoint Haltepunkt

bridge Brücke
bridge (to) überbrücken
bridging program Brückenprogramm, Überbrückungsprogramm
brightness Helligkeit
broadband Breitband
broadband communications Breitbandkommunikation
broadband network Breitbandnetz
broadband transmission Breitbandübertragung
Brook's law Brook'sches Gesetz
browsing Durchblättern
BSC = Binary Synchronous Communications
BSI = British Standards Institution
BSP = Business Systems Planning
BTx act BTx-Gesetz
BTx law BTx-Recht
BTx service BTx-Dienst
BTx telex service BTx-Telex-Dienst
BTx treaty BTx-Staatsvertrag
bubble chart Datenflußdiagramm
bubble memory Blasenspeicher
buffer Puffer
buffer (to) puffern
buffer memory Pufferspeicher
buffer stock Sicherheitsbestand
bug Programmfehler, Wanze
built-in check Selbstprüfung
bulletin Aushang
bulletin board Aushangbrett
bundling gebundene Strategie, Bündelung
bus line system Sammelleitungssystem
bus system Bussystem, Sammelsystem
bus topology Bustopologie
Business Administration Betriebswirtschaftslehre
business area Geschäftsbereich
business data processing betriebliche Datenverarbeitung, kommerzielle Datenverarbeitung
business function betrieblicher Funktionalbereich
business graphics Geschäftsgraphik
Business Informatics Betriebsinformatik
business information system betriebliches Informationssystem
business strategy Geschäftsstrategie
business transaction Geschäftsvorgang
busy belegt
button Taste
button feedback Tastenrückmeldung
buy Fremdbezug
by contract vertraglich
byte Byte

C

CA-Technologie = Computer Aided Technology
CAA = Computer Aided Assembling
cable Kabel
cable connection Kabelanschluß
cable duct Kabelkanal
cable laying Kabelverlegung
cable network Kabelnetz
cable television Kabelfernsehen
cable text Kabeltext
cabling Verdrahtung
cache memory Cache-Speicher
CAD = Computer Aided Design
CADD = Computer Aided Design and Drafting
CAE = Computer Aided Engineering
CAI = Computer Aided Industry
CAI = Computer Assisted Instruction
CAL = Computer Aided Learning
calculate (to) berechnen
calculation Berechnung, Kalkulation
calculation experiment Berechnungsexperiment
calculation program Berechnungsprogramm
calculator Rechenmaschine, Tischrechner
calculus Kalkül
calculus language Kalkülsprache
calendar management Terminkalender-Management
calendering Kalendermanagement
calibration Eichung, Kalibrierung
call Aufruf
call (to) abrufen, aufrufen
call diversion Anrufumleitung
call order Abrufauftrag
call request abgehender Ruf
call service Anrufwartung
called station Empfangsstation
CAM = Computer Aided Manufacturing
cancel (to) abbrechen, annullieren, stornieren
CAO = Computer Aided Office
CAP = Computer Aided Planning
CAP = Computer Aided Publishing
capability Fähigkeit
capacity Kapazität
capacity bottleneck Kapazitätsengpaß
capacity management Kapazitätsmanagement
capacity monitoring Kapazitätsüberwachung
capacity plan Kapazitätsplan
capacity planning Kapazitätsplanung
capacity scheduling Kapazitätsterminierung
capacity utilization Auslastung
capital letters Versalsatz
capitalization Großschreibung
capsule Kapsel
capture error Überlappungsfehler
CAQ = Computer Aided Quality Assurance
CAR = Computer Aided Retrieval
CAR = Computer Aided Robotics
carbonless paper Selbst-Durchschreibpapier
card driven payment system kartengesteuertes Zahlungssystem
card index box Karteikasten
card programmable calculator kartenprogrammierbarer Rechner
cardinal scale kardinale Skala
career Berufsbild, Karriere
career planning Karriereplanung
carriage space Zeilentransport
cartographic application kartographische Anwendung
cartridge Kassette, Magnetbandkassette
cartridge drive Kassettenlaufwerk
CAS = Computer Aided Strategy and Sales Controlling
CASE = Computer Aided Software Engineering
CASE = Computer Aided Systems Engineering
cash discount Skonto
cash dispenser Geldausgabe-Automat
cash management Währungs- und Devisenmanagement
cash register Registrierkasse
casual user gelegentlicher Benutzer
CAT = Computer Aided Testing
CAT = Computer Aided Training
CAT = Computer Aided Translation
catalog entry Katalogeintragung
catastrophe Katastrophe
catchword Schlagwort
category of users Benutzerklasse
cathode ray Elektronenstrahl
cathode ray tube Kathodenstrahlröhre
causal diagram Kausaldiagramm
causality Kausalität
cause Ursache
CAUSE = Computer Automated Software Engineering
cause/effectivity analysis Ursache/Wirkung-Analyse
cause/effectivity relation Ursache/Wirkung-Beziehung
CBA = Cost/Benefit Analysis

CBMS = Computer Based Message
System
CBT = Computer Based Training
CBX = Computerized Branch Exchange
CC = Cable Connector
CCD = Charge Coupled Device
CCIA = Computer and Communications
Industry Association
CCT = Cognitive Complexity Theory
CCTA = Central Computing and
Telecommunications Agency
CD = Cash Dispenser
CD = Compact Disk
CD technology CD-Technologie
CD-RAM = Compact Disk Random
Access Memory
CD-ROM = Compact Disk Read Only
Memory
CDE = Compact Disk Erasable
CECUA = Confederation of European
Computer Users Associations
CECUA model contract
CECUA-Modellvertrag
cell Zelle
center (to) einmitten, zentrieren
central department Hauptabteilung
central memory Zentralspeicher
central processing unit Zentraleinheit
central processor Zentralprozessor
central storage Zentralspeicher
centralization Zentralisation,
Zentralisierung
centralize (to) zentralisieren
centralized computer system zentrales
Computersystem
centralized data collection zentrale
Datenerfassung
centralized memory hierarchy
zentralisierte Speicherhierarchie
centronics interface
Centronics-Schnittstelle
CEO = Chief Executive Officer
CEP = Corporate Electronic Publishing
certificate of purchase Kaufschein
cession certificate Überlassungsschein
CGS = Computer Graphics Society
chain Kette
chained file organization verkettete
Dateiorganisation
chaining Verkettung
change Änderung, Veränderung
change (to) ändern, verändern
change alternative
Veränderungsalternative
change analysis Veränderungsanalyse
change code Änderungskennzeichen

change management
Änderungsmanagement
change process Veränderungsprozeß
change request Änderungsanforderung
changeability Änderbarkeit,
Veränderbarkeit
changeover Umstellung
changeover device
Umstellungseinrichtung
changeover plan Umstellungsplan
changeover sequence
Implementierungsreihenfolge
channel Kanal
channel capacity Kanalkapazität
channel command Kanalbefehl
Chapin chart Struktogramm
character Drucktype, Schriftzeichen,
Zeichen
character code chart
Zeichenverschlüsselungstabelle
character display Zeichenbildschirm
character error probability
Zeichenfehler-Wahrscheinlichkeit
character printer Zeichendrucker
character printing device
Zeichendruckwerk
character recognition
Schriftzeichenerkennung,
Zeichenerkennung
character resolution Zeichenauflösung
character set Zeichensatz, Zeichenvorrat
characteristic Charakteristik, Merkmal
characteristics Kenndaten
characters per line Zeichen pro Zeile
charge Gebühr
charge coupled device
Ladungstransport-Speicher
chargeout Belastung mit Kosten, mit
Gebühren
chart Diagramm
chart of accounts Kontenplan
chartered accountant Wirtschaftsprüfer
charting technique Diagrammtechnik
check Überprüfung
check (to) kontrollieren, prüfen
check bit Kontrollbit, Prüfbit
check code Prüfcode
check digit Kontrollzahl, Prüfziffer
check figure Prüfziffer
check keying Funktionstasten-Sicherung
check list Checkliste, Prüfliste
check number Prüfzahl
check number mode Prüfzahlverfahren
check of completeness
Vollständigkeitsüberprüfung
check sum Kontrollsumme
checking Kontrolle, Prüfung

checkpoint Fixpunkt, Prüfpunkt, Wiederanlaufpunkt
chief programmer Chefprogrammierer
chief programmer team Chef-Programmierer-Team
chip Halbleiterkristall
choice-set Alternativenmenge
CIM = Computer Input from Microfilm
CIM = Computer Integrated Manufacturing
CIO = Chief Information Officer
CIO = Computer Integrated Office
cipher (to) chiffrieren, verschlüsseln
ciphered data verschlüsselte Daten
ciphering Chiffrierung, Verschlüsselung
ciphering method Verschlüsselungsmethode
ciphering system Verschlüsselungssystem
ciphertext verschlüsselter Text
circle diagram Kreisdiagramm
circuit Schaltung
circuit switching digitale Vermittlungstechnik, Durchschaltevermittlung, Leitungsvermittlung
circuit-switching network leitungsvermittelndes Netz
circular Rundschreiben
circular causality Kreiskausalität
circulation slip Rundschreiben
CISC = Complex Instruction Set Computer
city radio call service Stadtfunk- und Rufdienst
clarity Klarheit
class of subscribers Teilnehmerklasse
classical ergonomics klassische Ergonomie
classification Klassifizierung
classification key klassifizierender Schlüssel
classification number Klassifizierungsnummer
classify (to) klassifizieren
clearing Verrechnungsverkehr
clerical staff Büropersonal
clerical task Sachbearbeitungsaufgabe
clerk Sachbearbeiter
CLG = Command Language Grammar
clipboard elektronische Pinwand, Zwischenablage
clock frequence Taktfrequenz
clock generator Taktgeber
clock speed Schrittgeschwindigkeit
clone Klone
closed circuit geschlossener Schaltkreis
closed decision table geschlossene Entscheidungstabelle

collection sheet

closed loop Regelkreis
closed shop geschlossener Betrieb
closed system geschlossenes System
closed task geschlossene Aufgabe
cluster Anhäufung, Klumpen
cluster analysis Clusteranalyse
CMOS = Complementary Metal-Oxide Semiconductor
CNC = Computerized Numerical Control
coax Koaxialkabel
coaxial cable Koaxialkabel
COBOL = Common Business Oriented Language
cobweb diagram Spinnennetz-Diagramm
COCOMO = Constructive Cost Model
CODASYL = Conference on Data Systems Languages
code Code
code checking Code-Prüfung
code inspection Code-Inspektion
code optimization Code-Optimierung
code transparent data transmission code-transparente Datenübermittlung
coded data codierte Daten
codetermination Mitbestimmung
Codetermination Act Mitbestimmungsgesetz
codetermine (to) mitbestimmen
CODIC = Computer Directed Communications
coding Codierung
coefficient Koeffizient
cognition Erkennung, Kognition
cognitive kognitiv
cognitive complexity theory Theorie der kognitiven Komplexität
cognitive decision style kognitiver Entscheidungsstil
cognitive dissonance kognitive Dissonanz
cognitive ergonomics kognitive Ergonomie
cognitive modelling kognitive Modellierung
cognitive process kognitiver Prozeß
cognitive science Kognitionswissenschaft
cognitive user interface kognitive Benutzerschnittstelle
COL = Computer Oriented Language
COL = Control Oriented Language
cold backup computing center kaltes Ausweich-Rechenzentrum
cold restart kalter Wiederanlauf
cold start Kaltstart
cold systems start kalter Systemstart
collaboration Mitarbeit
collection form Erfassungsbeleg
collection sheet Erfassungsbeleg

collective rating kollektives Rating
collision Kollision
color jet printer device Farbstrahldruckwerk
color screen Farbbildschirm
column Kolumne, Spalte
COM = Computer Output Microfilm
combinatorial optimization kombinatorische Optimierung
combinatorial search kombinatorische Suche
combined ciphering method kombinierte Verschlüsselungsmethode
combined costs distribution key kombinierter Verteilungsschlüssel
command Befehl, Kommando
command control Kommandosteuerung
command file Befehlsdatei, Kommandodatei
command key Befehlstaste
command language Befehlssprache, Kommandosprache
command mode Kommandomodus
comment Anmerkung, Bemerkung, Kommentar
comment (to) kommentieren
commitment Verpflichtung
commitment for involvement Beteiligungsbereitschaft
committee Ausschuß
common area gemeinsamer Bereich
common law öffentliches Recht
communicate (to) kommunizieren
communication Botschaft
communications Informationsaustausch, Kommunikation
communications analysis Kommunikationsanalyse
communications attribute Kommunikationseigenschaft
communications behavior Kommunikationsverhalten
communications chart Kommunikationsspinne
communications controller Fernbetriebseinheit
communications device Kommunikationseinheit
communications diagram Kommunikationsdiagramm
communications driver Leitungsanschluß
communications engineering Nachrichtentechnik
communications ergonomics Kommunikationsergonomie
communications gap Kommunikationslücke

communications group Kommunikationsverbund
communications integration Kommunikationsintegration
communications matrix Kommunikationsmatrix
communications network Kommunikationsnetz
communications process Kommunikationsprozeß
communications protocol Kommunikationsprotokoll
communications research Kommonikationsforschung
communications server Kommunikationsserver
communications service Transportdienst
communications subsystem Kommunikationssubsystem
communications system Kommunikationssystem
communications system study Kommunikationssystem-Studie
communications table Kommunikationstabelle
communications technology Kommunikationstechnik, Transporttechnik
commutation Vertauschung
compact dialing Kurzwahl
compact disk Kompaktplatte
compact disk erasable löschbare Kompaktplatte
comparative operation Vergleichsoperation
comparator Vergleicher
comparator check Prüfen durch Vergleich
compare (to) vergleichen
comparison Vergleich
comparison of organizations Betriebsvergleich
comparison of text Textvergleich
compatibility Austauschbarkeit, Kompatibilität, Vereinbarkeit, Verträglichkeit
compatibility device Verträglichkeitseinrichtung
compatible kompatibel
compete (to) in Wettbewerb treten, konkurrieren
competence Kompetenz, Zuständigkeit
competent kompetent, zuständig
competition Konkurrenz, Wettbewerb
competition analysis Wettbewerbsanalyse
competition law Wettbewerbsrecht

competitive advantage Wettbewerbsvorsprung, Wettbewerbsvorteil
competitive dynamic Wettbewerbsantrieb
competitive factor Wettbewerbsfaktor
competitive force Wettbewerbskraft
competitive impact Wettbewerbswirkung
competitive position Wettbewerbsposition
competitive response Wettbewerbsreaktion
competitive strategy Wettbewerbsstrategie
competitive threat Wettbewerbsbedrohung
competitive weapon Wettbewerbswaffe
competitiveness Wettbewerbsfähigkeit
competitor Konkurrent, Mitbewerber
compilation rate Übersetzungsrate
compiler Compiler, Kompilierer
complementary objective relation komplementäre Zielbeziehung
complete vollständig
complete prototype vollständiger Prototyp
complete survey Totalerhebung
completeness Vollständigkeit
complex ciphering method komplexe Verschlüsselungsmethode
complex decision style komplexer Entscheidungsstil
complex entity type komplexer Objekttyp
complexity Komplexität
component Komponente
composition Komposition
compound key Verbundschlüssel
compound numbering system Verbund-Nummernsystem
compress (to) komprimieren
compression Komprimierung
compression method Komprimierungsmethode
Compunication = Compu(ter and Commu)nication
computational precision Rechengenauigkeit
computational result Rechenergebnis
compute (to) rechnen
computer Computer, Rechenanlage, Rechner
computer abuse Computermißbrauch
computer aid Computerunterstützung
computer aided assembling computerunterstützte Montage
computer aided design computerunterstützte Konstruktion, computerunterstütztes Konstruieren
computer aided design and drafting computerunterstütztes Entwerfen und Zeichnen
computer aided engineering computerunterstütztes Engineering

computer aided instruction computerunterstützter Unterricht
computer aided learning computerunterstütztes Lernen
computer aided manufacturing computerunterstützte Fertigung
computer aided office computerunterstütztes Büro
computer aided planning computerunterstützte Planung
computer aided production planning and scheduling computerunterstützte Produktionsplanung und -steuerung
computer aided publishing computerunterstützte Druckvorlagenerstellung, computerunterstütztes Publizieren
computer aided quality assurance computerunterstützte Qualitätssicherung
computer aided software engineering computerunterstütztes Software Engineering
computer aided testing computerunterstütztes Testen
computer aided training computerunterstütztes Training
computer aided translation computerunterstütztes Übersetzen
computer animation Computeranimation
computer architecture Rechnerarchitektur
computer bureau Dienstleistungsrechenzentrum, externes Rechenzentrum
computer center Rechenzentrum
computer controlled dialog computergesteuerter Dialog
computer crime Computerverbrechen
computer criminality Computerkriminalität
computer directed communications computergeführte Kommunikation
computer evaluation Computerbewertung
computer family Rechnerfamilie
computer fraud Computerbetrug
computer graphics graphische Datenverarbeitung, Computergraphik
computer grouping Computerverbund
computer insurance Computerversicherung
computer linguistics Computerlinguistik
computer literacy Computerkompetenz
computer manipulation Computermanipulation
computer mouse Computermaus
computer network Rechnernetz, Rechnerverbund

computer oriented programming

computer oriented programming language maschinenorientierte Programmiersprache
computer output on microfilm Computerausgabe auf Mikrofilm
computer property insurance Computer-Sachversicherung
computer protection Computerschutz, Rechnerschutz
computer sabotage Computersabotage
Computer Science Computerwissenschaft, Informatik
computer security Computersicherheit
computer selection Rechnerauswahl
computer service center Dienstleistungsrechenzentrum, Service-Rechenzentrum
computer spying Computerspionage
computer strike Computerstreik
computer system Rechensystem
computer systems architecture Computersystem-Architektur
computer systems generation Computergeneration
computer virus Computervirus
computerization Computerisierung
computerized tomography Computertomographie
computervision Bildverstehen
computing center Rechenzentrum
computing service center externes Rechenzentrum, Dienstleistungsrechenzentrum
computing system Rechensystem
concentration Konzentration, Konzentrierung
concentrator Konzentrator
conception calculus Begriffskalkül
conceptual konzeptuell, konzeptionell
conceptual data model konzeptuelles Datenmodell
conceptual data structure konzeptuelle Datenstruktur
conceptual design konzeptueller Entwurf
conceptual knowledge konzeptuelles Wissen
conceptual model konzeptuelles Modell
conceptual modelling konzeptuelles Modellieren
conceptual schema konzeptuelles Schema
conciseness Kürze
concurrency Nebenläufigkeit
concurrent processing verzahnt ablaufende Verarbeitung
condition Bedingung
condition entry Bedingungsanzeiger
condition of measurement Meßbedingung

condition stub Bedingungsbezeichner
conditional jump bedingter Sprungbefehl
conditional statement bedingte Anweisung
conduit Kabelkanal
conference Konferenz, Kongreß
conference call Konferenzschaltung
conference conversation Konferenzgespräch
conference interview technique Konferenz-Interview-Technik
conference switching Konferenzschaltung
conferencing Konferenztechnik
confidential vertraulich
confidentiality Vertraulichkeit
confidentiality right Sperrecht
configurate (to) konfigurieren
configuration Ausrüstung, Konfiguration
configuration diagram Konfigurationsdiagramm
configuration management Konfigurationsmanagement
configuration manager Konfigurationsmanager
confirm (to) bestätigen
confirmation Bestätigung
conflict Konflikt
conflict management Konfliktmanagement
conflict potential Konfliktpotential
conflictary objective relation konfliktäre Zielbeziehung
conformity Konformität, Übereinstimmung
congestion Überlastung
conjunction Konjunktion
connect (to) durchschalten, verbinden
connect time Anschlußzeit
connection Verbindung
connectivity Konnektivität, Verbindbarkeit, Vernetzungsgrad
consequence Konsequenz
consistency Konsistenz, Widerspruchsfreiheit
consistency fault Konsistenzfehler
consistency rule Konsistenzregel
consistent konsistent, widerspruchsfrei
console Konsole
console operator Konsoloperator
consolidated decision table konsolidierte Entscheidungstabelle
consolidation Konsolidierung
constant Konstante
constraint Nebenbedingung, Restriktion
construct Konstrukt, konstruiertes Gebilde
construct validity Konstruktvalidität
constructional figure Gliederungszahl

constructional requirement
Baubestimmung
consult (to) beraten
consultant Berater
consulting company
Beratungsunternehmen
consulting firm Beratungsfirma
consulting service Beratungsservice
consulting system Beratungssystem
consumption of material
Materialverbrauch
container computing center
Behälter-Rechenzentrum
content addressable memory
inhaltsadressierbarer Speicher,
Assoziativspeicher
content analysis Aussagenanalyse,
Bedeutungsanalyse
content of dialog Dialoginhalt
content of goal Zielinhalt
content validity Inhaltsvalidität
content verification Inhaltsüberprüfung
context Kontext, Zusammenhang
context diagram Kontextdiagramm
contiguous angrenzend, benachbart
contingency Situationsabhängigkeit,
Kontingenz
contingency analysis Kontingenzanalyse
contingency plan Katastrophenplan,
Notfallplan
contingent situationsabhängig, situativ,
kontingent
continuous error Endlosfehler
continuous form Endlosformular
continuous form feed device
Endlosformularführung
continuous form stacker Endlosablage
continuous load Dauerbetrieb
continuous observation Dauerbeobachtung
continuous operation Dauerbetrieb
continuous pin-feed form Endlosformular
mit Führungslochung
continuous processing Dauerbetrieb
continuous tone Dauerton
continuous underscore
Dauerunterstreichung
contract Vertrag
contract clause Vertragsbestimmung
contract design Vertragsentwurf
contract law Vertragsrecht
contract negotiation Vertragsverhandlung
contracting parity Vertragspartner
contractor Auftragnehmer
contractual vertraglich
contractual obligation
Vertragsverpflichtung
contractual penalty Vertragsstrafe

contractual relationship
Vertragsverhältnis
contrast Kontrast
control Steuerung
control (to) kontrollieren, regeln, steuern
control break item Gruppenbegriff
control character Steuerzeichen
control characters Steuerungsdaten
control command Steuerbefehl
control computer Leitrechner,
Steuerrechner
control console Bedienerkonsole
control engineering Regelungstechnik,
Steuerungstechnik
control equipment Leiteinrichtung
control function Kontrollfunktion,
Steuerungsfunktion
control information Kontrollinformation,
Steuerungsinformation
control key Funktionstaste
control language Steuersprache
control level Gruppenstufe
control lever Steuerhebel
control line Regelstrecke
control loop Regelkreis
control mode Kontrollmodus
control panel Bedienungspult,
Bedienungstafel
control path Kontrollpfad
control program Steuerprogramm
control quantity Steuerungsgröße
control record Steuerungsdaten
control rule Steuerregel
control storage Kontrollspeicher
control structure Kontrollstruktur
control system Kontrollsystem
control unit Leitwerk, Steuereinheit,
Steuerwerk
control variable Laufvariable
controllability Steuerbarkeit
controlled cancellation kontrollierter
Abbruch
controlled system Regelstrecke
controller Controller
controller program Steuerungsprogramm
controlling Controlling
controlling element Stellglied
controlling technique Controllingmethode
conventional approach konventioneller
Ansatz
convergent decision style
konvergierender Entscheidungsstil
conversational mode Dialogbetrieb
conversational processing
Dialogverarbeitung
conversational system
Konversationssystem

conversion Umwandlung
convert (to) konvertieren
convertibility Austauschbarkeit
conviviality Konvivialität
cooperation Kooperation, Mitarbeit
cooperation aid Kooperationsunterstützung
cooperative dialog behavior kooperatives Dialogverhalten
cooperative dialog system kooperatives Dialogsystem
coordinate setting Punktsteuerung
coordination Koordination
coordination ability Koordinationsfähigkeit
coordinator Koordinator
copier Kopierer
copy Kopie
copy (to) kopieren, vervielfältigen
copy counter Kopienzähler
copy equipment Kopiergerät
copy management Kopiermanagement
copy program Kopierprogramm
copy protection Kopierschutz
copy stop Kopierstopp
copying carbon paper Durchschreibpapier
copyright Urheberrecht
CORAL = Computer Online Realtime Applications Language
core Kern
core activity Kerntätigkeit
core area Kernbereich
cornerstone Eckstein, Meilenstein
corporate culture Unternehmenskultur
corporate data base unternehmensweite Datenbasis
corporate goal Unternehmensziel
corporate identity Unternehmenspersönlichkeit
corporate level Unternehmensebene
corporate model Unternehmensmodell
corporate objective Unternehmensziel
corporate plan Unternehmensplan
corporate politics Unternehmenspolitik
corporate strategy Strategie der Unternehmung, Unternehmensstrategie
corporate success Unternehmenserfolg
correction privilege Richtigstellungsrecht
correction right Berichtigungsrecht
corrective job design korrigierende Arbeitsgestaltung
corrective maintenance korrigierende Wartung
correctness Korrektheit, Richtigkeit
correlation analysis Korrelationsanalyse
correlation matrix Korrelationsmatrix

COS = Corporation for Open Systems
cost accounting Betriebsbuchhaltung, Kosten- und Leistungsrechnung, Kostenträgerrechnung
cost allocation Kostenumlage, Kostenverteilung
cost allocation key Kostenverteilungsschlüssel
cost analysis Kostenanalyse
cost assessment Kostenabschätzung
cost avoidance Kostenvermeidung
cost center measurement Kostenstellenrechnung
cost chargeback Kostenverrechnung
cost chargeout Kostenverrechnung
cost comparison measurement Kostenvergleichsrechnung
cost conscious kostenbewußt
cost control Kostenüberwachung
cost cut Kostenabbau
cost displacement Kostenverlagerung, Kostenverschiebung
cost distribution Kostenumlage
cost effectiveness Kostenwirksamkeit
cost efficiency Kostenwirtschaftlichkeit
cost equalization Kostenausgleich
cost estimate Kostenschätzung
cost estimating Aufwandschätzung
cost factor Kostenfaktor
cost function Kostenfunktion
cost item Kostenart
cost item accounting Kostenartenrechnung
cost item measurement Kostenartenrechnung
cost justification Rechtfertigung von Kosten
cost lead Kostenvorsprung
cost leadership Kostenführerschaft
cost overrun insurance Mehrkosten-Versicherung
cost reduction Kostenabbau
cost sharing Kostenbeteiligung, Kostenteilung
cost structure Kostenstruktur
cost/benefit analysis Kosten/Nutzen-Analyse
cost/benefit ratio Kosten/Nutzen-Verhältnis
cost/benefit technique Kosten/Nutzen-Technik
cost/cost analysis Kosten/Kosten-Analyse
cost/effectiveness analysis Kosten/Wirksamkeits-Analyse
cost/value analysis Kosten/Wert-Analyse
costing Kostenrechnung
costs Kosten

counter Zählwerk
counter offer Gegenangebot
countermeasure Gegenmaßnahme
coupler Akustikmuff, Koppler
courseware Lernprogramm
cover Gehäuse
CPC = Card Programmed Calculator
CPE = Computer Performance Evaluation
CPF = Central Processing Facility
CPL = Characters Per Line
CPM = Critical Path Method
CP/M = Control Program for Microcomputers
cps = characters per second
cps = cycles per second
CPU = Central Processing Unit
CPU time CPU-Zeit
cracker Cracker
CRAM = Card Random Access Memory
crash Absturz, Zusammenbruch
crash program Absturzprogramm
CRBE = Conversational Remote Batch Entry
CRC = Cyclic Redundancy Check
creaping functionality Funktionsausbreitung
creative kreativ, schöpferisch
creative goal Gestaltungsziel
creativity Kreativität
creativity technique Kreativitätstechnik
credibility Glaubwürdigkeit, Zuverlässigkeit
credit symbol Habenzeichen
creditor accounting Kreditorenbuchführung
crime deliktische Handlung
criminal hacker Cracker
cripple (to) abklemmen
crisis management Krisenmanagement
criteria list Kriterienkatalog
criteria validity kriterienbezogene Validität
criteria weight Kriteriengewicht
criterion Kriterium
criterion of order Ordnungskriterium
critical competition factor kritischer Wettbewerbsfaktor
critical defect kritischer Defekt
critical error kritischer Fehler
critical event kritischer Vorgang
critical event warning Erfolgsfrühwarnung
critical path kritischer Weg
critical path method Methode des kritischen Wegs
critical success factor kritischer Erfolgsfaktor
criticism Kritik
criticism of fundamentals Grundsatzkritik
cross checking Querkontrolle
cross compiler Quer-Kompilierer
cross connection Querverbindung
cross impact analysis Cross-Impact-Analyse
cross reference Querverweis
cross reference list Kreuz-Referenz-Liste
cross reference table Zuordnungstabelle
crossfoot Quersumme
crossfoot check Summenkreuzprüfung
crossfooting Querrechnen, Quersummenkontrolle, Summenkreuzprüfung
crossfooting balance check Nullkontrolle
CRT = Cathode Ray Tube
cryo computer Tieftemperatur-Computer
crypto algorithm Kryptoalgorithmus
crypto analysis Kryptoanalyse
crypto hardware device Krypto-Hardware-Einheit
cryptogram verschlüsselter Text
cryptographic ciphering technique kryptographische Verschlüsselungsmethode
cryptographic key Chiffrierschlüssel
cryptography Kryptographie
cryptology Kryptologie
CSF = Critical Success Factors
CSI = Commercial System Integration
CSL = Computer Simulation Language
CSMA = Communication Systems Management Association
CSMA/CD = Carrier Sense Multiple Access/Collision Detection
CSP = Control Setting Panel
CTRL key Kontrolltaste
culture Kultur
cupboard software Schranksoftware
currency sign Währungszeichen
current data flow Ist-Datenfluß
current directory aktuelles Inhaltsverzeichnis
current fault aktiver Fehler
current file aktive Datei
current line aktive Zeile
current problem bestehendes Problem
current supply Netzanschluß
current system bestehendes System, Istzustand
current system-based approach istzustandsorientierter Ansatz

cursor Anforderungszeichen, Positionsmarke, Schreibmarke
cursor key Schreibmarken-Taste
curve diagram Kurvendiagramm
curve digitizer Kurvenleser
custom-tailored software Individualsoftware
customer Kunde
customer account Kundenkonto
customer dependent integrated circuit kundenspezifische integrierte Schaltung
customer order Kundenauftrag
customer service Kundendienst
customer service level Lieferbereitschaft
customer support Kundenunterstützung
customer terminal Teilnehmerendgerät
customization Kundenanpassung
customize (to) anpassen

customized angepaßt, kundenspezifisch
customized command symbolics Freihand-Symbolik
customized standard software organisationsangepaßte Standardsoftware
customizing method Anpassungsmethode
cut (to) ausschneiden
cutover Umstellung
cybernetic principle kybernetisches Prinzip
cybernetic thinking kybernetisches Denken
cybernetics Kybernetik
cycle time Zykluszeit
cyclic flowchart zyklisches Ablaufdiagramm
cylinder Zylinder
cypher text Schlüsseltext

D

DAI = Distributed Artificial Intelligence
daily backup volume täglicher Sicherungsdatenträger
daisy wheel Schreibrad, Typenrad
daisy wheel printer Typenraddrucker
DAL = Design Analysis Language
DAM = Direct Access Method
damage Schaden
DAP = Distributed Array Processor
DAT = Digital Audio Tape
data Daten
data abstraction Datenabstraktion
data abuse insurance Datenmißbrauch-Versicherung
data access Datenzugriff
data access diagram Datenzugriffsdiagramm
data administration Datenverwaltung
data administrator Datenadministrator, Datenverwalter
data analysis Datenanalyse
data assurance Datensicherung
data assurance measure Datensicherungsmaßnahme
data bank (external) Datenbank
data bank service Datenbankdienst
data base Datenbasis
data base access Datenbankzugriff
data base administrator Datenbank-Administrator
data base architecture Datenbank-Architektur
data base computer Datenbankrechner
data base definition Datenbankdefinition
data base description Datenbank-Beschreibung
data base description language Datenbank-Beschreibungssprache
data base design Datenbankentwurf
data base language Datenbanksprache
data base machine Datenbankmaschine
data base management Datenbankmanagement
data base management system Datenbank-Managementsystem, Datenbank-Verwaltungssystem
data base model Datenbankmodell
data base of organization Organisationsdatenbank
data base schema Datenbankschema
data base selection criterion Datenbank-Auswahlkriterium
data base structure diagram Datenbank-Strukturdiagramm
data base system Datenbanksystem
data block Datenblock
data boundary Datengrenze
data bus Datenbus
data bus line Daten-Sammelleitung
data capsule Datenkapsel
data capturing Datenerfassung
data capturing system Datenerfassungssystem
data capturing technique Datenerfassungsmethode
data carrier Datenträger
data check Datenprüfung
data ciphering key datenchiffrierender Schlüssel
data collection Datenerfassung
data collection form Datenerfassungsbeleg
data collection platform Datenerfassungsstelle
data collection sheet Datenerfassungsbeleg
data collection system Datenerfassungssystem
data collection technique Datenerfassungsmethode
data communications Datenkommunikation, Datenübermittlung
data communications control Datenübermittlungssteuerung
data communications service Datenübermittlungsdienst
data communications standards Datenübermittlungsverordnung
data communications system Datenübermittlungssystem
data compression Datenkomprimierung, Datenverdichtung
data concentrator Datenkonzentrator
data concept Datenkonzept
data consistency Datenkonsistenz
data control Datensteuerung
data conversion Datenkonvertierung
data conversion error Datenkonversionsfehler
data correction Datenkorrektur
data declaration Datenvereinbarung
data definition language Datendefinitionssprache
data description Datenbeschreibung
data description language Datenbeschreibungssprache
data design Datenentwurf
data dictionary Datenkatalog, Datenwörterbuch
data dictionary system Datenkatalog-System

data driven approach datenorientierter Ansatz
data driven forward chaining datengetriebene Vorwärtsverkettung
data element Datenelement
data encoding Verschlüsselung
data encryption Datenverschlüsselung
data encryption standard Datenverschlüsselungsnorm
data entry location Datenerfassungsstelle
data flow Datenfluß
data flow arrow Datenflußpfeil
data flow chart Datenflußplan
data flow computer Datenflußrechner
data flow control Datenflußsteuerung
data flow diagram Ablaufdiagramm, Datenflußdiagramm
data flow oriented detailed analysis datenflußorientierte Feinstudie
data flow oriented testing datenbezogenes Testen
data format Datenformat
data format specification Datenformatangabe
data gram Datenpaket
data group Datengruppe
data independence Datenunabhängigkeit
data input Dateneingabe
data integration Datenintegration
data integrity Datenintegrität
data item Datenfeld, Datengröße, Datum
data key Datentaste
data legal protection insurance Datenrechtsschutz-Versicherung
data lexicon Datenlexikon
data liability insurance Datenhaftpflicht-Versicherung
data link Übermittlungsabschnitt
data link control Datenübertragungssteuerung
data link layer Verbindungsschicht
data loss Datenverlust
data management Datenverwaltung
data manipulation Datenmanipulation
data manipulation language Datenmanipulationssprache
data matrix Datenmatrix
data medium Datenträger
data medium archive Datenträger-Archiv
data medium exchange Datenträgeraustausch
data medium management Datenträger-Verwaltung
data memory Datenspeicher
data mirroring Datenspiegelung
data model Datenmodell
data model design Datenmodellentwurf

data network Datennetz
data of order Ordnungsdaten
data organization Datenorganisation
data orientation Datenorientierung
data oriented approach datenorientierter Ansatz
data oriented auditing datenorientierte Prüfung
data output Datenausgabe
data packet Datenpaket
data path Datenweg
data preparation Datenaufbereitung, datentechnische Vorbereitung
data privacy Datenschutz
data privacy act Datenschutzgesetz
data privacy committee Datenschutzkommission
data privacy council Datenschutzrat
data processing Datenverarbeitung
data processing center Datenverarbeitungszentrum
data processing department Datenverarbeitungsabteilung
data processing equipment Datenverarbeitungsanlage
data processing profession Datenverarbeitungsberuf
data processing register Datenverarbeitungsregister
data processing registration number Datenverarbeitungsregister-Nummer
data processing system Datenverarbeitungssystem
data protection Datenschutz
data protection act Datenschutzgesetz
data protection measure Datenschutzmaßnahme
data protection officer Datenschutzbeauftragter
data protection report Datenschutzbericht
data protection right Datenschutzrecht
data rate Datenrate
data record Datensatz
data recovery Datenrekonstruktion
data reduction program Datenreduktionsprogramm
data redundancy Datenredundanz
data relationship Datenbeziehung
data resource management Datenmanagement
data routing Datenwegleitung
data scope Dataskop
data secrecy Datengeheimnis
data security Datensicherheit
data set Datenbestand, Datei
data sharing Datenverbund
data sink Datensenke

data source Datenquelle
data stack Datenkeller
data structure Datenstruktur
data structuring Datenstrukturierung
data system Datensystem
data telephone Datentelephon
data terminal Datenendeinrichtung, Datenendgerät, Datenstation
data theft Datendiebstahl
data throughput Datendurchsatz
data track Datenspur
data transfer Datenübertragung
data transfer rate Datentübertragungsrate
data transmission Datenübertragung
data transmission equipment Datenübertragungseinrichtung
data transmission line Datenübertragungsleitung, Datenübertragungsweg
data transmission medium Datenübertragungsmedium
data transmission mode Datenübertragungsmodus
data transmission rate Datenübertragungsrate
data transmission speed Datenübertragungsgeschwindigkeit
data type Datenbauart, Datentyp
data typist Datentypist
data validation Datenprüfung
data verification Datenprüfung
data view Datensicht
data volume Datenumfang, Datenvolumen
dataphone Datentelephon
date Datum
date of movement Entnahmedatum
DATEL = Data Telecommunications
DATEL service DATEL-Dienst
db = Dezibel
DBA = Data Base Administrator
DB/DC System = Data Base/Data Communications System
DBMS = Data Base Management System
DCS = Distributed Computing System
DD = Data Dictionary
DD = Double Density
DDB = Distributed Data Base
DDL = Data Description Language
DDP = Decentralized Data Processing
DDP = Distributed Data Processing
DDS = Data Dictionary System
dead costs Leerkosten
deadline Stichtag
deadlock gegenseitige Blockierung, Stillstand, Verklemmung
debit accounting Debitorenbuchhaltung

debitor Schuldner
debug (to) austesten
debugger Diagnoseprogramm, Fehlersuchprogramm
debugging Fehlerbeseitigung
debugging aid Testhilfe
debugging program Fehlersuchprogramm
debugging support Testunterstützung
DEC = Data Exchange Control
decentralization Dezentralisation, Dezentralisierung
decentralized data collection dezentrale Datenerfassung
decentralized data processing dezentrale Datenverarbeitung
decibel Dezibel
decide (to) entscheiden
decimal digit Dezimalziffer
decipher (to) dechiffrieren, entschlüsseln
deciphering Entschlüsselung
decision Entscheidung
decision analysis Entscheidungsanalyse
decision competence Entscheidungsbefugnis
decision criterion Entscheidungskriterium
decision field Entscheidungsfeld
decision level Entscheidungsebene
decision maker Entscheidungsträger
decision making Entscheidungsfindung
decision making approach entscheidungsorientierter Ansatz
decision making behavior Entscheidungsverhalten
decision making conference Entscheidungskonferenz
decision matrix Entscheidungsmatrix
decision model Entscheidungsmodell
decision phase Entscheidungsphase
decision principle Entscheidungsprinzip
decision process Entscheidungsprozeß
decision rule Entscheidungsregel
decision scope Entscheidungsspielraum
decision style Entscheidungsstil
decision support system Entscheidungsunterstützungssystem
decision table Entscheidungstabelle
decision table technique Entscheidungstabellentechnik
decision table with extended entries Entscheidungstabelle mit erweiterten Eintragungen
decision table with limited entries Entscheidungstabelle mit einfachen Eintragungen
decision tableau Entscheidungstableau
decision technique Entscheidungstechnik
decision theory Entscheidungstheorie

decision tree Entscheidungsbaum
decision tree method
Entscheidungsbaumverfahren
decision threshold Entscheidungsschwelle
decision value Entscheidungswert
declaration Deklaration, Vereinbarung
declaration partition Vereinbarungsteil
declarative knowledge representation
deklarative Wissensdarstellung
declarative programming deklarative
Programmierung
declarative programming language
deklarative Programmiersprache
decline of performance Leistungsabfall
decode (to) dekodieren, dechiffrieren,
entschlüsseln
decoding Dekodierung, Dechiffrierung,
Entschlüsselung
decompose (to) zerlegen
decomposition Dekomposition, Zerlegung
decomposition diagram
Zerlegungsdiagramm
decompression Dekomprimierung
deconcentration Dekonzentration
decouple (to) entkoppeln
decoupling Entkopplung
dedicated dediziert, zweckbestimmt
dedicated connection Standleitung
dedicated line Standleitung
dedicated system dediziertes System,
zweckbestimmtes System
dedicated user group geschlossene
Benutzergruppe
deducible ableitbar
deduction Ableitung, Deduktion
deductive system Deduktionssystem
default value Ausgangswert, Defaultwert,
Standardwert
defective fehlerhaft
defensive strategy defensive Strategie
deferred restart verzögerter
Wiederanlauf
define (to) definieren
degree of automation
Automatisierungsgrad
degree of centralization/decentralization
Distribuierungsgrad
degree of co-ordination
Koordinierungsgrad
degree of decomposition Zerlegungsgrad
degree of insertion Einfügungsgrad
degree of interaction Dialogisierungsgrad
degree of interconnectivity
Verbindungsgrad
degree of participation
Partizipationsdimension

degree of penetration
Durchdringungsgrad
degree of relationship Beziehungsgrad
degree of reliability
Zuverlässigkeitsgrad
degree of structuring
Strukturierungsgrad
delay Verzögerung
delete (to) löschen
deletion privilege Löschungsrecht
delimiter Begrenzer
delivery Auslieferung, Lieferung
delivery service Lieferservice
delivery service flexibility
Lieferflexibilität
delivery service quality
Lieferbeschaffenheit, Lieferqualität
delivery time Anlieferungszeit, Lieferzeit
Delphi method Delphi-Methode
demodulate (to) demodulieren,
gleichrichten
demodulation Demodulation, Gleichrichten
demoscopy Demoskopie
density of characters Zeichendichte
department Fachabteilung
department coordinator
Abteilungskoordinator
departmental detailed analysis
abteilungsorientierte Feinstudie
departmental level Abteilungsebene
dependability Abhängigkeit
dependency analysis Dependenzanalyse
dependent abhängig
dependent job control abhängige
Auftragskontrolle, abhängige
Auftragssteuerung
dependent variable abhängige Variable
deposit of source program
Quellprogramm-Hinterlegung
depreciable costs abschreibbare Kosten
depreciation method
Abschreibungsmethode
depth-first search Tiefensuche
derivation Ableitung
derived abgeleitet
DES = Data Encryption Standard
DES algorithm DES-Algorithmus
descending key absteigender
Sortierbegriff
descending order absteigende Folge
descending sequence absteigende
Reihenfolge
descramble (to) entwürfeln
descrambler Entwürfler
describe (to) beschreiben
description Beschreibung
description error Beschreibungsfehler

description language Beschreibungssprache
description model Beschreibungsmodell
description of process Prozeßbeschreibung
description rule Beschreibungsregel
description technique Beschreibungstechnik
description tool Beschreibungsmittel
descriptive data beschreibende Daten
descriptive feature Beschreibungsmerkmal
descriptor Beschreiber, Deskriptor, Schlagwort
design alternative Gestaltungsalternative
design category Entwurfsdimension
design data base Entwurfsdatenbank
design document Entwurfsdokument
design function Entwurfsfunktion
design guideline Entwurfsrichtlinie
design language Entwurfssprache
design matrix Entwurfsmatrix
design phase Entwurfsphase
design principle Entwurfsprinzip
design review Entwurfsinspektion
design scope Gestaltungsspielraum
design specification Entwurfsbeschreibung
design technique Entwurfsmethode
design test Designtest, Entwurfstest
design tool Entwurfswerkzeug
desired value Sollwert
desk test Schreibtischtest
desktop publishing computerunterstütztes Publizieren, Publizieren vom Schreibtisch
destination Bestimmungsort
destructive readout löschendes Lesen, zerstörungsfreies Lesen
destructive strategy destruktive Strategie
DETAB = Decision Table
detailed analysis Detailanalyse, Feinanalyse
detailed design Detailentwurf, Feinentwurf
detailed study Detailstudie, Feinstudie
detailed survey Detailstudie, Feinstudie
detailed systems design Feinprojektierung
determinism Determinismus
determinism hypothesis Determinismus-Hypothese
deterministic deterministisch
deterministic heuristics deterministische Heuristik
develop (to) entwickeln
developer Entwickler

development Entwicklung
development administrator Entwicklungsadministrator
development backlog Entwicklungsrückstau
development computer Entwicklungsrechner
development cycle Entwicklungszyklus
development data base Entwicklungsdatenbank
development library Entwicklungsbibliothek
development strategy Entwicklungsstrategie
development testing Entwicklungstest
development tool Entwicklungswerkzeug
deviation Abweichung
deviation analysis Abweichungsanalyse
deviation report Abweichungsbericht
device Gerät
device certificate Geräteschein
device independence Geräteunabhängigkeit
device number Gerätenummer
device specification Geräteschein
DFD = Data Flow Diagram
DIA = Distributed Intelligent Agent
diagnose (to) diagnostizieren
diagnosis Diagnose
diagnostic function Diagnosefunktion
diagnostic map Diagnosemappe
diagnostic model Diagnosemodell
diagnostic program Diagnostikprogramm
diagnostic rule Diagnoseregel
diagram Diagramm
diagramming technique Diagrammtechnik
dial (to) anwählen
dialog Dialog
dialog ability Dialogfähigkeit
dialog control Dialogführung, Dialogsteuerung
dialog design Dialoggestaltung
dialog flexibility Dialogflexibilität
dialog generator Dialoggenerator
dialog interface Dialogoberfläche, Dialogschnittstelle
dialog job Dialogauftrag
dialog language Dialogsprache
dialog medium Dialogmedium
dialog partner model Dialogpartnermodell
dialog stacking Dialogkellerung
dialog structure Dialogstruktur
dialog switching Dialogwechsel
dialog system Dialogsystem
dialog technique Dialogtechnik

dialup connection Wählleitung
dialup network Wähldatennetz
diameter Durchmesser
DIANE = Direct Information Access Network for Europe
dictation machine Diktiergerät
dictionary Wörterbuch
differentiation Differenzierung
differentiated internal pricing differenzierter Verrechnungspreis
differentiation Differenzierung
difficulty Kompliziertheit
diffuse reflection diffuse Reflexion
digit Ziffer
digit block Ziffernblock
digit key Zifferntaste
digital digital
digital/analog converter Digital/Analog-Umsetzer
digital audio tape digitales Kassettenband
digital communications system digitales Kommunikationssystem
digital computer Digitalrechner
digital data digitale Daten
digital local area network digitales Ortsnetz
digital network architecture digitale Netzarchitektur
digital optical computer digitaler optischer Computer
digital representation digitale Darstellung
digital signature digitale Unterschrift
digitize (to) digitalisieren
digitizer Digitalisierer, Tablett, Zeichentablett
digitizer board Digitalisierbrett, Digitalisiertablett
direct direkt
direct (to) anweisen
direct access direkter Zugriff
direct access memory Direktzugriffsspeicher
direct changeover Direktumstellung
direct connection direkte Verbindung
direct costing Teilkostenrechnung
direct costs direkt zurechenbare Kosten
direct current Gleichstrom
direct data entry Datendirekteingabe
direct data network Direktdatennetz
direct input Direkteingabe
direct knowledge representation direkte Wissensdarstellung
direct labor cost Fertigungslohn
direct lightning direkter Blitzeinschlag
direct line Direktanschluß

direct manipulation direkte Manipulation
direct memory access Direktzugriffsspeicher
direct participation direkte Partizipation
direct positioning direktes Positionieren
direct query Direktabfrage
directional gerichtet
directory Inhaltsverzeichnis
disable (to) abschalten, deaktivieren
disable the line Abschalten der Leitung
disaster Katastrophe
disaster management Katastrophenmanagement
disaster plan Katastrophenplan
disaster protection Katastrophenschutz
disconnection Leitungsunterbrechung
discontinuity Diskontinuität
discrete optimization diskrete Optimierung
discrete simulation diskrete Simulation
discriminant analysis Diskriminanzanalyse
disjunction Disjunktion
disk Platte
disk access Plattenzugriff
disk error Plattenfehler
disk operating system Plattenbetriebssystem
disk pack Plattenstapel
disk storage Plattenspeicher
disk storage drive Plattenspeicherlaufwerk
disk track Plattenspur
disk unit Platteneinheit
dispatch (to) abfertigen, ingangsetzen
dispatcher Verteiler
dispatching Auftragseinplanung
dispatching queue Bereitschaftswarteschlange
display Anzeige, Datensichtgerät
display (to) anzeigen, ausgeben
display device Bildschirmgerät
display form Bildschirmformular
display graphics Bildschirmgraphik
display mask Bildschirmmaske
display phone Fernzeichner
display size Bildschirmgröße
display station Datensichtstation
display table Bildschirmformular
display unit Bildschirmeinheit
display window Bildschirmfenster
disposition Disposition, Vorkehrung
dissatisfaction Unzufriedenheit
distance Abstand
distribute (to) verteilen
distributed artificial intelligence verteilte künstliche Intelligenz

distributed computer system verteiltes Computersystem
distributed data base verteilte Datenbank, verteilte Datenbasis
distributed data processing verteilte Datenverarbeitung
distributed intelligence verteilte Intelligenz
distributed knowledge base verteilte Wissensbasis
distributed program verteiltes Programm
distribution Auslieferung, Distribuierung, Verteilung
distribution channel Absatzweg
distribution list Verteilerliste
distribution logistics Vertriebslogistik
disturbance Störgröße, Störung
disturbance variable Störgröße
divergent decision making behavior divergierender Entscheidungsstil
division remainder Divisionsrest
DL/1 = Data Language One
DMA = Direct Memory Access
DML = Data Manipulation Language
DNA = Digital Network Architecture
DNC = Direct Numerical Control
DNIC = Data Network Identification Code
document Beleg, Dokument, Schriftstück
document analysis Dokumentenauswertung
document date Dokumentdatum
document delivery Dokumentenanlieferung
document design Beleggestaltung
document dissemination Dokumenteverteilung
document distribution Dokumenteverteilung
document feed Einzelblatteinzug
document log Dokumentprotokoll
document management Dokumenteverwaltung
document preparation Belegaufbereitung
document printer Belegdrucker
document processing Belegverarbeitung, Dokumenteverarbeitung
document reader Belegleser, Formularleser, Klarschriftleser
document retrieval Dokumente-Wiedergewinnung
document system Belegsystem
document transport Belegdurchlauf
documentation Dokumentation
documentation guide Dokumentationshandbuch
documentation handbook Dokumentationshandbuch
documentation language Dokumentationssprache
documentation process Dokumentieren
documentation standard Dokumentationsstandard
documentation system Dokumentationssystem
domain Bereich, Domäne, Wertebereich
domain of attribute Attribute-Wertebereich
domain of common law öffentlicher Rechtsbereich
domain of goal Zielausmaß
domain of private law privater Rechtsbereich
DOS = Disk Operating System
dot matrix Punktmatrix
double covering Zweifachbelegung
double linked data organization doppelt gekettete Dateiorganisation
double precision doppelte Genauigkeit
double recording density doppelte Schreibdichte
double sided zweiseitig
double sided printer Zwillingsdrucker
double strike Doppeldruck
double word Doppelwort
downline loading Fernladen
download Herunterladen
downsizing Größenreduzierung
downtime Ausfallzeit, Stillstandzeit
downtime insurance Ausfallschaden-Versicherung
downward communication Abwärtskommunikation
DP = Data Processing
DP = Document Publishing
DP auditor DV-Revisor
DP committee DV-Ausschuß
DP coordinator DV-Koordinator
DP manager DV-Manager
dpi = dots per inch
DQ = Draft Quality
draft contract Vertragsentwurf
draft quality Entwurfsqualität, Konzeptqualität
DRAM = Dynamic Random Access Memory
drap door Falltür
drawer plan Schubladenplan
drawing Zeichnung
drawing reader Zeichnungsleser
3D terminal Stereo-Bildbetrachter
drive Laufwerk
driver Treiber
DRM = Data Resource Management
drop in performance Leistungsverlust

drop-in signal Störsignal
drum plotter Trommelplotter
drum printer Trommeldrucker
dry running Trockenlauf
dry testing Trockentest
DSE = Distributed System Environment
DSS = Decision Support System
DTP = Desktop Publishing
dual keying Funktionstasten-Sicherung
dummy Platzhalter
dump Speicherauszug
duplex communications Duplexverbindung
duplex mode Duplexbetrieb, Gegenbetrieb
duplex operation Duplexbetrieb, Gegenbetrieb
duplex system Duplexsystem
duplex telephone system Gegensprechanlage
duplicate (to) vervielfältigen
duplication of software Vervielfältigen von Software
dx = duplex
dynamic dynamisch

dynamic authorizing dynamische Autorisierung
dynamic data structure dynamische Datenstruktur
dynamic file backup dynamische Dateisicherung
dynamic help system dynamisches Hilfesystem
dynamic instrumentation dynamische Instrumentierung
dynamic memory dynamischer Speicher
dynamic memory management dynamische Speicherverwaltung
dynamic program analysis dynamische Programmanalyse
dynamic quality measure dynamisches Qualitätsmaß
dynamic read-write memory dynamischer Lese-Schreibspeicher
dynamic resource allocation dynamische Systemmittelzuordnung
dynamic sitting dynamisches Sitzen
dynamic system dynamisches System
dynamic testing dynamisches Testen
dynamic topology dynamische Topologie

E

EAPROM = Electrically Alterable Programmable Read Only Memory
earliest begin date frühester Anfangstermin, frühester Beginntermin
earliest end date frühester Endtermin
earliest start date frühester Beginntermin, frühester Starttermin
early sales warning Umsatzfrühwarnung
early success warning Erfolgsfrühwarnung
early warning Frühwarnung
early warning function Frühwarnfunktion
early warning system Frühwarnsystem
EARN = European Academic and Research Network
EAROM = Electrically Alterable Read Only Memory
ease of development Entwicklungsmöglichkeit
ease of usage Benutzbarkeit
ease of use Benutzungsfreundlichkeit
easiest first strategy Easiest-first-Strategie
easy to use benutzungsfreundlich
EBCDIC = Extended Binary Coded Decimal Interchange Code
ECC = Error Correcting Code
ECCAI = European Committee for Artificial Intelligence
ECITIC = European Committee for Information Technology Certification
ECMA = European Computer Manufacturers Association
ECMA symbolics ECMA-Symbolik
ecological information system Umweltinformationssystem
economic benefits wirtschaftlicher Nutzen
economic impact wirtschaftliche Auswirkung
economic informatics Wirtschaftsinformatik
economic value wirtschaftlicher Wert
EDC = Error Dedecting Code
EDFD = Entity Data Flow Diagram
edge Kante
edge model Kantenmodell
EDI = Electronic Data Interchange
EDIF = Electronic Design Interchange Format
EDIFACT = Electronic Data Interchange for Administration, Commerce and Transport
edit (to) überarbeiten
edited item druckaufbereitendes Datenfeld
editing Ausgabeaufbereitung
editor Ausgabeaufbereiter, Dateiaufbereiter
EDP = Electronic Data Processing
EDP consultant EDV-Berater
EDP department EDV-Abteilung
EDP expert EDV-Sachverständiger
EDP function EDV-Funktion
EDP masterplan EDV-Rahmenplan
EDP oriented approach EDV-orientierter Ansatz
EDS = Electronic Data Switching
EEPROM = Electrically Erasable and Programmable Read Only Memory
EEROM = Electrically Erasable Read Only Memory
effect Wirkung
effect of integration Integrationswirkung
effective wirksam, wirkungsvoll
effective range Meßbereich
effectiveness Wirksamkeit
effectiveness analysis Wirksamkeitsanalyse
effectiveness level Wirkungsebene
effectiveness relation Wirkungsbeziehung
effectivity Effektivität
effectivity chain Wirkungskette
effectivity network Wirkungsnetzwerk
efficiency Effizienz, Wirtschaftlichkeit
efficiency analysis Wirtschaftlichkeitsanalyse
efficiency calculus Wirtschaftlichkeitsrechnung
efficiency measure Wirtschaftlichkeitskennzahl
efficient wirtschaftlich
effort Aufwand
effort estimate Aufwandschätzung
EFTS = Electronic Funds Transfer System
EIA = Electronic Industries Association
EIM = Enterprise Information Management
EIS = Executive Information System
EISA = Extended Industry Standard Architecture
ELAN = Elementary Language
elapsed time Belegungszeit
elapsed time measurement Fortschrittszeit-Messung
elasticity Elastizität
electrically alterable programmable read only memory elektrisch änderbarer programmierbarer Festwertspeicher

electrically alterable read only memory
elektrisch änderbarer Festwertspeicher
electro-engraving printer
Elektro-Erosionsdrucker
electro-magnetic pollution
elektromagnetische Umweltverschmutzung
electro-optical transformer
elektro-optischer Wandler
electro-photographic printer
elektrofotografischer Drucker
electron beam addressable memory
Elektronenstrahlspeicher
electronic book elektronisches Buch
electronic calender elektronischer Kalender
electronic cash payment elektronisches Bezahlen
electronic commercial panel elektronisches Handelspanel
electronic conference room elektronischer Konferenzraum
electronic copier elektronischer Kopierer
electronic data processing elektronische Datenverarbeitung
electronic data processing equipment elektronische Datenverarbeitungsanlage
electronic dictionary elektronisches Wörterbuch
electronic funds transfer system elektronisches Zahlungssystem
electronic garbage bin elektronischer Papierkorb
electronic mail elektronische Post
electronic mailbox elektronischer Briefkasten
electronic paint box elektronischer Malkasten
electronic post box elektronisches Postfach
electronic printer elektronischer Drucker
electronic stylus Lichtstift
electronic telephone book elektronisches Telephonbuch
electronic wastebasket elektronischer Papierkorb
electrostatic plotter elektrostatischer Plotter
electrostatic print unit elektrostatisches Druckwerk
element Element
elementary item Datenelement
ELSE statement Sonst-Anweisung
E-Mail = Electronic Mail
embossing terminal Prägeterminal
emergency Notfall
emergency cutoff Notabschaltung
emergency operation Notbetrieb

emergency plan Notfallplan
emergency planning Notfallplanung
emergency power device Notstromgerät
emergency service Notdienst
emergency signal Notsignal
emergency switch Notschalter
emergency system Notfallsystem
emotional process emotionaler Prozeß
empirical empirisch
empirical finding empirischer Befund
empirical testing empirisches Testen
empirism Empirismus
employ (to) beschäftigen
employee roster Stellenbesetzungsplan
employment Beschäftigung
empty-shell backup computing center kaltes Rechenzentrum
emulate (to) nachahmen
emulation Emulation, Nachahmung
emulator Emulator, Nachahmer
enable (to) freischalten
encode (to) chiffrieren, verschlüsseln
encoded data verschlüsselte Daten
encoding Verschlüsselung
encoding method Verschlüsselungsmethode
encryption Verschlüsselung
end of block Blockende
end of conversation Gesprächsende
end of file Dateiende
end of message Nachrichtenende
end of tape Bandende
end of text Textende
end of transmission Übertragungsende
end of transmission block Ende des Übertragungsblocks
end of volume label Bandkennsatz
end product Endprodukt
end-to-end ciphering Ende-zu-Ende-Verschlüsselung
end-user Benutzer, Endanwender, Endbenutzer
end-user behavior Benutzerverhalten
end-user computing benutzergesteuerte Datenverarbeitung
end-user independence Benutzerunabhängigkeit
end-user language Benutzersprache
end-user support Benutzerunterstützung
end-user system Benutzersystem, Endbenutzersystem
end-user tool Benutzerwerkzeug
enforce (to) durchsetzen
enforcement Durchsetzung
enter (to) eingeben
enter key Eingabetaste, Rücksprungtaste
enterprise Unternehmen

enterprise (to) unternehmen
enterprise area Unternehmensbereich
enterprise-wide information management unternehmensweites Informationsmanagement
entity Entität, Objekt
entity key Objektschlüssel
entity model Objektmodell
entity relationship Objektbeziehung
entity relationship diagram Objekt-Beziehung-Diagramm, Objekt-Struktur-Diagramm
entity relationship principle Objekt-Beziehung-Prinzip
entity set Objektmenge
entity type Objekttyp
entity type approach Objekttypen-Ansatz
entity type graph Objekttypen-Zusammenhangsgraph
entity type representation Objekttyp-Darstellung
entity usage analysis Objekt-Verwendungsanalyse
entry point Eingangsstelle
environment Umgebung
environmental condition Umgebungsbedingung, Umweltbedingung
environmental requirement Umgebungsanforderung, Umweltanforderung
EOB = End of Block
EOF = End of File
EOJ = End of Job
EOM = End of Message
EOR = End of Reel
EOT = End of Tape
EOT = End of Text
EOT = End of Transmission
EOV = End of Volume
EP = Electronic Publishing
EPROM = Erasable Programmable Read Only Memory
ER = Externer Rechner
equal sign Gleichheitszeichen
equality of structure Strukturähnlichkeit
equipment Anlage
equipment maintenance Anlageninstandhaltung
equipment requirements Technikbedarf
equipment selection Anlagenauswahl
equipment type Techniktyp
equivalence Äquivalenz
ER-Diagramm = Entity-Relationship-Diagramm
erasable programmable read only memory feldprogrammierbarer Festwertspeicher, löschbarer Festwertspeicher
erasable storage löschbarer Speicher
ergonomics Ergonomie
ergonomics of work area Arbeitsplatzergonomie
ERM = Entity Relationship Model
ERMES = European Radio Message System
error Fehler
error avoidance Fehlerumgehung
error burst Fehlerhäufung
error checking code Fehlerprüfcode
error classification Fehlerklassifikation
error control Fehlerschutz, Fehlerüberwachung
error control unit Fehlerüberwachungseinheit
error correcting code fehlerkorrigierender Code, selbstprüfender Code
error correction Fehlerbeseitigung, Fehlerkorrektur
error correction code Fehlerkorrekturcode
error correction feature Fehlerkorrektureinrichtung
error detecting Fehlererkennung
error detection code Fehlererkennungscode
error estimation Fehlerabschätzung
error frequency Fehlerhäufigkeit
error handling Fehlerbehandlung
error in estimating Schätzfehler
error isolation Fehlereingrenzung
error log Fehlerprotokoll
error logging Fehlererfassung
error message Fehlermeldung, Fehlernachricht
error parity Paritätsfehler
error probability Fehlerwahrscheinlichkeit
error rate Fehlerrate
error recording Fehleraufzeichnung
error report Fehlerbericht, Fehlerliste
error tolerance Fehlerunempfindlichkeit
ESC = Escape
ESPRIT = European Strategic Programme for Research in Information Technology
ESS = Executive Support System
estimate Schätzung
estimate (to) schätzen
estimate error Schätzfehler
estimate function Schätzfunktion
estimate of costs Kostenvoranschlag
estimate procedure Schätzverfahren
estimate scale Schätzskala
estimated benefits geschätzter Nutzen

estimated costs

estimated costs geschätzte Kosten
estimation Abschätzung, Schätzung
estimation of benefits Nutzenschätzung
estimation of costs Kostenschätzung
estimator Schätzer
ETB = End of Transmission Block
ETHICS = Effective Technical and Human Implementation of Computerbased Systems
EUC = End-User Computing
Euclidean distance Euklidischer Abstand
Euro signal Eurosignal
European Product Code Europaeinheitliche Artikelnummer
evaluate (to) bewerten
evaluation Bewertung, Evaluierung
evaluation criterion Bewertungskriterium
evaluation of alternatives Alternativenbewertung
evaluation procedure Bewertungsverfahren
evaluation process Bewertungsprozeß
evaluation technique Bewertungsmethode
even geradzahlig
even parity geradzahlige Parität
even parity check Prüfung auf geradzahlige Parität
event Ereignis
event buffer Ereignispuffer
event chain Ereigniskette
event driven monitoring Ereignismessung
event node network plan Ereignisknoten-Netzplan
event type Ereignistyp
evolution Evolution, Entfaltung
evolution matrix Evolutionsmatrix
evolution theory Evolutionstheorie
evolutionary prototyping evolutionäres Prototyping
evolutionary software development evolutionäre Software-Entwicklung
evolvability Entwicklungsfähigkeit
EwIM = Enterprise-wide Information Management
EX = Execute
EXAPT = Exact Automatic Programming of Tool
exception condition Ausnahmebedingung
exception handling Ausnahmebehandlung
exchange Vermittlung
exchange mode Vermittlungsart
exclusive right of use ausschließliches Nutzungsrecht
executable ausführbar
executable program ablauffähiges Programm, ausführbares Programm
execute (to) ausführen

executing the order Auftragsdurchführung
execution error Ausführungsfehler
execution information Ausführungsinformation, Durchführungsinformation
execution time Ausführungszeit, Durchlaufzeit
executive leitender Angestellter
exhaustive search erschöpfende Suche
exhaustive testing vollständiges Testen
exhibition Messe
existing system Istzustand, Istsystem
exit Ausgang
expand (to) ausbauen, erweitern
expandability Ausbaufähigkeit, Erweiterbarkeit
expansion board Erweiterungsplatine
expectation Erwartung
expedited data flow beschleunigter Datenfluß
expenditure Ausgabe von Geld
experience Erfahrung
experience curve Erfahrungskurve
experience curve concept Erfahrungskurvenkonzept
experiment Experiment, Versuch
experimental prototyping experimentelles Prototyping
expert Gutachter, Sachverständiger
expert knowledge Expertenwissen, Sachwissen
expert mode Expertenmodus
expert opinion Gutachten, Sachverständigengutachten
expert questioning Expertenbefragung
expert support system Expertenunterstützungssystem
expert system Expertensystem
expertise Sachverständigengutachten
expiration date Verfallsdatum
explanation Erklärung
explanatory model Erklärungsmodell
explicit warranty ausdrückliche Garantie
exploration Erkundung
exploratory data analysis explorative Datenanalyse
exploratory experiment Erkundungsexperiment
exploratory prototyping exploratives Prototyping, erforschendes Prototyping
explosion Auflösung
exponential smoothing exponentielle Glättung
expression Ausdruck
extend (to) erweitern

extended binary-coded decimal interchange code erweiterter Binärcode für Dezimalziffern
extended main memory erweiterter Hauptspeicher
extended menu erweitertes Menü
extension Nebenanschluß
extent of damage Schadensausmaß
external auditing externe Revision
external bridge externe Brücke
external computer externer Rechner
external conflict Außenkonflikt
external data externe Daten
external data base externe Datenbank
external data processing Datenverarbeitung außer Haus
external interrupt externe Unterbrechung
external memory externer Speicher
external model externes Schema
external printer externer Drucker
external priority externe Priorität
external restart externer Wiederanlauf
external schema externes Schema
external software Fremdsoftware
external storage externer Speicher
extract management Extraktmanagement
extragenetic information extragenetische Information
extrasomatic information extrasomatische Information

F

face Drucktype
facilities planning Anlagenplanung
facility Anlage, Betriebsmittel
facsimile Faksimile, Nachbildung
facsimile machine Fernkopierer
facsimile service Faksimiledienst
facsimile technology Faksimiletechnik
facsimile transmission Faksimileübertragung, Fernkopieren
fact Faktum, Tatsache
factor analysis Faktorenanalyse
factory accounting Betriebsbuchhaltung
factory automation Fabrikautomation
factory data collection Betriebsdatenerfassung
factory of the future Fabrik der Zukunft
factory overhead costs Betriebsgemeinkosten
factory terminal Betriebsdaten-Erfassungsgerät
facts data base Fakten-Datenbank
failure Ausfall
failure frequency Ausfallhäufigkeit
failure rate Ausfallrate
failure stop permanente Fehlerunterdrückung
falsification Falsifizierung
FAM = Fast Access Memory
fan Gebläse
fanfolded zickzackgefaltet
fanfold paper zickzack gefaltetes Endlospapier
fast access memory Speicher mit schnellem Zugriff
fastener Verschluß
fatigue factor Ermüdungsfaktor
fault Fehler
fault analysis Fehleranalyse
fault diagnosis Fehlerdiagnose
fault free operation störungsfreier Betrieb
fault indication Fehleranzeige
fault indicator Fehleranzeiger
fault interrupt routine Fehlerunterbrechungsprogramm
fault liability Fehleranfälligkeit
fault rate Ausfallrate
fault security Ausfallsicherheit
fault suppression Fehlerunterdrückung
fault tolerance Fehlertoleranz
fault tolerant fehlertolerant
fault tolerant system fehlertolerantes System
fault tree Fehlerbaum
fault tree analysis Fehlerbaumanalyse

fault type Fehlerart
faulted line gestörte Leitung
faulty fehlerhaft
fax card Faxkarte
fax machine Fernkopierer
FCS = Frame Check Sequence
FDM = Frequency Division Multiplexing
FDMA = Frequency Division Multiplex Access
fdx = full duplex
feasibility Durchführbarkeit
feasibility study Durchführbarkeitsstudie, Machbarkeitsstudie
feasible durchführbar
feasible solution durchführbare Lösung
feature charakteristisches Merkmal, Hauptmerkmal
feature analysis Merkmalanalyse
federal data protection law Bundesdatenschutzgesetz
federal data protection officer Bundesdatenschutzbeauftragter
fee Gebühr
fee for administrative handling Bearbeitungsgebühr
fee schedule Gebührenverzeichnis
feed Vorschub
feed forward Vorkopplung
feed hole Führungsloch im Papier
feedback Rückkopplung, Rückmeldung
feedback control Regelung
feedback control system Regelsystem
feedback diagram Rückkopplungsdiagramm
FEP = Front End Processor
FET = Field Effect Transistor
FET technology FET-Technologie
fetch (to) abrufen
FF = Form Feed
fiber optics Glasfaserkabel, Lichtwellenleiter
fibre Faser
field Feld
field description Feldbeschreibung
field experiment Feldexperiment
FIFO = First In First Out
figure of order Ordnungsbegriff
file Datei
file access Dateizugriff
file assurance Dateisicherung
file change Dateiänderung
file comparator Dateivergleicher
file compression Dateikomprimierung
file design Dateientwurf
file directory Dateiverzeichnis
file editor Dateiaufbereiter

foreground programm

file generating Dateigenerierung
file label Dateikennsatz
file locking Dateisperre
file maintenance Dateiwartung
file management Dateiverwaltung
file name Dateiname
file organization Dateiorganisation
file processing Dateiverarbeitung
file profile Dateiprofil
file protection Dateischutz
file recovery Dateiwiederherstellung
file segment Dateisegment
file transfer Dateitransfer
file transmission Dateiübertragung
filing hole Abheftloch
filing holes Abheftlochung
filler Füllzeichen
filter Filter
filtering Filterung
final assembly Fertigmontage
final delivery Endauslieferung
final report Schlußbericht
final test Abschlußtest
finance Finanzierung
finance and accounting Finanz- und Rechnungswesen
finding Befund
fine design Feinentwurf
finish date Fertigstellungsdatum
finished goods Fertigerzeugnis
finished goods inventory Fertigwarenbestand
finished product Fertigware
finite element method Finite-Elemente-Methode
finite number endliche Anzahl
fire insurance Brandversicherung
fire prevention Brandverhütung
fire warning device Brandmelder
first normal form erste Normalform
fit in (to) einfügen
fitness Eignung
fixed assets Anlagevermögen
fixed assets accounting Anlagenbuchhaltung
fixed costs fixe Kosten
fixed data fixe Daten
fixed day changeover Stichtagsumstellung
fixed disk drive Festplattenspeicher
fixed document reader stationärer Belegleser
fixed length record Satz fester Länge
fixed picture storage Festbildspeicher
fixed point presentation Festkommadarstellung, Festpunktdarstellung

fixed program computer festprogrammierter Computer
fixed programming Festprogrammierung
fixed sitting statisches Sitzen
flag Kennzeichen
flag bit Kennzeichenbit
flat display flache Anzeige
flexibility Beweglichkeit, Flexibilität
flexible flexibel
flexible automation flexible Automation
flexible disk flexible Magnetplatte
flexible disk desk Diskettenlaufwerk
flexible manufacturing cell flexible Fertigungszelle
flexible manufacturing system flexibles Fertigungssystem
flexible strategy flexible Strategie
flexible working hours Gleitzeit
flexitime Gleitzeit
flicker (to) flackern, flimmern
floating decimal Gleitpunkt
floating point Gleitpunkt
floating point presentation Gleitkommadarstellung
floppy disk Diskette, flexible Magnetplatte
flow Ablauf
flow control Ablaufsteuerung
flow diagram Flußdiagramm
flow interrupt Ablaufunterbrechung
flow language Fließsprache
flow line Ablauflinie
flow of control Kontrollfluß, Steuerfluß
flowchart Ablaufdiagramm, Flußdiagramm
flowchart symbol Flußplansymbol
Floyd's method Floyd's Methode
flush (to) unterbrechen durch Operatoreingriff
flying print fliegender Druck
FMS = Flexible Manufacturing System
FO = Fiber Optic
font Schriftart
font generator Schriftgenerator
footer Fußzeile
forced ending erzwungenes Ende
forecast error Vorhersagefehler
forecasting Prognose, Vorhersage
forecasting computation Prognoserechnung
forecasting method Prognose, Prognosemethode
forecasting of need Bedarfsvorhersage
foreground Vordergrund
foreground job Vordergrundauftrag
foreground program Vordergrundprogramm

141

foreign key Fremdschlüssel
form design Formularentwurf
form Formular
form control Formularsteuerung
form feed Formularvorschub
form generator Formulargenerator
form letter Serienbrief
form reader Formularleser
form set Formularsatz
formal job situation formale Arbeitssituation
formal language formale Sprache
formal method formale Methode
formal notation formale Notation
formal organization formale Organisation
formal participation formale Partizipation
formal requirement formale Anforderung
formal specification formale Spezifikation
formal specification method formale Spezifikationsmethode
formalization Formalisierung
formalize (to) formalisieren
formalized problem Formalproblem
format Format
format error Formatfehler
formatted data formatierte Daten
formatting Formatieren
formatting program Formatierer
FORTRAN = FORmula TRANslator
forward chaining Vorwärtsverkettung
forward controlled inferencing vorwärtsgesteuertes Schlußfolgern
forward documentation Vorwärtsdokumentation
fourth generation language Sprache der vierten Generation
fragmentation Fragmentierung, Zerstückelung
FRAM = Ferroelectronic Random Access Memory
frame Rahmen
framework Rahmenkonzept
fraud Betrug
free formed character offener Schrifttyp
free stock balance verfügbarer Bestand
freehand shape Freihandzeichen
frequency Frequenz, Häufigkeit
frequency analysis Häufigkeitsanalyse
frequency distribution Häufigkeitsverteilung
frequency division multiplexing Frequenzmultiplexing

FROM = Factory Read Only Memory
FROM = Fusible Read Only Memory
front end processor Kommunikationsrechner, Vorfeldrechner, Vorrechner, Vorschaltrechner
FSK = Frequency Shift Keying
FSS = Full Software Service
FTAM = File Transfer Access Management
full duplex vollduplex
full file search Durchsuchen der gesamten Datei
full screen Gesamtbildschirm
full screen editor Gesamtbildschirm-Editor
full text data base Volltext-Datenbank
fully formed character geschlossener Schrifttyp
fully optional frei wählbar
fully qualified name voll gekennzeichneter Name
function Funktion
function assurance Funktionssicherung
function/event matrix Funktion/Ereignis-Matrix
function key Funktionstaste
function oriented system funktionsorientiertes System
function point Funktionspunkt
function point model Function-Point-Verfahren
function sharing Funktionsverbund
function test Funktionstest
functionability Funktionsbereitschaft
functional analysis Funktionsanalyse
functional cohesion funktionaler Zusammenhang
functional dependency funktionale Abhängigkeit
functional design funktioneller Entwurf
functional diagram Funktionsdiagramm
functional programming funktionale Programmierung
functional requirement Funktionsanforderung
functional testing funktionsbezogenes Testen
functional unit Funktionseinheit
functionality Funktionalität
functioning Arbeitsweise, Funktionsweise
future analysis Zukunftsanalyse
future research Zukunftsforschung
future technology Zukunftstechnologie

G

G = Giga
game theory Spieltheorie
gamma change Gamma-Veränderung
GAN = Global Area Network
Gantt chart Gantt-Diagramm
gap Lücke
gap analysis Lückenanalyse
gate Gatter
gateway Anpassungsschaltung, Netzkonverter
GB = Gigabyte
Gbit = Gigabit
GCS = Generally Accepted Principles of Computer Security
GDSS = Group Decision Support System
general account Sachkonto
general accounting Sachkontenbuchführung
general conditions of contract allgemeine Vertragsbedingungen
general design Grobprojektierung
general diagram Übersichtsdiagramm
General Economic Informatics Allgemeine Wirtschaftsinformatik
general goal Rahmenziel
general guidelines for EDP contracts allgemeine EDV-Vergaberichtlinien
general ledger Finanzbuchhaltung, Sachkontenbuchführung
general purpose computer Universalcomputer
general purpose operating system allgemeines Betriebssystem
general reference to standards allgemeine Verweisung auf Normen
generality Allgemeingültigkeit
generalization Generalisierung, Verallgemeinerung
generalize (to) generalisieren
generally accepted accounting guidelines Grundsätze ordnungsmäßiger Buchführung
generally accepted data processing guidelines Grundsätze ordnungsmäßiger Datenverarbeitung
generally accepted data protection guidelines Grundsätze ordnungsmäßigen Datenschutzes
generally accepted storage accounting guidelines Grundsätze ordnungsmäßiger Speicherbuchführung
generation Generation
generation principle Generationsprinzip
generator Generator
geometric modelling system geometrisches Modelliersystem
German Research Network Deutsches Forschungsnetz
gestalt psychology Gestaltpsychologie
GIGO = Garbage In - Garbage Out
giving the order Auftragserteilung
GKS = Graphical Kernel System
global umfassend
global design umfassender Entwurf
global job evaluation summarische Arbeitsplatzbewertung
goal Sachziel, Ziel
goal achievement Zielerreichung
goal conflict Zielkonflikt
goal criterion Zielkriterium
goal driven backward chaining zielgetriebene Rückwärtsverkettung
goal gap Ziellücke
goal identification Zielfindung
goal oriented observation zielgerichtete Beobachtung
goal production Zielertrag
goal program Zielprogramm
goal relationship Zielbeziehung
goal setting Zielsetzung
goal setting analysis Zielsetzungsanalyse
goal setting planning Zielplanung
goal standard Zielmaßstab
goal system Zielsystem
goods inwards inspection Wareneingangsprüfung
goods received Wareneingang
Gozinto graph Gozinto-Graph
GPIB = General Purpose Interface Bus
GPL = Graphic Programming Language
GPSS = General Purpose Systems Simulator
GRAF = Graphic Addition to FORTRAN
grammar Grammatik
grandfather-father-son principle Großvater-Vater-Sohn-Prinzip
grapevine informelles Berichtssystem
graph Graph
graph theory Graphentheorie
graphical data processing graphische Datenverarbeitung
graphical description graphische Beschreibung
graphical kernel system graphisches Kernsystem
graphical model graphisches Modell
graphical presentation graphische Darstellung
graphical processor graphischer Prozessor

graphical programming language
graphische Programmiersprache
graphical representation graphische Darstellung
graphical tablet graphisches Tablett, Graphiktablett
graphics Graphik
graphics printer Graphikdrucker
grid Raster
gross design Grobentwurf
gross income Umsatz
gross pay Bruttolohn
ground wire Massenkabel
group Gruppe
group assignment Gruppenzuordnung
group change Gruppenwechsel
group computing center Gemeinschafts-Rechenzentrum
group decision support system Entscheidungsunterstützungssystem für Gruppen, Gruppen-Entscheidungsunterstützungsystem
group dynamics Gruppendynamik
group interview Gruppeninterview
group technology Gruppentechnologie
grouping Verbund
growth Wachstum
growth rate Wachstumsrate, Zuwachsrate
guideline Grundsatz, Richtlinie
guillotine Schneideeinrichtung

H

hacker Hacker
half duplex halbduplex
half duplex mode Halbduplexbetrieb
half tone Halbton
hand held computer Handcomputer
hand held scanner Lesepistole
hand rest Handauflage
handbook Handbuch
handiness Handhabbarkeit
handle (to) bearbeiten
handling Handhabung
handshaking Quittungsbetrieb
handsheld tragbarer PC
hard copy Computerausgabe auf Papier
hard copy of screen Kopie des Bildschirminhalts
hard core Perfektionskern
hard disk Platte
hard wired fest verdrahtet
hardest first strategy Hardest-first-Strategie
hardware Geräteausstattung
hardware compatibility Hardware-Kompatibilität, Hardware-Verträglichkeit
hardware configuration Hardware-Konfiguration
hardware environment Hardware-Umgebung
hardware ergonomics Hardware-Ergonomie
hardware interface Hardware-Schnittstelle
hardware malfunction Maschinenfehler
hardware monitoring Hardware-Überwachung
hardware preparation gerätetechnische Vorbereitung
hardware protection Hardware-Schutz
hardware selection Anlagenauswahl
harmonization Harmonisierung
hash function Speicherfunktion
hash total Abstimmsumme, Prüfsumme
hashing Zugriffsfunktion
HCI = Human Computer Interaction
HDLC = High Level Data Link Control
HDR = Head Record
head crash Headcrash, Landen
header Kennsatz, Kopfzeile
header label Anfangskennsatz
header record Leitsatz
helm Führung
help function Hilfefunktion
help information Hilfeinformation
help system Hilfesystem

heterogeneous modelling heterogene Modellierung
heuristic algorithm heuristischer Algorithmus
heuristic forecasting heuristische Prognose
heuristic programming heuristische Programmierung
heuristic search heuristisches Suchen
heuristics Heuristik
hexadecimal hexadezimal
HFS = Hierarchical File System
hidden observation verdeckte Beobachtung
hierarchical data model hierarchisches Datenmodell
hierarchical decomposition hierarchische Zerlegung
hierarchical file system hierarchisches Dateisystem
hierarchical level of department Abteilungsebene
hierarchical level of position Arbeitsplatzebene
hierarchical network hierarchisches Netz
hierarchical structure hierarchische Struktur
hierarchical structuring hierarchische Strukturierung
hierarchically structured check list hierarchisch strukturierte Prüfliste
hierarchy Hierarchie, Rangordnung
hierarchy diagram Hierarchiediagramm
hierarchy of keys Schlüsselhierarchie
high level language Hochsprache
high level programming language höhere Programmiersprache
high performance computer Hochleistungscomputer
high speed computer Hochgeschwindigkeitscomputer
high speed memory Schnellspeicher
high speed printer Schnelldrucker
HIPO = Hierarchy plus Input, Process and Output
histogram Histogramm
history map historische Mappe
HLL = High Level Language
holism Ganzheitslehre, Holismus
holistic ganzheitlich
holistic design ganzheitliches Gestalten
holistic thinking ganzheitliches Denken
hologram Ganzheitsbild, Hologramm
holographic memory holografischer Speicher
holography Holografie
home banking Homebanking

home computer

home computer Heimcomputer
home position Grundstellung
home worker Heimarbeiter
homomorphism Homomorphismus
homonym Homonym
host Host, Arbeitsrechner, Verarbeitungsrechner
host computer zentraler Arbeitsrechner, Gastrechner, Wirtsrechner
host language Gastsprache, Wirtssprache
host program Wirtsprogramm
hot backup computing center heißes Rechenzentrum
hub Netzknoten
human Mensch

human asset Humanvermögen
human engineering Arbeitsplatzgestaltung
human resource management Menschenführung, Personalführung
hx = halbduplex
hybrid computer Hybridrechner
hybrid dialog control hybride Dialogführung
hybrid modelling hybride Modellierung
hyper text Hypertext
hypermedia system Hypermedia-System
hyphenation Silbentrennung
hypothesis Hypothese

I

IBC = Integrated Broadcast Communication
IC = Information Center
IC = Integrated Circuit
ICAI = Intelligent Computer Assisted Instructions
ICAM = Integrated Computer Aided Manufacturing
ICASE = Integrated CASE
iceberg effect Eisbergeffekt
iconograph Bildsymbol, Ikonogramm
iconological data ikonische Daten
ICP = Intelligent Copier/Printer
ID = Identification
idea generating Ideenfindung
ideation Ideenbildung
ident number Identnummer
identification card Identifikationskarte, Identkarte
identification check Identifikationsprüfung
identification experiment Erkennungsexperiment, Identifikationsexperiment
identification key Identifikationsschlüssel
identification number Identifizierungsnummer
identification of risk Risikoerkennung
identification of speaker Sprecheridentifikation
identification of synonyms Synonymerkennung
identifier Bezeichner
identify (to) bezeichnen, identifizieren
identity card Ausweis
identity verification Identitätsüberprüfung
idle time Leerzeit
IDM = Information Display Matrix
IDMS = Integrated Database Management System
IDN = Integrated Digital Network
IE = Industrial Engineering
IE = Information Engineering
IEC = International Electronical Commission
IEEE = Institute of Electrical and Electronics Engineers
IFIP = International Federation for Information Processing
IGES = Initial Graphics Exchange Standard
ill-structured problem schlecht strukturiertes Problem
illuminance Beleuchtungsstärke

IM = Information Management
image Bild
image grabber Bildbearbeiter
image mode Abbildungsmodus
image processing Abbildungsverarbeitung, Bildverarbeitung
image resolution Bildauflösung
image set Bildmenge
image storage Abbildungsspeicher
imaging Abbilden
IMAIL System = Intelligent Mail System
IMIS = Integrated Management Information System
immediate access Sofortzugriff
immediate cancel sofortiger Abbruch
immediate data entry Daten-Direkteingabe
IMP = Interface Message Processor
impact Auswirkung, Einfluß
impact analysis Auswirkungsanalyse, Wirkungsanalyse
impact printer Anschlagdrucker, mechanischer Drucker
imperative programming imperative Programmierung
impersonal account Sachkonto
implement (to) implementieren, einführen
implementation Implementierung, Einführung
implementation costs Implementierungskosten, Einführungskosten
implementation language Implementierungssprache
implementation method Implementierungsmethode
implementation of prototype Musterimplementierung
implementation phase Realisierungsphase
implementation scheduling Implementierungsplanung, Einführungsplanung
implementation technique Implementierungstechnik
implementation time Implementierungszeit, Einführungszeit
implosion Verwendungsnachweis
improve (to) verbessern
inability Unfähigkeit
inadequate unangemessen
incentive Leistungsanreiz
incoming mail Posteingang
incompatibility Unvereinbarkeit
incompatible unvereinbar
incomplete unvollständig

incomplete prototype unvollständiger Prototyp
incompleteness Unvollständigkeit
inconsistency Inkonsistenz, Widersprüchlichkeit
inconsistent widersprüchlich
increase in costs Kostenerhöhung
increase in performance Leistungsteigerung
increase in productivity Produktivitätssteigerung
increase in revenue Erlössteigerung
increment Inkrement, Zuwachs
incremental compiler inkrementeller Kompilierer
incumbent Stelleninhaber
independent unabhängig
independent variable unabhängige Variable, variable Stellgröße
indeterminism Indeterminismus
index Index, Sachregister, Verzeichnis
index card Karteikarte
index figure Indexzahl
index table Indextabelle
indexed file organization indizierte Dateiorganisation
indexed sequential access method indexsequentielle Zugriffsmethode
indexed sequential file organization indexsequentielle Dateiorganisation
indexing Indexieren
indicator Indikator
indifference Indifferenz
indifferent objective relation indifferente Zielbeziehung
indirect costs nicht direkt zurechenbare Kosten
indirect knowledge representation indirekte Wissensdarstellung
indirect lightning indirekter Blitzeinschlag
indirect participation indirekte Partizipation
indirect positioning indirektes Positionieren
individual Individuum
individual goal Individualziel
individual interview Einzelinterview
individual rating individuelles Rating
individual user einzelner Benutzer
individual workplace Einzelarbeitsplatz
induction Induktion
induction system Induktionssystem
inductive inferencing induktives Schlußfolgern
industrial law Arbeitsrecht
industrial police Werkschutz

industrial psychology Arbeitspsychologie, Organisationspsychologie
industrial roboter Industrieroboter
industrial sociology Arbeitssoziologie, Betriebssoziologie
industry Branche, Industrie
industry-specific standard software Branchensoftware
ineffective unwirksam
inefficiency Unwirtschaftlichkeit
inefficient unwirtschaftlich
infect (to) infizieren
inference Inferenz, Ableitung, Schlußfolgerung
inference (to) schlußfolgern
inference pattern Inferenzmuster, Schlußfolgerungsmuster
inference rule Inferenzregel, Schlußfolgerungsregel
inference system Inferenzsystem, Schlußfolgerungssystem
inflexibility Inflexibilität, Starrheit
influence quantity Einflußgröße
informal organization informale Organisation
informal participation informale Partizipation
informal specification informale Spezifikation
information Information
information advisor Informationsberater
information age Informationszeitalter
information and communications function Informations- und Kommunikationsfunktion
information and communications system Informations- und Kommunikationssystem
information and communications technology Informations- und Kommunikationstechnologie
information architecture Informationsarchitektur
information assessment Informationsbewertung
information assurance Informationssicherung
information base Informationsbank
information behavior Informationsverhalten
information broker Informationsvermittler
information brokering Informationsvermittlung
information category Informationskategorie
information center Benutzerservice-Zentrum, Informationszentrum

information chain Informationskette
information class Informationsklasse
information cluster Informationsblock
information costs Informationskosten
information demand
Informationsnachfrage
information display matrix
Informationstafel
information distortion
Informationsdeformation
information distribution
Informationsverteilung
information economics
Informationswirtschaft
information efficiency
Informationswirtschaftlichkeit
information engineering
Informationsmanagement-Technik
information exchange
Informationsaustausch
information exchange process
Informationsaustauschprozeß
information fee Auskunftsgebühr
information flow Informationsfluß
information flow diagram
Informationsflußdiagramm
information flow model
Informationsflußmodell
information for decision making
Entscheidungsinformation
information function Informationsfunktion
information function structuring
Stellenbildung Informationsfunktion
information gap Informationslücke
information gate Informationsschleuse
information hiding principle
Geheimnisprinzip, Prinzip des
Information Hiding
information infrastructure
Informationsinfrastruktur
information intensity
Informationsintensität
information law Informationsrecht
information logistics Informationslogistik
information manager
Informationsmanager
information modelling
Informationsmodellierung
information need Informationsbedürfnis
information oriented business
management informationsorientierte
Unternehmensführung
information overload
Informationsüberlastung
information process Informationsprozeß
information processing
Informationsverarbeitung

information processor
Informationsverarbeiter
information procurement
Informationsbeschaffung
information production
Informationsproduktion
information profit Informationserlös
information protection Informationsschutz
information provider
Informationsanbieter
information requirement
Informationsbedarf
information requirements analysis
Informationsbedarfsanalyse
information resource management
Informationsmanagement
information retailer Informationshändler
information retailing Informationshandel
information retrieval
Informationswiedergewinnung
information right Auskunftsrecht
Information Science
Informationswissenschaft
information security
Informationssicherheit
information self-determination
informationelle Selbstbestimmung
information service Informationsdienst
information shock Informationsschock
information strategy
Informationsstrategie
information strategy planning
Informationsstrategie-Planung
information system Informationssystem
information system analysis
Informationssystem-Analyse
information system architecture
Informationssystem-Architektur
information system design
Informationssystem-Entwurf
information system development
Informationssystem-Entwicklung
information system implementation
Informationssystem-Einführung
information system study
Informationssystem-Studie
information systems department
Abteilung
Datenverarbeitung/Organisation
information systems department
Abteilung Informations- und
Kommunikationssysteme
information technology
Informationstechnik,
Informationstechnologie

information technology assessment
informationstechnologische Wirkungsforschung
information theory Informationstheorie
information trace Informationsspur
information transfer Informationstransfer
information transmission Informationsübermittlung
information type Informationsart
information value Informationswert
information value analysis Informationswert-Analyse
infrared detector Infrarotdetektor
infrared radiation Infrarotstrahlung
infrared transmission Infrarotübertragung
infrastructure Infrastruktur
infrastructure planning Infrastruktur-Planung
inherent necessity Sachzwang
inherent reliability Entwurfszuverlässigkeit
inheritance Vererbung
inhouse BTx innerbetriebliches BTx
inhouse integration innerbetriebliche Integration
inhouse system innerbetriebliches System
initial study Vorstudie
initial value Anfangswert
initialize (to) einleiten, initialisieren
initiate (to) anlaufen
initiate time Anlaufzeit
ink jet plotter Tintenspritzplotter
ink jet printer Tintenstrahldrucker
inline comment Inline-Kommentar
inline documentation Inline-Dokumentation, projektbegleitende Dokumentation, Selbstdokumentation
innovation Innovation
innovation strategy Innovationsstrategie
innovation technique Innovationstechnik
inplant innerbetrieblich
input Eingabe
input (to) eingeben
input data Eingabedaten
input device Eingabegerät
input document Eingabebeleg
input error Eingabefehler
input error checking Prüfung auf Eingabefehler
input job queue Eingabewarteschlange
input manipulation Inputmanipulation
input medium Eingabemedium
input protection Eingabeschutz
input rate Eingabegeschwindigkeit
input technology Eingabetechnik
input unit Eingabeeinheit, Eingabewerk

input/output analysis Input/Output-Analyse
input/output control system Eingabe-/Ausgabesteuerungssystem
input/output diagram Eingabe/Ausgabe-Diagramm
input/output mapping Formulartechnik
input/output processor Eingabe-/Ausgabeprozessor
input/output protection Eingabe-/Ausgabeschutz
inscription position Beschriftungsstelle
insert Einschub
insert (to) einfügen
insertion Einfügung
inside out approach Inside-Out-Ansatz
instability Instabilität, Labilität
install (to) installieren, aufstellen
installation Installation, Aufstellung
installation instructions Installationsanleitung
instant camera for screen Bildschirmrecorder
instant changeover sofortige Umstellung
instruct (to) anleiten
instruction Anweisung, Befehl, Instruktion
instruction language Befehlssprache
instruction set Befehlssatz, Befehlsvorrat
instruction technique Anweisungs-Technik
instruction type Befehlstyp
instruction word Befehlswort
instrumentation technique Instrumentierungstechnik
insular solution Insellösung
insurance Versicherung
insurance against abuse Mißbrauch-Versicherung
insurance against computer abuse Computermißbrauch-Versicherung
insurance against damage of confidence Vertrauensschaden-Versicherung
insurance against data privacy violation Datenschutz-Versicherung
insurance against loss of data Datenträger-Versicherung
intangible nicht erfaßbar, nicht quantifizierbar
intangible benefits nicht erfaßbarer Nutzen, nicht quantifizierbarer Nutzen
intangible costs nicht erfaßbare Kosten, nicht quantifizierbare Kosten
integer ganze Zahl, ganzzahlige Darstellung
integrate (to) integrieren, zusammenschließen

Integrated Broadband Telecommunications Network Integriertes Breitband-Fernmeldenetz
integrated ciphering system integriertes Verschlüsselungssystem
integrated circuit integrierte Schaltung
Integrated Circuit Digital Network Dienstintegriertes Digitalnetz
integrated data processing integrierte Datenverarbeitung
integrated management information system integriertes Management-Informationssystem
Integrated Services Network Integriertes Dienstnetz
integrated system integriertes System
integration Integration, Zusammenschluss
integration ability Integrationsfähigkeit
integration mode Integrationsform
integration of activities Vorgangsintegration
integration of application Anwendungsintegration
integration of functions Funktionsintegration
integration of security measures Sicherungsintegration
integration of tasks Aufgabenintegration
integration principle Integrationsprinzip
integration test Integrationstest
integrity Integrität
integrity checked dialog control integritätsbestimmte Dialogführung
integrity constraint Integritätsbedingung
integrity verification Integritätsüberprüfung
intelligence Intelligenz
intelligent intelligent
intelligent copier intelligenter Kopierer
intelligent courseware intelligentes Lehrsystem
intelligent data terminal intelligente Datenstation
intelligent support system intelligentes Unterstützungssystem
Intelsat = International Telecommunications Satellite Organization
intention Absicht
interact (to) interagieren
interaction Interaktion, Wechselbeziehung
interaction language Interaktionssprache
interaction tool Interaktionswerkzeug
interactive interaktiv
interactive data collection Dialogdatenerfassung
interactive debugging tool interaktive Testhilfe
interactive diagram Interaktionsdiagramm
interactive job Dialogauftrag
interactive mode interaktiver Betrieb, Dialogbetrieb
interactive programming interaktive Programmierung
interactive programming language interaktive Programmiersprache
interactive system interaktives System
interactive videotex Bildschirmtext
interactive videotex law Bildschirmtextgesetz
interactive videotex treaty Bildschirmtext-Staatsvertrag
interblock gap Blockzwischenraum
intercept (to) abfangen
interchange standard Austauschformat
interdependence gegenseitige Abhängigkeit, Interdependenz
interface Nahtstelle, Schnittstelle
interface ergonomics Schnittstellenergonomie
interface hardware Verbindungsgeräte
interface message processor Knotenrechner
interface technology Schnittstellentechnik
interference Störung
interference factor Störgröße
interference suppression Funkentstörung
interior test Strukturtest
interleaving Verschränkung
intermediate language Zwischensprache
intermediate layer Zwischenschicht
intermediate storage Zwischenspeicher
intermediate transfer paper Zwischenträgerpapier
intermittent observation unterbrochene Beobachtung
internal auditing interne Revision
internal bridge interne Brücke
internal conflict Innenkonflikt
internal data interne Daten
internal memory interner Speicher
internal model internes Schema
internal operation interne Operation
internal price Verrechnungspreis
internal restart interner Wiederanlauf
internal schema internes Schema
internal storage interner Speicher
interoffice slip Laufzettel
interoperation time Übergangszeit
interorganizational collaboration zwischenbetriebliche Zusammenarbeit

interorganizational information system
betriebsübergreifendes
Informationssystem
interorganizational integration
zwischenbetriebliche Integration
interperse (to) dazwischenschreiben
interpretation Auswertung
interpreter Interpretierer
interrelation Wechselbeziehung,
Zusammenhang
interrogation Befragung, Rückfrage
interrupt Unterbrechung
interrupt (to) unterbrechen
interrupt of operation
Betriebsunterbrechung
interval timer Zeitgeber
interviewing method Interviewmethode
interviewing technique Interviewtechnik
interworking Dienstübergang
intransparency Intransparenz
intrusion Intrusion, Eindringen
intrusion protection Intrusionsschutz,
Objektschutz
intrusion signal facility
Intrusionsmeldeanlage
intrusion technology Intrusionstechnik
invalid ungültig
invalid address ungültige Adresse
invalid combination of characters
ungültige Zeichenkombination
inventory Bestand, Inventar, Inventur
inventory activity Lagerbewegung
inventory control Bestandsüberwachung
inventory data Bestandsdaten
inventory depletion Lagerabgang
inventory holding costs
Lagerhaltungskosten
inventory management Lagerhaltung
inventory record Artikelbestandssatz
inventory shrinkage Schwund
inventory turnover Lagerumschlag
inversed type Negativschrift
invert (to) invertieren, umkehren
inverted file invertierte Datei
inverted representation invertierte
Darstellung, Negativdarstellung
investigate (to) untersuchen
investigation Erhebung
investigation of current system
Istzustandserhebung
investment Investition
investment costs Investitionskosten
investment failure Fehlinvestition
invitation to tender Angebotseinholung

invoice Rechnung
invoice amount Rechnungsbetrag
invoicing Fakturierung,
Rechnungserstellung
involuted relationship rekursive
Beziehung
I/O device E/A-Gerät
IOCS = Input/Output Control System
ion printer Ionendrucker
IPL = Initial Program Load
IPO chart EVA-Diagramm
IPO = Input/Processing/Output
IPO-Diagramm =
Input/Processing/Output-Diagramm
**IPSE = Integrated Project Support
Environment**
**IRM = Information Resource
Management**
**IRM-Committee = Information Resource
Management Committee**
I/S department Informatikabteilung,
IKS-Abteilung
**I/S Management = Information Systems
Management**
I/S service Informatikdienst
**ISAM = Indexed Sequential Access
Method**
**ISDN = Integrated Services Digital
Network**
**ISDOS = Information System Design and
Optimization System**
ISN = Integrated Services Network
**ISO = International Organization for
Standardization**
ISO architecture model
ISO-Architekturmodell
ISO layer model ISO-Schichtenmodell
ISO reference model ISO-Referenzmodell
ISO-7-bit code ISO-7-Bit-Code
isomorphism Isomorphismus
ISP = Information Strategy Planning
**ISPBX = Integrated Services Private
Branch Exchange**
ISS = Information System Study
ISS = Intelligent Support System
italic Kursivschrift
iteration Iteration, Wiederholung
iteration loop Iterationsschleife,
Wiederholungsschleife
iterative refinement iterative
Verfeinerung
iterative test Wiederholungstest
**ITU = International Telecommunication
Union**

J

Jackson design methodology
Jackson-Methode
Jackson diagram Jackson-Diagramm
JAD = Joint Application Design
JCL = Job Control Language
JDS = Job Diagnostic Survey
JiT = Just-in-Time
job Auftrag
job accounting Auftragsabrechnung
job analysis Arbeitsanalyse
job around time Verweilzeit
job assignment Aufgabenzuweisung
job calculation Auftragsrechnung
job chain Auftragskette
job content Arbeitsinhalt, Aufgabeninhalt
job control Auftragssteuerung
job control language Auftragssprache, Auftragskontrollsprache, Kommandosprache
job description Arbeitsplatzbeschreibung, Stellenbeschreibung, Tätigkeitsbeschreibung
job design Arbeitsgestaltung
job designation Arbeitsplatzbezeichnung
job dissatisfaction Arbeitszufriedenheit
job enlargement Arbeitserweiterung, Arbeitsvergrößerung, Aufgabenerweiterung, horizontale Arbeitsstrukturierung
job enrichment Arbeitsbereicherung, Aufgabenbereicherung, vertikale Arbeitsstrukturierung
job evaluation Arbeitsbewertung
job grading Arbeitsbewertung
job holder Stelleninhaber
job identification Auftragskennzeichen
job information Arbeitsinformation

job management Auftragsverwaltung
job motivation Arbeitsmotivation
job name Auftragsname
job number Auftragsnummer
job order Arbeitsauftrag
job partitioning Arbeitsteilung
job plan Arbeitsplan
job preparation Arbeitsvorbereitung
job priority Auftragspriorität
job productivity Arbeitsproduktivität
job queue Auftragswarteschlange
job release Auftragsfreigabe
job requirement Arbeitsanforderung
job rotation Arbeitswechsel, Aufgabenwechsel, Tätigkeitswechsel
job satisfaction Arbeitszufriedenheit
job scheduling Auftragseinplanung
job scope Tätigkeitsspielraum
job selection Auftragsauswahl
job sequence Arbeitsfolge
job situation Arbeitssituation
job specification Arbeitsplatzbeschreibung
job step Auftragsschritt
job structuring Arbeitsstrukturierung
job technique Arbeitstechnik
joint fixed costs nicht aufteilbare Fixkosten
joint venture Arbeitsgemeinschaft
joy stick Steuerhebel, Steuerknüppel
JSD = **Jackson Structured Design**
JSP = **Jackson Structured Programming**
just-in-time production Just-in-Time-Produktion, zeitgerechte Produktion
justification Rechtfertigung
justified text Blocksatz
justify (to) zentrieren

K

K-interface K-Schnittstelle
KB = Kilobyte
Kbit = Kilobit
KBS = Knowledge-Based System
kernel Kern
key Schlüssel, Taste
key attack Schlüsselangriff
key attribute Schlüsselattribut
key ciphering key schlüsselchiffrierender Schlüssel
key factor Schlüsselfaktor
key factor analysis Schlüsselfaktoren-Analyse
key number Schlüsselzahl
key role Schlüsselrolle
key sequence Tastenfolge
key technology Schlüsseltechnologie
key term Schlüsselbegriff
key touch Tastenanschlag
key variable Schlüsselgröße
keyboard Tastatur
keyboard encoder Tastaturverschlüsseler
keyboard selection Tastaturauswahl
keyboard template Tastaturschablone
keyboard with function keys Funktionstastatur
keypad Tastatur
keystroke Tastendruck
keyword Schlagwort, Schlüsselwort
keyword technique Schlüsselwort-Technik
kill criterion Muß-Kriterium
Kimball tag Kimball-Etikette
kind of fault Fehlerart
kind of type Schriftart
KIP = Knowledge Information Processing
KIPS = Kilo Instructions Per Second
kit Ausrüstung
Kiviath graph Kiviath-Graph
KMS = Knowledge Management System
know how Erfahrungswissen
know how data base Wissensdatenbank
knowledge Wissen
knowledge acquisition Wissensakquisition, Wissenserwerb
knowledge base Wissensbasis
knowledge based design wissensbasierter Entwurf
knowledge based man-machine interface wissensbasierte Benutzerschnittstelle
knowledge based system wissensbasiertes System
knowledge coordinator Wissenskoordinator
knowledge data base Wissens-Datenbank
knowledge editor Wisenseditor
knowledge engineer Wissensingenieur
knowledge management system Wissensverwaltungssystem
knowledge processing Wissensverarbeitung
knowledge representation Wissensdarstellung
knowledge transfer Wissensübertragung
knowledge work wissensbasierte Arbeit
k.o. criterion K.-o.-Kriterium
KOPS = Kilo Operations Per Second
KR = Knowledge Representation
kryo computer Kryo-Computer
KSR = Keyboard Send Receive

L

label Etikett, Kennsatz, Marke
label printer Etikettendrucker
label printing Etikettendruck
label reader Etikettenleser
labor agreement Betriebsvereinbarung
labor constitution Betriebsverfassung
Labor Constitution Act Betriebsverfassungsgesetz
labor costs Arbeitskosten
labor council Betriebsrat
labor law Arbeitsrecht, Arbeitsverfassungsgesetz
labor science Arbeitswissenschaft
labor union Gewerkschaft
laboratory experiment Laborexperiment
LAN = Local Area Network
landscape printing Ausdruck im Querformat
language Sprache
language compatibility Sprachen-Kompatibilität
language subset Sprachteil
language translation Sprachübersetzung
laptop tragbarer PC
Laser = Light Amplification of Stimulated Emission of Radiation
laser beam Laserstrahl
laser card Laserkarte
laser disk Laserplatte
laser printer Laserdrucker
laser technology Lasertechnik
last issue letztes Abgangsdatum
latency Latenzzeit
latest start date spätester Beginntermin
launching costs Anlaufkosten
law Recht
law informatics Rechtsinformatik
Law on Radio Amateur Operations Gesetz über den Amateurfunk
layer Schicht
layer model user interface Schichtenmodell Benutzerschnittstelle
LCD = Liquid Crystal Display
LCD keyboard LCD-Tastatur
LCS = Liquid Crystal Shutter
LCS printer LCS-Drucker
lead time Auftragsdurchlaufzeit
leader Führer
leadership Führerschaft
leadership attidude Führungsverhalten
leadership style Führungsstil
leading Durchschuß
leading graphics führende Zeichen
leading sign Vorzeichen
leading zeros führende Nullen

learnability Erlernbarkeit, Lernbarkeit
learning Lernen
learning from examples induktives Schlußfolgern
lease (to) mieten
lease certificate Mietschein
lease contract Mietvertrag
leased equipment Mietgerät
leased line festgeschaltete Leitung, gemietete Leitung
leasing Anlagenmiete
leaving check Abgangskontrolle
LED = Light Emitting Diode
left aligned linksbündig
left justified linksbündig
legal integration juristische Integration
legal protection Rechtsschutz
legal protection insurance Rechtsschutz-Versicherung
legal requirement rechtliche Anforderung
legibility Lesbarkeit
LEMP = Lightning Explosion Magnetic Power
lens Leuchtknopf, Linse
letter Brief, Buchstabe
letter opening machine Brieföffnungsmaschine
letter quality Briefqualität
letter quality printer Korrespondenzdrucker, Schönschreibdrucker
level Ebene
level concept Ebenen-Konzept
level of abstraction Abstraktionsebene
level of control Kontrollebene
lexical order lexikographische Ordnung
LF = Line Feed
liability Haftpflicht, Verbindlichkeit
liability insurance Haftpflicht-Versicherung
library Bibliothek
library management program Bibliotheksverwaltungsprogramm
licence Lizenz
licence program Lizenzprogramm
life cycle Lebenszyklus
life cycle analysis Lebenszyklus-Analyse
life cycle concept Phasenkonzept
life cycle management Lebenszyklus-Management
life cycle model Lebenszyklus-Modell, Phasenmodell
life cycle schema Phasenschema
life expectancy voraussichtliche Lebensdauer
life of contract Vertragsdauer
LIFO = Last In First Out

light beam Lichtstrahl
light emitting diode Leuchtdiode, Licht emittierende Diode
light pen Lichtstift, Leuchtstift
light pen detect Lichtstifteingabe
light sensitivity Lichtempfindlichkeit
light stylus Lichtgriffel
light wave Lichtwelle
light wave cable Glasfaserkabel
lightning arrester Blitzschutzvorrichtung
lightning damage Blitzschaden
lightning explosion magnetic power Überspannung durch Blitzentladung
likelihood Wahrscheinlichkeit
limit Grenzwert
limitational criterion Limitierungskriterium
line Leitung
line charge Leitungsgebühr
line chart Liniendiagramm
line ciphering Leitungsverschlüsselung
line conditioner magnetischer Konstanthalter
line display Zeilendisplay
line efficiency Leitungsausnutzung
line feed Zeilenvorschub
line management Linienmanagement
line model Drahtmodell, Linienmodell
line of business Geschäftszweig
line of code Programmzeile
line printer Zeilendrucker
line production Fließbandfertigung
line space Zeilenabstand
line switching Leitungsvermittlung
line transmission error Übertragungsfehler
linear optimization lineare Optimierung
linguistic data processing linguistische Datenverarbeitung
linguistics Linguistik
link Verbindung, Verbindungsglied
link (to) verbinden
link line Verbindungsleitung
link procedure Übermittlungsvorschrift
link protocol Übermittlungsvorschrift
link time Verbindungszeit
linkage Verkettung
linkage editor Binder
linkage loader Bindelader
linkage program Brückenprogramm
linked file organization gekettete Dateiorganisation
linked network Verbundnetz
LIPS = Logical Inferences Per Second
liquid crystal display Flüssigkeitskristall-Anzeige

liquidity early warning Liquiditätsfrühwarnung
LISP = List Processing Language
LISP machine LISP-Maschine
list Liste
list of components Komponentenliste
list of experts Sachverständigenliste
list of systems strengths Stärkenkatalog
list of systems strengths/weaknesses Stärken-/Schwächen-Katalog
list of systems weaknesses Schwächenkatalog
list of work elements Tätigkeitenkatalog
list operation Listenoperation
list processing Listenverarbeitung
listen in (to) abhören
listening device Abhörvorrichtung
listening security Abhörsicherheit
listening technique Abhörmethode
literacy Bildung, Fähigkeit, Literacy
LMS = Logico Mathematical Structur
load Belastung
load (to) laden
load carrying ability Belastbarkeit
load dependent job release belastungsorientierte Auftragsfreigabe
load sharing Lastverbund
load chart Belastungsdiagramm
loadable program ladefähiges Programm
loader Lader, Ladeprogramm
loading operating system Betriebssystem laden
LoB = Line of Business
LoC = Line of Code
local lokal, örtlich
local area lokaler Bereich
local area network lokales Netz
local bridge lokale Brücke
local connection Ortsverbindung
local mode Lokalbetrieb, Ortsbetrieb
local network örtliches Netz, Ortsnetz
local output lokale Ausgabe
local printer attachement Direktanschluß für Drucker
locality Lokalität
localization Lokalisierung
location Standort
lock (to) sperren
lock word Kennwort
log Logbuch, Protokolldatei
log file Log-Datei, Protokolldatei
log-off Abmeldung
log-off (to) abmelden
log-on Anmeldung
log-on (to) anmelden
log-on mode Anmeldemodus
log-out (to) abmelden

logging Aufzeichnen,
Ereignisaufzeichnung
logging file Protokolldatei
logic Logik
logic device Schaltwerklogik
logic diagram Logikdiagramm
logical logisch
logical bomb logische Bombe
logical chain logische Kette
logical data definition language logische
Datendefinitionssprache
logical description logische Beschreibung
logical design logischer Entwurf
logical data flow diagram logisches
Datenflußdiagramm
logical data independence logische
Datenunabhängigkeit
logical data model logisches Datenmodell
logical data security measure logische
Datensicherungsmaßnahme
logical data structure logische
Datenstruktur
logical data structuring logische
Datenstrukturierung
logical data view logische Datensicht
logical deletion logisches Löschen
logical information systems design
logischer Informationssystem-Entwurf
logical knowledge representation logische
Wissensdarstellung
logical level logische Ebene
logical memory logischer Speicher
logical model logisches Modell
logical programming logische
Programmierung
logical record logischer Satz
logical test Schreibtischtest
logical testing logisches Testen

logical validity logische Validität
logistics Logistik
logistics chain Logistikkette
logistics information system
Logistik-Informationssystem
logistics philosophy Logistikdenken
logistics system Logistiksystem
logo Firmenzeichen
logogram Logogramm, Wortzeichen
long distance network Fernnetz
long range planning langfristige
Planung
long time memory Langzeitgedächtnis
loop Ringleitung, Schleife
loop flowchart zyklisches
Ablaufdiagramm
loop topology Sternring-Topologie
looping error Endlosfehler
loss Verlust
loss of information Informationsverlust
loss of performance Leistungsverlust
loss rate Verlustrate
lot quantity Losgröße
LOTOS = Language Of Temporal
Ordering Specification
low level graphics Halbgraphik
low level programming language niedere
Programmiersprache
lower case character Kleinbuchstabe
lower case printing Drucken von
Kleinbuchstaben
LPC = Linear Predictive Coding
LPS = Lines Per Second
LQ = Letter Quality
LSI = Large Scale Integration
luminescense Leuchtdichte
luminosity Leuchtstärke

M

machine Maschine
machine code Maschinencode
machine hour rate Maschinenstundensatz
machine instruction Maschinenbefehl
machine language Maschinensprache
machine language program Maschinenprogramm
machine learning maschinelles Lernen
machine oriented maschinenorientiert
machine readable maschinenlesbar
machine serial number Maschinennummer
machine tool Werkzeugmaschine
machine tool control Werkzeugmaschinen-Steuerung
machine-machine-communications Maschine-Maschine-Kommunikation
macro Makro
macro command Makrokommando
macro instruction Makrobefehl
macro protection Grobschutz
magnetic bubble memory Magnetblasenspeicher
magnetic card Magnetkarte
magnetic card memory Magnetkartenspeicher
magnetic disk Magnetplatte
magnetic disk management Magnetplattenverwaltung
magnetic disk memory Magnetplattenspeicher
magnetic disk pack Magnetplattenstapel
magnetic ink Magnettinte
magnetic layer memory Magnetschichtspeicher
magnetic ledger card feature Magnetkonto
magnetic printer Magnetdrucker
magnetic recording magnetische Aufzeichnung
magnetic recording technique magnetisches Aufzeichnungsverfahren
magnetic stripe card Magnetstreifenkarte
magnetic tape Magnetband
magnetic tape clearing Magnetband-Clearing-Verfahren
magnetic tape deck Magnetbandlaufwerk
magnetic tape management Magnetbandverwaltung
magnetic tape security Magnetbandsicherung
magnetic tape storage Magnetbandspeicher
magnetic writing reader Magnetschriftleser

magnify (to) vergrößern
magnitude Mächtigkeit
mail Postsendung
mail survey Erhebung durch Briefpost
mailbox Mailbox, Briefkasten
mailer Adressiermaschine
main department Hauptabteilung
main function Hauptfunktion
main goal Hauptziel
main memory Hauptspeicher
main program Hauptprogramm
main routine Hauptprogramm
main station for speed call Hauptanschluß für Direktruf
main storage Hauptspeicher
mainframe Großrechner, Universalcomputer
maintain (to) warten
maintainability Wartbarkeit
maintenance Instandhaltung, Pflege, Wartung
maintenance agreement Wartungsvereinbarung
maintenance by patching Wartung durch Flickarbeit
maintenance certificate Pflegeschein, Wartungsschein
maintenance charges Wartungsgebühren
maintenance console Wartungskonsole
maintenance contract Wartungsvertrag
maintenance costs Wartungskosten
maintenance documentation Wartungsdokumentation
maintenance goal Erhaltungsziel
maintenance period Wartungszeit
maintenance processor Wartungsprozessor
maintenance rate Wartungszeitraum
maintenance request Wartungsanforderung
maintenance schedule Wartungsplan
maintenance test Wartungstest
major requirement Hauptanforderung
make operational (to) operationalisieren
make or buy Eigenerstellung oder Fremdbezug
malfunction Fehlfunktion, Fehlverhalten
MAN = Metropolitan Area Network
man Mensch
man computer interaction Mensch-Computer-Interaktion
man computer interface Mensch-Computer-Schnittstelle
man year Mannjahr
man year's effort Aufwand an Mannjahren

manageability Beherrschbarkeit, Hantierbarkeit
management Führung, Management
management advisor Betriebsberater
management consultant Betriebsberater, Organisationsberater, Unternehmensberater
management consulting Unternehmensberatung
management control Organisationskontrolle
management graphics Managementgraphik
management information system Führungsinformationssystem, Management-Informationssystem
management potential analysis Management-Potential-Analyse
management principle Managementprinzip
management science Managementlehre
management support system Management-Unterstützungssystem
management task Führungsaufgabe
management technique Managementtechnik
manager Führungskraft
managerial function Führungsfunktion
managerial level Führungsebene
managerial technique Führungsmethode
mandant system Mandantensystem
mandatory verpflichtend, zwingend
mandatory criterion Muß-Kriterium
mandatory disconnection zwingender Verbindungsabbruch
mandatory feature K.-o.-Kriterium
mandatory field Mußfeld, Pflichtfeld
mandatory requirement Muß-Anforderung
man-machine communications Mensch-Maschine-Kommunikation
man-machine interface Benutzerschnittstelle, Mensch-Maschine-Schnittstelle
manner of usage Nutzungsform
manual Handbuch
manual procedure manuelles Verfahren
manufacturer Hersteller
manufacturing Fertigung
manufacturing automation Fertigungsautomatisierung
manufacturing automation protocol Schnittstelle für Fabrikautomatisierung
manufacturing cell Fertigungszelle
manufacturing center Bearbeitungszentrum
manufacturing control Fertigungssteuerung

manufacturing information and control system Fertigungsinformations- und -steuerungssystem
many-to-many relationship m:n-Beziehung
many-to-one relationship m:1-Beziehung
MAP = Manufacturing Automation Protocol
margin Seitenrand Druckpapier
marginal condition Randbedingung
marginal costs Grenzkosten
mark scanning Zeichenabfühlung
mark sensing Zeichenabfühlung
mark sensing document Markierungsbeleg
mark sensing reader Markierungsleser
mark sheet Markierungsbeleg
marker Markierer
market research Marktforschung
market share Marktanteil
marketing information system Marketing-Informationssystem
mask Maske
mask (to) maskieren
mask design Maskengestaltung
mask generator Maskengenerator
mask identification Maskenkennzeichnung
mask programming Maskenprogrammierung
mask technique Maskentechnik
mass communications Massenkommunikation
mass data Massendaten
mass memory Massenspeicher
mass of numbers Zahlenmeer
mass store Massenspeicher
master control program Hauptsteuerprogramm
master data Stammdaten
master file Stammdatei
master plan Rahmenplan
master processor Hauptprozessor
master station Hauptanschluß
master system Herrensystem, übergeordnetes System
master tape Hauptband
match (to) abgleichen
match code Abgleichcode, Matchcode
material availability date Verfügbarkeitstermin des Materials
material inventory planning Nettobedarfsermittlung
material requirements planning Materialbedarfsplanung
materials defect liability Sachmängelhaftung

materials delivering Materialausgabe
materials distribution Materialausgabe
materials flow Material- und Warenfluß, Warenfluß
materials management Materialbewirtschaftung
mathematical model mathematisches Modell
matrix Matrix, Raster
matrix analysis Matrixanalyse
matrix calculus Matrizenkalkül
matrix notation Matrizenschreibweise
matrix of variances Varianzmatrix
matrix organization Matrixorganisation
matrix printer Matrixdrucker
matrix printing device Matrixdruckwerk
matrix project organization Matrix-Projektorganisation
matrix representation Matrizendarstellung
maximum stock Höchstbestand
MBA = Master of Business Administration
MBI = Master of Business Information
Mbit = Megabit
MBMS = Model Base Management System
MbO = Management by Objectives
MbS = Management by Strategies
Mbyte = Megabyte
MCBF = Mean Computation Before Failure
MCD = Master Clerical Data
MCI = Man Computer Interaction
MCP = Master Control Program
mean access time mittlere Zugriffszeit
mean error mittlerer Fehler
mean value Mittelwert
means Hilfsmittel
meantime between failures mittlere Zeitspanne zwischen Ausfällen
meantime to repair mittlere Reparaturzeit
measurable meßbar
measurable benefits meßbarer Nutzen
measurable costs meßbare Kosten
measure Maßnahme
measure (to) messen
measure system Maßsystem
measurement Messung
measuring device Meßgerät
measuring entitiy Meßobjekt
measuring error Meßfehler
measuring figure Meßgröße
measuring goal Meßziel
measuring platform Meßstation
measuring point Meßort, Meßpunkt

measuring procedure Meßvorschrift
measuring program Meßprogramm
measuring result Meßergebnis
measuring scale Meßskala
measuring technique Meßmethode
measuring theory Meßtheorie
measuring tool Meßinstrument
measuring value Meßwert
mechanical mouse mechanische Maus
mechanistic model mechanistisches Modell
media clash analysis Medienbruch-Analyse
medium Medium, Mittel
member Mitglied, Zugehöriger
membership Zugehörigkeit
memory Gedächtnis, Speicher
memory access Speicherzugriff
memory card Speicherkarte
memory configuration Speicherauslegung
memory management Hauptspeicherverwaltung, Speicherverwaltung
memory protection Speicherschutz
memory screen Speicherbildschirm
memory typewriter Speicherschreibmaschine
mental mental, geistig
mental model mentales Modell
mental models research Mentale-Modelle-Forschung
mental objective mentales Ziel
menu Menü
menu based menügesteuert
menu control Menüsteuerung
menu controlled menügesteuert
menu driven menügesteuert
menu mask Menümaske
menu selection Menüauswahl
menu selection technique Menü-Selektionstechnik
menu type Menütyp
mesh Masche
mesh network Maschennetz
mesh topology Maschentopologie
message Botschaft, Meldung, Nachricht
message channel Nachrichtenkanal
message flow Nachrichtenfluß
message overload Nachrichtenüberlastung
message rating Mitteilungsrating
message source Nachrichtenquelle
message switching Nachrichtenvermittlung, Meldevermittlung
message transmission Nachrichtenübertragung

meta meta
meta communications Metakommunikation
meta data Metadaten
meta knowledge Metawissen
meta language Metasprache
meta software Metasoftware
metaphor Methapher
method Methode
method of parametric estimate equation Methode der parametrischen Schätzgleichungen
method oriented programming methoden-orientiertes Programmieren
method system Methodensystem
methodism methodisches Verfahren
methodology Methodik
methodology of organizing Organisationsmethodik
methodology of planning Planungsmethodik
methods administrator Methodenadministrator
methods analysis Methodenanalyse
methods base Methodenbank, Methodenbasis
methods base management system Methodenbankverwaltungssystem
methods base system Methodenbanksystem
methods deficiency Methodenmangel
methods description language Methodenbeschreibungssprache
methods integration Methodenintegration
methods management system Methodenverwaltungssystem
methods model Methodenmodell
metra potential method Metra-Potential-Methode
metropolitan area network Netz für Ballungsgebiete
MFLOPS = Million Floating Point Operations Per Second
MFM = Modified Frequency Modulation
MHS = Message Handling System
MIC = Microwave Integrated Circuit
micro mikro
micro circuit card Speicherkarte
micro instruction Mikrobefehl
micro protection Feinschutz
microchip Mikrochip
microcode protection Mikrocodeschutz
microcomputer Mikrocomputer
microfiche Mikrofiche
microfilm Mikrofilm
microfilm device Mikrofilmgerät
microfilm reader Mikrofilmleser

microfilming Mikroverfilmung
microprocessor Mikroprozessor
microprogram Mikroprogramm
microprogram memory Mikroprogramm-Speicher
microprogramming Mikroprogrammierung
microwave identification Mikrowellen-Identifikation
microwave integrated circuit mikrowellenintegrierte Schaltung
mid run explanation Erklärung mitten im Ablauf
MIDAS = Management Information Dataflow System
milestone Meilenstein
milli milli
MIMD = Multiple Instruction/Multiple Data
minimum run time Mindestbearbeitungszeit
minimum stock Mindestbestand
MIPS = Million Instructions Per Second
mirror-disk concept Spiegelplatten-Konzept
mirroring Spiegelung
MIS = Management Information System
miscellaneous function Zusatzfunktion
mission Hauptzweck
mix Mischung
mixed environment gemischte Systemauslegung
mixed hardware gemischte Hardware
mixed software gemischte Software
mnemonic abbreviation mnemotechnische Abkürzung
mnemonic name Merkname
mnemonics Mnemotechnik
MNP = Microcom Networking Protocol
mobile communications mobile Kommunikation
mobile data collection mobile Datenerfassung
mode Betriebsart, Modus
mode error Modusfehler
model Leitbild, Modell, Schema
model application Modellanwendung
model design Modellentwurf
model development Modellentwicklung
model experiment Modellexperiment
model generating system Modellgenerierungssystem
model of architecture Architekturmodell
model of user view Benutzermodell
model principle Modellprinzip
model representation Modelldarstellung
model type Modelltyp

modelling Modellbildung, Modellieren
modelling approach modellbildender Ansatz
modelling end-user modellierender Benutzer
modem = modulator/demodulator
moderate strategy gemäßigte Strategie
moderator Moderator, Diskussionsleiter
modifiability Änderbarkeit, Modifizierbarkeit
modification Veränderung
modify (to) ändern, verändern
modular program Modularprogramm
modular programming modulare Programmierung
modularity Modularität
modularization Modularisierung
modulate (to) modulieren
modulation Modulation
module Modul, Baustein
module correspondence Baustein-Korrespondenz
module design Modulentwurf
module principle Baukastenprinzip, Modularisierungsprinzip
module test Komponententest, Modultest
modulo method Divisionsrest-Verfahren, Modulo-Verfahren
modulo n check Modulo-N-Kontrolle
momentum strategy Momentum-Strategie
monitor Überwacher
monitor (to) überwachen
monitoring Überwachung
monitoring device Überwachungseinrichtung
monitoring procedure Monitoring-Verfahren
monochrome screen monochromer Bildschirm
monotonic inferencing monotones Schlußfolgern
Monte Carlo analysis Monte-Carlo-Analyse
MOPS = Million Operations Per Second
MOSFET = Metal Oxide Semi-Conductor Field Effect Transistor
morphological analysis morphologische Analyse
morphological box morphologischer Kasten
MOS = Metal Oxide Semiconductor
mosaic graphics Mosaikgraphik
mosaic printer Mosaikdrucker
motivate (to) motivieren
motivation Motivation
motivation of achievement Leistungsmotivation

motivational-conative process motivational-konativer Prozeß
motive Motiv, Trieb
motive for user commitment Beteiligungsmotiv
mouse Maus
mouse pointer Mauszeiger
moving line Fließband
MPA = Management Potential Analysis
MPM = Metra Potential Method
mpx = multiplex
MRP = Materials Requirement Planning
MS-DOS = Microsoft Disk Operating System
MSI = Medium Scale Integration
MSS = Management Support System
MTBF = Mean Time Between Failures
MTBM = Meantime Between Malfunctions
MTM = Methods Time Measurement
MTTF = Mean Time To Failure
MTTR = Mean Time To Repair
multiaddress message Rundsenden
multiattribute search Suchen mit Mehrfachbegriffen
multicolor printer Mehrfarbendrucker
multicomputer system Mehrrechnersystem
multifont printer Mehrschriftendrucker
multifont reader Mehrschriftenleser
multifunctional mehrfunktional
multifunctional workplace mehrfunktionaler Arbeitsplatz
multilevel model Mehrebenenmodell
multilingual software mehrsprachige Software
multimedial document mehrmediales Dokument
multiorganizational application system mehrorganisationales Anwendungssystem
multiple access Mehrfachzugriff
multiple choice Mehrfachauswahl
multiple connection Mehrfachverbindung
multiple copies Mehrfachkopien
multiple error Mehrfachfehler
multiple menu multiples Menü
multiple part forms Mehrfachformularsatz
multiple requesting Mehrfachaufforderung
multiple usage Mehrfachbenutzung, Mehrfachverwendung
multiple work station Mehrfacharbeitsplatz
multiple way ciphering Mehrwegverschlüsselung
multiplex channel Multiplexkanal
multiplex operation Multiplexbetrieb

multiplexing Mehrfachnutzung, Multiplexbetrieb
multiplexing access Vielfachzugriff
multiplier technique Multiplikatormethode
multipoint connection Mehrpunktverbindung
multiprocessor system Mehrprozessorsystem
multiprogramming Mehrprogrammverarbeitung
multiprogramming mode Mehrprogrammbetrieb
multistage rating Mehrstufenrating
multistation system Mehrplatzsystem
multistep pop-up menu mehrstufiges Pop-up-Menü
multitasking gleichzeitige Mehrfachverarbeitung
multiuser mode Mehrbenutzerbetrieb
multiuser system Mehrbenutzersystem
multivariable forecasting multivariable Prognose
multivendor Mehrhersteller
multivendor environment Mehrhersteller-Umgebung
MUMPS = Massachusetts General Hospital Utility Multiprogramming System
mutating virus mutierender Virus
mutation Änderung, Mutation
mutilate (to) verstümmeln
MVS = Multiple Virtual Operating System

N

naive end-user naiver Benutzer
named benannt
narrative Anmerkung (in DFD), verbale Beschreibung
Nassi-Shneiderman chart Nassi-Shneiderman-Diagramm, Struktogramm
natural language natürliche Sprache
natural language dialog natürlich-sprachlicher Dialog
natural language processing Verarbeitung natürlicher Sprache
NBS = National Bureau of Standards
NC = Numeric Control
NCC = National Computing Centre
NCGA = National Computer Graphics Association
NCR paper = non carbon required paper
near letter quality beinahe Briefqualität
need Bedarf, Bedürfnis
need forecast Bedarfsvorhersage
need hierarchy Bedürfnishierarchie
needle printer Nadeldrucker
needle printing device Nadeldruckwerk
negation Negation, Verneinung
neighborhood work center Nachbarschaftsbüro
NEMP = Nuclear Explosion Magnetic Power
nesting Schachtelung
net change Nettoabweichung
net change principle Prinzip der Nettoabweichung
net filter Netzfilter
net pay Nettolohn
netting Netting
network Netz, Netzwerk
network architecture Netzarchitektur
network configuration Netzkonfiguration, Netzstruktur
network control Netzsteuerung
network control program Netzsteuerungsprogramm
network heterodyning Netzüberlagerung
network information center zentrale Netzinformation
network interface unit Netz-Zugangseinheit
network layer Netzschicht
network level Netzebene
network management Netzmanagement
network management program Netzsteuerungsprogramm
network model Netzmodell
network node Netzknoten
network operating system Netzbetriebssystem
network optimization Netzoptimierung
network plan Netzplan
network planning technique Netzplantechnik
network speed Netzgeschwindigkeit
network structure Netzstruktur
network technology Netztechnik
network topology Netztopologie
network user Netzteilnehmer
network user address Netzteilnehmer-Aadresse
network user identification Netzteilnehmer-Erkennung
network workload Netzlast
neural network neuronales Netz
new media neue Medien
new technology neue Technologie
news Botschaft
next executable statement nächste auszuführende Anweisung
NIP = Non Impact Printer
NKRO = N-Key-Roll-Over
NL = Natural Language
NLP = Natural Language Processing
NLQ = Near Letter Quality
node Knoten
noise peak Störspitze
noise protection Lärmschutz
noise reduction Schalldämpfung
noise source Störquelle
nominal scale nominale Skala
nomogram Funktionsnetz
non-administrative data processing technische Datenverarbeitung
non-carbon required paper Selbstdurchschreibepapier
non-destructive readout zerstörungsfreies Lesen
non-impact printer anschlagfreier Drucker, nicht mechanischer Drucker
non-impact printing device nicht mechanisches Druckwerk
non-linear optimization nicht lineare Optimierung
non-monotonic inferencing nicht monotones Schlußfolgern
non-numeric nicht numerisch
non-operation Nulloperation
non-permanent menu nicht dauerhaftes Menü
non-personal conflict objektiver Konflikt
non-procedural programming nicht prozedurale Programmierung

non-procedural programming language nicht prozedurale Programmiersprache
non-redundant storage redundanzfreie Speicherung
non-sharable nicht gemeinsam benutzbar
non-standardized interview nicht standardisiertes Interview
non-stop computer unterbrechungsfreier Computer
non-stop processing unterbrechungsloser Betrieb
non-volatile memory nicht flüchtiger Speicher, permanenter Speicher
norm Norm, Richtschnur
norm conflict Normenkonflikt
norm/value system Norm-/Wertsystem
normalization Normalisierung
normalization process Normalisierungsprozeß
normalize (to) normalisieren
normalized form Normalform
notation Notation, Schreibweise
notice Aushang
notice board Aushangbrett
notice of contestation Bestreitungsvermerk
notification Benachrichtigung, Mitteilung
NOP = Non Operation
novice mode Anfängermodus, Laienmodus
novice user ungeübter Benutzer
NPV = Net Present Value
NRZ = Non Return to Zero

NS-Diagramm = Nassi-Shneidermann-Diagram
NUA = Network User Address
nuclear explosion magnetic power Überspannung durch Nuklearexplosion
nucleus Kernprogramm
NUI = Network User Identification
number Nummer
number (to) numerieren
number of order Ordnungsnummer
number of tests performed Anzahl Testläufe
number representation Zahlendarstellung
number system Zahlensystem
number type Nummernart
numbered entity Nummerungsobjekt
numbering Nummerung
numbering schema Nummernschema
numbering system Nummernsystem
numeric numerisch
numeric address numerische Adresse
numeric analysis numerische Analyse
numeric control numerische Steuerung
numeric control device Handhabungssystem
numeric controlled machine tool numerisch gesteuerte Werkzeugmaschine
numeric data numerische Daten
numeric data base numerische Datenbasis
numeric keyboard numerische Tastatur
numeric keypad Blocktastatur, Zehnerblock

O

O & M department organization and methods department
object code Objektcode, Zielsprache
object computer Zielcomputer
object language Objektsprache, Zielsprache
object of contract Vertragsgegenstand
object of testing Testling, Testobjekt
object oriented programming objektorientierte Programmierung
object program Objektprogramm
object system Objektsystem
object time Programmlaufzeit
objective objektiv, Ziel
objective information requirement objektiver Informationsbedarf
objective job situation objektive Arbeitssituation
objectivity Objektivität
obligation of abstention Enthaltungspflicht
obligatory verpflichtend
observation Beobachtung
observation experiment Beobachtungsexperiment
observation interview Beobachtungsinterview
OCR = Optical Character Recognition
OCR A font Schriftart A
OCR B font Schriftart B
OCR document Klarschriftbeleg
OCR document reader Klarschriftbeleglser
octal number Oktalziffer
odd ungeradzahlig
odd parity ungeradzahlige Parität, Ungleichheit
odd parity check Prüfung auf ungeradzahlige Parität
ODETTE = Organization for Data Exchange by Tele Transmission in Europe
ODF = On Demand Publishing
ODIF = Office Document Interchange Format
OEM = Original Equipment Manufacturer
offhook condition Zustand 'Hörer abgehoben'
office Büro
office automation Büroautomation
office communications Bürokommunikation
office communications system Bürokommunikationssystem
office composition Bürosatz
office computer Bürocomputer
office equipment Büroausstattung
office function Sekretariatsfunktion
office furniture Büromöbel
office information system Büroinformationssystem
office technology Bürotechnik
office telewriting Bürofernschreiben
office trigger system Bürovorgangssystem
office work Büroarbeit
office work analysis Büroarbeitsanalyse
office work area Büroarbeitsplatz
officer in charge Sachbearbeiter
offline nicht direkt verbunden
offshade processing Fehlfarbenverarbeitung
OIS = Office Information System
one-for-one changeover Stichtagsumstellung
one-to-many relationship 1:m-Beziehung
one-to-one communications Individualkommunikation
one-to-one relationship 1:1-Beziehung
ongoing-operating costs laufende Betriebskosten
ongoing running costs laufende Betriebskosten
onhook condition Zustand 'Hörer aufgelegt'
onion model Zwiebelmodell
online direkt verbunden
online data entry Direktdatenerfassung
online documentation Online-Dokumentation
ONP = Open Network Provision
open communications offene Kommunikation
open communications system offenes Kommunikationssystem
open loop offener Regelkreis, offene Schleife
open network offenes Netz
open observation offene Beobachtung
open query freie Abfrage
open shop operation offener Betrieb
open system offenes System
open systems interconnection ISO-Schichtenmodell
open task offene Aufgabe
open wire line Freileitung
operability Hantierbarkeit
operating costs Betriebskosten
operating indicator Betriebsanzeige
operating instructions Betriebsanweisung, Betriebsvorschrift, Bedienungsanleitung

operating sequence
Bearbeitungsreihenfolge
operating system Betriebssystem
operating time Bearbeitungszeit,
Betriebszeit
operating time per unit Bearbeitungszeit
operation duration Arbeitsgangdauer
operation principle Arbeitsprinzip
operation step Arbeitsgang,
Arbeitsvorgang
operational einsatzfähig, operational
operational guidance Bedienerführung
operational guidance indicator
Bedienerführungsanzeige
operational mode Betriebsart,
Betriebsform, Systembetrieb
operational readiness
Betriebsbereitschaft
operational status Betriebszustand
operations manual Bedienungshandbuch
operations research Operations Research,
Unternehmensforschung, Optimalplanung
operations scheduling Arbeitsplanung,
Arbeitsvorbereitung
operative goal operatives Ziel
operative information management
operatives Informationsmanagement
operative management operatives
Management
operative test Betriebstest
operative test planning operative
Testplanung
operator Anlagenbediener, Bediener,
Operator
operator command Bedienerbefehl
operator console Bedienerkonsole
operator convenience
Bedienerfreundlichkeit
operator initiated termination vom
Bediener eingeleiteter Abbruch
operator interface Bedieneroberfläche
operator message Bedienernachricht
opinion poll Meinungsumfrage
opinion research Demoskopie
opportunity costs Opportunitätskosten
OPT = Optimized Production Technology
optical character Klarschriftzeichen
optical character recognition optische
Zeichenerkennung
optical computer optischer Computer
optical disk optische Speicherplatte,
Bildplatte
optical fiber Glasfaserkabel,
Lichtwellenleiter
optical message transmission optische
Nachrichtenübertragung
optical reader optischer Leser

optimization experiment
Optimierungsexperiment
optimization model Optimierungsmodell
optimization of benefit
Nutzenoptimierung
optimization of current system
Optimieren des Istzustands
optimize (to) optimieren
optimizing compiler optimierender
Compiler
optimizing of current system
Istzustandsoptimierung
optimum value Optimalwert
option Auswahlmöglichkeit, Wahl
optional wählbar, wahlweise, zusätzlich
optional word Wahlwort
opto computer Opto-Computer
opto-electrical transformer
opto-elektrischer Wandler
OR = Operations Research
oral questioning mündliche Befragung
order Auftrag, Bestellung, Ordnung
order (to) bestellen, veranlassen
order acknowledgement
Auftragsbestätigung
order backlog Auftragsrückstand
order confirmation Auftragsbestätigung
order control Auftragssteuerung,
Bestellüberwachung
order data Auftragsdaten, Bestelldaten
order disposition Bestelldisposition
order entry Auftragseingang
order form Bestellformular
order number Auftragsnummer
order of rank Rangordung
order placement Auftragsvergabe
order point Bestellpunkt
order priority Auftragspriorität
order procedure Bestellverfahren
order processing Auftragsabwicklung,
Auftragsverarbeitung
order processing subsystem
Auftragsinformationssystem
order quantity Bestellmenge
order servicing Auftragsbearbeitung
orderer Auftraggeber, Besteller
orderly Ordnungsmäßigkeit
orderly close down planmäßiger
Abschluß
ordinal scale ordinale Skala
organization Organisation
organization and methods department
Organisationsabteilung
organization chart Organigramm
organization of work Arbeitsorganisation
organizational analysis
Organisationsanalyse

organizational change organisatorischer Wandel
organizational control Organisationskontrolle
organizational culture Organisationskultur
organizational demoscopy Organisationsdemoskopie
organizational design alternative organisatorische Gestaltungsalternative
organizational development Organisationsentwicklung
organizational ergonomics Organisationsergonomie
organizational form Organisationsform
organizational function Organisationsfunktion
organizational goal Organisationsziel
organizational interface organisatorische Schnittstelle
organizational integration organisatorische Integration
organizational learning process organisatorischer Lernprozeß
organizational model Organisationsmodell
organizational plan Organisationsplan
organizational planning Organisationsplanung
organizational power organisatorische Macht
organizational preparation organisatorische Vorbereitung
organizational principle Organisationsgrundsatz, Organisationsprinzip
organizational research Organisationsforschung
organizational structure Aufbauorganisation, Organisationsstruktur, Strukturorganisation
organizational system Organisationssystem
organizational teachings Organisationslehre
organizational techniques Organisationsmittel
organizational technology Organisationstechnologie
organizational theory Organisationstheorie
organizational type Organisationstyp
organizational unit Struktureinheit
organize (to) organisieren
organizer Organisator
organizing user involvement Beteiligungsorganisation
organizing scope Organisationsspielraum

orientation Orientierung
orientation hypothesis Orientierungshypothese
original Orginal, Vorlage
original document Originalbeleg, Urbeleg
original equipment manufacturer Hersteller eines Originalsystems
organogram Organigramm
OROM = Optical Read Only Memory
orthogonal design Orthogonalentwurf
OS = Open System
OS = Operating System
Osborn alienation Osborn-Verfremdung
OSF = Open Software Foundation
OSI = Open Systems Interconnection
OSI model OSI-Modell
OTA = Office of Technology Assessment
out of line Abweichung vom Normalen
outage Ausfall
outage time Ausfallzeit
outgoing mail Postausgang
outline guide Umrißplan
outline proposal Rahmenvorschlag
outlook Vorschau
output Ausgabe, Ausstoß, Ergebnis
output (to) ausgeben
output class Ausgabeklasse
output command Ausgabebefehl
output data Ausgabedaten
output data set Ausgabedatei
output device Ausgabegerät
output document Ausgabebeleg
output driven ergebnisorientiert
output driven design ergebnisorientierter Entwurf
output error Ausgabefehler
output manipulation Outputmanipulation
output medium Ausgabemedium
output operation Ausgabeoperation
output protection Ausgabeschutz
output queue Ausgabewarteschlange
output rate Ausgabegeschwindigkeit
output record Ausgabesatz
output stream Ausgabestrom
output technology Ausgabetechnik
output transfer rate Ausgaberate
output unit Ausgabeeinheit, Ausgabewerk
outside in approach Outside-in-Ansatz
overall internal price summarischer Verrechnungspreis
overcapacity Überkapazität
overflow Überlauf
overflow indication Kapazitätsüberwachung
overhead Gemeinkosten, Mehraufwand
overhead systems engineering Gemeinkosten-System-Engineering

overhead value analysis
Gemeinkosten-Wertanalyse
overlap Überlappung
overlay Überlagerung
overlay (to) überlappen, überlagern
overload Überlastung, Bereichsüberschreitung
overload (to) überlasten
overload capacity Überlastbarkeit
overtime Überstunden

overview Überblick
overvoltage Überspannung
overvoltage protection
Überspannungsschutz
overvoltage protection device
Überspannungsschutz-Element
overwork Arbeitsüberlastung
owner Eigner
owner/member relationship
Eigner/Zugehöriger-Beziehung

P

PA = Public Access
PABX = Private Automatic Branch Exchange
pacemaker technology Schrittmachertechnologie
packet Paket
packet assembly/disassembly Paketanordnung und -auflösung
packet switching Paketvermittlung
packet switching network Paketvermittlungsnetz
packing density Packungsdichte
PAD = Packet Assembler/Disassembler
padding Auffüllen (mit Zeichen)
paddle Drehknopf
page Seite
page (to) blättern
page break Seitenumbruch
page description language Seitenbeschreibungssprache
page down (to) vorwärts blättern
page feed Seitenvorschub
page frame Seitenrahmen
page heading Seitenüberschrift
page length Seitenlänge
page makeup Seitenumbruch
page mapping Seitenaustausch
page printer Seitendrucker
page reader Blattleser, Seitenleser
page replacement Seitenersetzung
page up (to) rückwärts blättern
pages per minute Seiten pro Minute
pagination Seitenumbruch
paging Ein-/Auslagern, Seitenaustausch
paging algorithm Seitenaustauschverfahren
paired comparison Paarvergleich
panel questioning Panelbefragung
panning Schwenken
paper Papier
paper feed Papiereinzug, Papiervorschub
paper form Formular
paper size Papierformat
paper width Papierbreite
paperless papierlos
paperless office papierloses Büro
PAQ = Position Analysis Questionnaire
paradigm Paradigma
parallel changeover Parallelumstellung
parallel computer Parallelcomputer
parallel dialog paralleler Dialog
parallel distributed processing parallele verteilte Verarbeitung
parallel key Parallelschlüssel
parallel mode Parallelbetrieb

parallel numbering system Parallel-Nummernsystem
parallel operation Parallelbetrieb
parallel printer Paralleldrucker
parallel printing device Paralleldruckwerk
parallel processing Parallelverarbeitung, parallele Verarbeitung
parallel programming parallele Programmierung
parallel session Parallelsitzung
parallel test Paralleltest
parameter Parameter
parameter estimation Parameterschätzung
parameterization Parametrisierung
parameterize (to) parametrisieren
parameterizing end-user parametrisierender Benutzer
parametric estimate equation parametrische Schätzgleichung
parametric query parametrisierte Abfrage
parametric rating Parameterschätzung
paranthesis Klammer
PARC = Palo Alto Research Center
Pareto analysis Pareto-Analyse
parity Gleichheit, Parität
parity bit Gleichheitsbit, Paritätsbit
parity check Gleichheitsprüfung
parity error Gleichheitsfehler
part Teil
part-period balancing Stück-Perioden-Ausgleich
partial changeover Teilumstellung
partial strategy Teilstrategie
partial survey Teilerhebung
participant Beteiligter, Mitwirkender, Teilnehmer
participate (to) beteiligen, mitwirken
participation Beteiligung, Mitwirkung, Partizipation, Teilnahme
participation objective Partizipationsziel
participative approach Partizipationsansatz
partitioning Aufteilung
partitioning system Teilsystembildung
partitioned data base aufgeteilte Datenhaltung
parts list Stückliste
passive help system passives Hilfesystem
passive observation passive Beobachtung
password Kennwort, Paßwort
password algorithm Paßwort-Algorithmus
paste (to) einfügen

PATBX = Private Automatic Telex Branch Exchange
patent protection Patentschutz
pattern Muster
pattern matching Mustervergleich
pattern recognition Mustererkennung
PAX = Private Automatic Exchange
payment Zahlung
payments system Zahlungsverkehr
payroll Gehaltsabrechnung
payroll accounting Lohn- und Gehaltsverrechnung
PBX = Private Branch Exchange
PC = Parity Check
PC = Personal Computer
PC = Personal Computing
PC = Plug Compatible
PC-DOS = Personal Computer Disk Operating System
PCM = Plug Compatible Manufacturer
PCM = Pulse Code Modulation
PD-Software = Public Domain Software
PDF = Program Development Facility
PDL = Page Description Language
peak load Spitzenbelastung
PEARL = Process and Experiment Automation Realtime Language
pen plotter Stiftplotter
penetrate (to) durchdringen, penetrieren
penetration Durchdringung, Penetrierung
penetration strategy Durchdringungsstrategie
percentage rate method Prozentsatzmethode
perception Perzeption, Wahrnehmung
perfective maintenance Perfektionswartung
perform (to) leisten
performability Leistungsbereitschaft
performance Leistung
performance ability Leistungsfähigkeit
performance analysis Leistungsanalyse
performance appraisal Leistungsbeurteilung
performance attribute Leistungsmerkmal
performance characteristics Leistungsdaten
performance comparison Leistungsvergleich
performance criterion Leistungskriterium
performance engineering Technikanalyse
performance evaluation Leistungsbewertung
performance index Leistungskenngröße
performance level Leistungsgrad
performance link Leistungsverbund
performance measure Leistungskennzahl

performance measurement Leistungsmessung
performance measurement technique Methode der Leistungsmessung
performance objective Leistungsziel
performance principle Leistungsprinzip
performance requirement Leistungsanforderung
performance specification Leistungsprofil
performance standard Leistungsstandard
performance synthesis Leistungssynthese
performance test Leistungstest
perimeter system Perimetersystem
periodic interference symmetrische Störung
periodic procedure order Bestellrhythmusverfahren
peripheral connection Peripherieanschluß
peripheral device Peripheriegerät
peripheral equipment Peripherie
peripheral unit periphere Einheit
peripherals Peripherie
permanent fortdauernd, permanent
permanent data Stammdaten
permanent menu dauerhaftes Menü, permanentes Menü
permanent test Dauerversuch
permission of usage Werknutzungsbewilligung
personal persönlich
personal checkword persönliches Kennwort
personal computer persönlicher Computer
personal computing individuelle Informationsverarbeitung
personal conflict subjektiver Konflikt
personal data personenbezogene Daten
personal identification number persönliche Identifikationsnummer, Personenkennzeichen
personal information management persönliches Informationsmanagement
personal password persönliches Paßwort
personal time management persönliche Arbeitstechnik
personnel Personal, Personalbestand
personnel administration Personalverwaltung
personnel allocation Personalzuordnung
personnel costs Personalkosten
personnel deployment Personaleinsatz
personnel development Personalentwicklung
personnel file Personalakte
personnel information system Personalinformationssystem
personnel intensive personalintensiv

171

personnel management

personnel management Personalwesen
personnel planning Personalplanung
personnel procurement
Personalbeschaffung
personnel record Personalakte
personnel recruitment
Personalbeschaffung
personnel reduction Personalabbau
personnel reporting
Personalberichtswesen
personnel requirements Personalbedarf
personnel requirements planning
Personalbedarfsplanung
personnel turnover Personalumschichtung
PERT = Program Evaluation and
Review Technique
Petri net Petri-Netz
PH = Page Heading
phase of production Produktionsgang
phased changeover phasenweise
Umstellung
photo typesetting Photosatz
photocopying paper Photokopierpapier
physical real
physical address reale Adresse
physical attribute physisches Attribut
physical cancellation physisches Löschen
physical characteristic technische
Eigenschaft
physical data assurance measurement
physische Datensicherungsmaßnahme
physical data definition language
physische Datendefinitionssprache
physical data flow diagram physisches
Datenflußdiagramm
physical data independence physische
Datenunabhängigkeit
physical data structure physische
Datenstruktur
physical data view physische Datensicht
physical deficiency technischer Mangel
physical layer Geräteschicht
physical life technische Nutzungsdauer
physical memory Realspeicher
physical model physikalisches Modell,
physisches Modell
physical operating system reales
Betriebssystem
physical process realer Prozeß
physical unit Baueinheit
physiological need physiologisches
Bedürfnis
PIA = Peripheral Interface Adapter
pick (to) auswählen, picken
pico piko
pictograph Bildzeichen, Piktogramm
picture Bild

picture check Maskenprüfung
picture communications
Festbildkommunikation
picture element Bildelement, Bildpunkt
picture phone Bildtelephon
picture processing Bildverarbeitung
picture set Bildmenge
picture window Bildfenster
pie chart Tortendiagramm
pilot project Pilotprojekt
pilot record Leitsatz
PIM = Personal Information Managment
PIN = Personal Identification Number
pinch off (to) abklemmen
pipeline concept Pipeline-Konzept
pipelining Pipeline-Verarbeitung,
Fließbandverarbeitung
PIPO = Parallel In Parallel Out
pirated copy Raubkopie
PISO = Parallel In Serial Out
pixel Bildelement, Bildpunkt, Pixel
PLA = Programmable Logic Array
plain text Klartext, Normalschrift
plain writing reader Handschriftenleser
plan Plan
plan (to) planen
plan design Planentwurf
planned quantity geplante Menge
PLANNET-Technik =
PLANning-NETwork-Technique
planning Planung
planning approach Planungsansatz
planning costs Planungskosten
planning goal Planungsziel
planning horizon Planungszeitraum
planning information
Planungsinformation
planning modelling language
Planungssprache
planning process Planungsprozeß
plant Betrieb
plant organization Betriebsorganisation
plasma display Plasmabildschirm
plasma screen Plasmabildschirm
plastic card Plastikkarte
plausibility Glaubwürdigkeit,
Plausibilität
plausibility check Plausibilitätskontrolle
PL/1 = Programming Language One
plot (to) graphisch darstellen
plotter Koordinatenschreiber,
Kurvenschreiber, Planzeichner, Plotter,
Zeichenmaschine
plug Stecker
plug compatibility Stecker-Kompatibilität
plug compatible steckerkompatibel
pneumatic postal system Rohrpost

172

P.O. = Post Office
pocket telephone Taschentelephon
point of sale Verkaufspunkt
point of sale banking Bankgeschäft am Verkaufspunkt
point of sale terminal Datenkasse am Verkaufspunkt, Kassenterminal
point plotting punktförmiges Zeichen
point-to-point connection Punkt-zu-Punkt-Verbindung, Zweipunktverbindung
pointer Zeiger
pointer array Kettenspur
pointing device Zeigeinstrument
polar coordinate Polarkoordinate
polarity profile Polaritätsprofil
polling Sendeaufruf
polling mode Aufrufbetrieb
polling technique Abruftechnik, Polling
pollution Umweltverschmutzung
POM = Purchase Order Management
pooling Zusammenfassen von Geldbeträgen
poorly documented schlecht dokumentiert
POP = Point Of Purchase
pop Ausfügeoperation
port Steckerbuchse
portability Portabilität, Portierbarkeit, Tragbarkeit, Übertragbarkeit
portable tragbar, übertragbar
portable computer tragbarer Computer
portable document reader Handleser
portable memory mobiler Speicher
portation Übertragung
portfolio Portfolio
portfolio analysis Portfolioanalyse
POS = Point Of Sale
POS-Banking = Point Of Sale Banking
POS-Terminal = Point Of Sale Terminal
position Stelle
positional parameter Positionsparameter
positioning Positionierung
post office Postamt
post office box Postfach
postal scanner Adressenleser
postal service Postdienst
postaudit nachträgliche Überprüfung
postcompletion documentation nachträgliche Dokumentation
postcondition Folgebedingung
postprocessor Auswerteprogramm
postreview nachträgliche Überprüfung
potential of benefit Nutzenpotential
potential of usage Nutzungspotential
power Mächtigkeit, Macht, Strom
power amplifier Leistungsverstärker
power breakdown Netzausfall

power circuit Stromkreis
power consumption Stromverbrauch
power failure Stromausfall
power of language Sprachmächtigkeit, Sprachumfang
power rate Belastbarkeit
power supply Netzversorgung, Stromversorgung
power supply interference Netzstörung
power supply interruption Netzunterbrechung
power supply undervoltage Netzunterspannung
power supply unit Stromversorgungsgerät
power switch Netzschalter
power transient transienter Störer
PPM = Pages Per Minute
PPX = Private Packet Switching Exchange
practicability Praktikabilität
pragmatics Pragmatik
precedence analysis Präzedenzanalyse
precision Genauigkeit
precompiler Vorübersetzer
predecessor Vorgänger
predecessor count Anzahl Vorgänger
predicate calculus Prädikatenkalkül
predicative programming prädikative Programmierung
preference Vorziehenswürdigkeit, Präferenz
preference matrix Präferenzmatrix
preference order Präferenzordnung
preliminary analysis Grobanalyse
preliminary design Grundkonzeption, Grobentwurf, Vorentwurf
preliminary study Vorstudie
premise Prämisse, Voraussetzung
preparation for implementation Vorbereiten der Implementierung, Implementierungsvorbereitung
preparing test data Testdatenerstellung
preprocessor Präprozessor, Vorlaufprogramm, Vorprozessor
prerequisite Vorbedingung
presentation Darstellung
presentation graphics Präsentationsgraphik
presentation layer Darstellungsschicht
presentation method Darstellungsmethode
presentation technique Darstellungstechnik, Präsentationstechnik, Vortragstechnik
presentation with icons ikonische Darstellung

Prestel = Press button on telephone lines
preventive job design vorbeugende Arbeitsgestaltung
preventive maintenance vorbeugende Wartung
previous statement vorherige Anweisung
price assessment Preisbeurteilung
price determining Preisbildung
price lookup automatische Preiszuordnung, Preisabfrage
price of benefit Nutzenpreis
pricing Preisbildung
primary key Primärschlüssel
primitive function Grundfunktion
principle Grundsatz, Prinzip
principle of abstraction Abstraktionsprinzip, Prinzip der Abstraktion
principle of data abstraction Prinzip der Datenabstraktion
principle of functional design Prinzip des funktionellen Entwurfs
principle of hierarchical structuring Prinzip der hierarchischen Strukturierung
principle of integrated documentation Prinzip der integrierten Dokumentation
principle of locality Prinzip der Lokalität
principle of multiple usage Prinzip der Mehrfachverwendung
principle of remote concentration Prinzip der dezentralen Konzentration
principle of stepwise refinement Prinzip der schrittweisen Verfeinerung
principle of structured programming Prinzip der strukturierten Programmierung
print (to) drucken
print chain Druckkette
print device Druckwerk
print head Druckkopf
print mask Druckmaske
print medium Druckmedium
print output Druckausgabe
print quality Druckqualität
print ribbon Druckband
print screen (to) Bildschirminhalt drucken
print server Druckserver
print span Druckbreite
print unit Druckwerk
print view Druckbild
print wheel Druckrad, Typenrad
print width Druckbreite
printed circuit gedruckte Schaltung
printed form Vordruck
printed matter Drucksache
printer Drucker
printer buffer Druckpuffer
printer capacity Druckerkapazität
printer control character Druckersteuerzeichen
printer cover Druckerverkleidung
printer driver Druckertreiber
printer terminal Druckerterminal
printing Drucken
printing rate Druckgeschwindigkeit
prioritize (to) bevorzugen
prioritizing goals Zielpriorität festlegen
priority Priorität, Vorrang, Vorzug
priority aging Altern der Priorität
priority analysis Prioritätsanalyse
priority control Prioritätensteuerung
priority rule Prioritätsregel
prisoner's dilemma Gefangenendilemma
privacy Privatsphäre
private automatic branch exchange Fernsprech-Nebenstellenanlage, Telephon-Nebenstellenanlage
private branch exchange private Nebenstellenanlage, Nebenstellenanlage
private ciphering private Verschlüsselung
private law Privatrecht
probabilistic probabilistisch
probability Wahrscheinlichkeit
probability calculus Wahrscheinlichkeitsrechnung
probability of failure Ausfallwahrscheinlichkeit
probability theory Wahrscheinlichkeitstheorie
problem Problem
problem analysis Problemanalyse
problem co-ordinator Problemkoordinator
problem data base Problemdatenbank
problem definition Problemerkennung, Problemdefinition
problem description Problembeschreibung
problem description language Problembeschreibungssprache
problem formulation Problemformulierung
problem management Fehlerverwaltung, Problemmanagement
problem oriented programming language problemorientierte Programmiersprache
problem report Problembericht
problem sensing Problemerfassung
problem solution Problemlösung
problem solving Problemlösen

problem solving data base Problemlösungs-Datenbank
problem solving system Problemverarbeitungssystem
problem statement language Problembeschreibungssprache
problem text Problemtext
problem tracking Problemverfolgung
PROCAL = Programmable Calculator
procedural prozedural
procedural knowledge representation prozedurale Wissensdarstellung
procedural programming language prozedurale Programmiersprache
procedure Prozedur, Verfahren
procedure design Verfahrensentwurf
procedure manual Verfahrenshandbuch
procedure partition Prozedurteil
procedure specification Verfahrensbeschreibung
process Prozeß
process (to) verarbeiten
process analysis Prozeßanalyse, Verfahrenskritik
process automation Prozeßautomatisierung
process call Prozeßaufruf
process computer language Prozeßrechnersprache
process control Prozeßsteuerung
process control computer Prozeßrechner
process control computing Prozeßdatenverarbeitung
process driven approach ablaufgesteuerter Ansatz
process environment Prozeßumgebung
process flow Arbeitsablauf
process integration Ablaufintegration
process management Prozeßmanagement
process model Ablaufmodell
process monitoring Prozeßüberwachung
process of data processing Datenverarbeitungsprozeß
process of information and communications Informations- und Kommunikationsprozeß
process organization Ablauforganisation, Prozeßorganisation
process orientation Prozeßorientierung
process oriented approach ablauforientierter Ansatz
process oriented sequential control prozeßabhängige Ablaufsteuerung
process owner Prozeßverantwortlicher
process under control beherrschter Prozeß
processing Verarbeitung

processing error Verarbeitungsfehler
processing performance Verarbeitungsleistung
processing rule Verarbeitungsregel
processing technology Verarbeitungstechnik
processor Prozessor, Verarbeiter
PROCOL = Process Control Oriented Language
procurement Beschaffung
procurement costs Beschaffungskosten
procurement guideline Beschaffungsrichtlinie
procurement planning Beschaffungsplanung
product Produkt
product code Artikelnummer
product development Produktentwicklung
product development process Produktentwicklungsprozeß
product liability Produkthaftung
product life cycle Produktlebenszyklus
product management system Produktverwaltungssystem
production Leistungserstellung, Produktion
production capacity Produktionskapazität
production control Produktionssteuerung
production costs Betriebskosten, Fertigungskosten
production line Fließband
production management Produktionsleitung
production manager Betriebsleiter
production operation Produktionsbetrieb
production output Produktionsmenge
production planning Produktionsplanung
production planning and scheduling Produktionsplanung und -steuerung
production plant Fertigungsbetrieb, Produktionsstätte
production resources Produktionsmittel
production rule Produktionsregel
production schedule Arbeitsplan
production scheduling Fertigungsvorbereitung
production step Produktionsgang
production system Produktionssystem
production time Betriebszeit
production unit Fertigungsinsel
productive produktiv
productive application system produktives Anwendungssystem
productive capacity Produktionskapazität
productivity Produktivität, Leistungsfähigkeit

productivity improvement Produktivitätssteigerung
productivity measure Produktivitätskennzahl
profile diagram Profildiagramm
profile of benefit Nutzenprofil
profit Gewinn
profit center Ertragszentrum
profit margin Gewinnspanne
program Programm
program (to) programmieren
program adaption Programmadaption
program analyzer Programmanalysator
program architecture Programmstruktur
program auditor Programmrevisor
program backup Programmsicherung
program barrier Programmsperre
program code Programmcode
program code generating Programmcode-Generierung
program compiling Programmübersetzung
program construction Programmkonstruktion
program control Programmsteuerung
program convention Programmkonvention
program conversion Programmumwandlung
program crash Programmabbruch
program data Programmdaten
program derivation Programmableitung
program description Programmbeschreibung
program design Programmentwurf
program documentation Programmdokumentation
program error Programmfehler
program execution Programmausführung
program flag data Programmkenndaten
program flow Programmablauf
program flow chart Programmablaufplan
program flow control Programmablaufsteuerung
program for stress testing Streßprogramm
program generator Programmgenerator
program innovation Programminnovation
program inspection Programminspektion
program instrumentation Programminstrumentierung
program instrumentation technique Programm-Instrumentierungstechnik
program interrupt Programmunterbrechung
program library Programmbibliothek
program loader Programmlader
program maintenance Programmpflege

program management Programmverwaltung
program manipulation Programmanipulation
program module Programmbaustein
program package Programmpaket
program preparation programmtechnische Vorbereitung
program protection Programmschutz
program quality Programmqualität
program release Programmfreigabe
program run Programmlauf
program segmentation Programmsegmentierung
program specification Programmbeschreibung, Programmspezifikation
program storage Programmspeicher
program support Programmunterstützung
program test Programmtest
program testing Programmprüfung, Programmtesten
program theft Programmdiebstahl
program type Programmtyp
program verification Programmüberprüfung
programmable programmierbar
programmable calculator programmierbare Rechenmaschine
programmable decision programmierbare Entscheidung
programmable read only memory programmierbarer Festwertspeicher
programmed instruction programmierter Unterricht
programmed query vorprogrammierte Abfrage
programmer Programmierer, **Programmiergerät**
programmer team organization Organisationsform Programmierteam
programmer workbench Programmier-Arbeitsplatz
programming Programmierung
programming aid Programmierhilfe
programming behavior Programmierverhalten
programming bureau Programmierbüro
programming environment Programmierumgebung
programming language Programmiersprache
programming language generation Sprachgeneration
programming language translator Sprachübersetzer

programming method
Programmiermethode
programming specification
Programmiervorgabe
programming support
Programmierunterstützung
programming tool Programmierwerkzeug
project Projekt
project (to) entwerfen, planen,
projektieren
project achievement Projektfortschritt
project administration Projektverwaltung
project assistant Projektassistent
project audit Projektrevision
project call Projektaufforderung
project controlling Projektkontrolle,
Projektsteuerung
project coordinator Projektkoordinator
project costs Projektkosten
project diary Projekttagebuch
project documentation
Projektdokumentation
project estimating
Projekt-Aufwandschätzung
project goal Projektziel
project leader Projektführer
project leadership Projektführerschaft
project library Projektbibliothek
project life cycle Projektlebenszyklus
project management Projektmanagement
project management tool
Projektmanagement-Werkzeug
project manager Projektleiter
project manual Projekthandbuch
project monitoring Projektüberwachung
project organization Projektorganisation
project plan Projektplan
project portfolio Projektportfolio
project progress Projektfortschritt
project proposal Projektvorschlag
project ranking Projektordnung
project redevelopment Projektsanierung
project review Projektüberprüfung
project scheduling Projektplanung
project secretary Projektsekretär
project selection Projektauswahl
project task Projektaufgabe
project team Projektgruppe, Projektteam
project termination Projektbeendigung
project tracking Projektverfolgung
projection Hochrechnung
PROLOG = PROgramming in LOGic
PROM = Programmable Read Only Memory
prompter Anforderungszeichen,
Aufforderungszeichen

prompting Bedienerführung,
Eingabeaufforderung
prompting character Abfragezeichen,
Eingabe-Abfragezeichen
property sheet Eigenschaften-Fenster
proportional figure Verhältniszahl
proportional scale Verhältnisskala
proportional spacing Proportionalabstand
proportional writing Proportionalschrift
proposal Angebot, Vorschlag
proposition Antrag, Vorschlag
prosody Prosodie
prospective job design vorausschauende
Arbeitgestaltung
protected file geschützte Datei
protection technology Schutztechnik
protective measure Schutzmaßnahme
protocol Protokoll
protocol adaption Protokollanpassung
protocol converter Anpassungsrechner,
Protokollkonverter
prototype Modell, Prototyp
prototype contract Modellvertrag,
Mustervertrag
prototype design Prototyp-Entwurf
prototyping Prototyping
PSA = Problem Statement Analyzer
PSDA = Problem Statement and Design Analyzer
pseudo code Pseudo-Code
pseudo graphics Pseudo-Graphik
PSL = Problem Statement Language
Psychology Psychologie
psychology of software development
Software-Psychologie
psychosocial factor psycho-sozialer
Faktor
psychosomatic disturbance
psychosomatische Störung
psychosomatics Psychosomatik
public access öffentlicher Zugriff
public administration öffentliche
Verwaltung
public administration informatics
Verwaltungsinformatik
public data freie Daten
public domain öffentlicher Bereich
public domain category allgemeine
Benutzerklasse
public domain software nicht durch
Copyright geschützte Software
public key system offenes
Verschlüsselungssystem
public network öffentliches Netz
public service öffentlicher Dienst
public switched network öffentliches
Fernsprechnetz

publish (to) publizieren
publishing on demand Publizieren auf Anforderung
pull down menu herabziehbares Menü
pull system Holsystem
pull tractor Zugtraktor
punched tape Lochstreifen
purchase (to) einkaufen
purchase order disposition Einkaufsdisposition
purchase order number Bestellnummer

purchase price Einkaufspreis
purchased software Fremdsoftware
purchasing Einkauf
purpose orientation Zweckbezogenheit
purposefulness Zweckhaftigkeit
purposiveness Zweckmäßigkeit
push Einfügeoperation
push button Drucktaste
push system Bringsystem
push tractor Schubtraktor
PWS = Personal Workstation

Q

QA = Quality Assurance
QBE = Query By Example
QL = Query Language
quadrant Quadrant
qualification Eignung, Fähigkeit, Qualifikation
qualifier Kennzeichner, Qualifikationsbegriff
qualify (to) qualifizieren
qualitative evaluation qualitative Bewertung
quality Qualität, Güte
quality assurance Qualitätssicherung
quality assurance system Qualitätssicherungssystem
quality audit Qualitätskontrolle
quality circle Qualitätszirkel
quality control Qualitätsteuerung, Qualitätslenkung
quality criterion Gütekriterium
quality goal Formalziel
quality improvement Qualitätssteigerung
quality measure Qualitätsmaß
quality of work Arbeitsqualität
quality of working life Humanisierung der Arbeit
quantifiable quantifizierbar
quantification Quantifizierung
quantify (to) quantifizieren

quantitative evaluation quantitative Bewertung
quantity Größe
quantity discount Mengenstaffel
quantity requirements Mengengerüst
quasi parallel program quasi-paralleles Programm
query Abfrage
query language Abfragesprache, Datenbank-Abfragesprache
query mode Abfragemodus
query with update Abfrage mit Fortschreibung
query/reply communications Abfrage-/Antwort Kommunikation
questionnaire Fragebogen
questionnaire technique Fragebogenmethode
questioning Befragung
questioning experiment Befragungsexperiment
questioning interview Befragungsgespräch
queue Warteschlange
queue name Warteschlangenname
queue time Wartezeit
quotation Kostenvoranschlag, Preisangabe
quotation mark Anführungszeichen
QWERTY keyboard QWERTY-Tastatur
QWERTZ keyboard QWERTZ-Tastatur

R

R & D = Research and Development
radiation protection Strahlenschutz
radio beam Richtfunk
radio beam transmission Richtfunkübertragung
radio link Funkverbindung
radio telephone drahtloses Telephon
radio telephone service Funkrufdienst
radio transmission drahtlose Übertragung
radius Radius
RAM = Random Access Memory
random direkt, wahlfrei
random access wahlfreier Zugriff, direkter Zugriff
random access memory Speicher mit wahlfreiem Zugriff
random error Zufallsfehler
random file organization gestreute Dateiorganisation
random generator Zufallsgenerator
random interference asymmetrische Störung
random number generator Zufallszahlen-Generator
range Bereich
range check Bereichsprüfung
range of a variable Bereich einer Variablen
range of functions Funktionsumfang
range of numbers Nummernbereich
rank Rangordnung
ranking Rangordung
rapid prototyping schnelles Prototyping
raster Raster
raster display Rasterbildschirm
raster graphics Rastergraphik
raster image processing Rasterbildverarbeitung
rate Häufigkeit
rate (to) beurteilen
rate of change Änderungsrate
rate of growth Wachstumsrate
rating scale Rating-Skala
rating technique Rating-Methode
ratio figure Verhältniszahl
ratio of test coverage Test-Abdeckungsgrad
rational problem solving rationales Problemlösen
rationalism Rationalismus
rationalization Rationalisierung, Vereinfachung
rationalize (to) rationalisieren
raw material Rohmaterial

raw material inventory Rohmaterialbestand
RBMS = Report Base Management System
reaction Reaktion
reaction time Ansprechzeit
read (to) auslesen
read head Lesekopf
read in (to) einlesen
read only memory Nur-Lese-Speicher, Festspeicher, Festwertspeicher
read password Kennwort für Lesen
read pen Lesestift
read/write head Lese-/Schreibkopf
read/write memory Lese-/Schreibspeicher
readability Lesbarkeit
ready for operation betriebsbereit
ready list Bereitliste
ready to receive empfangsbereit
real real, wirklich
real problem Realproblem
reality Wirklichkeit
reality experiment Realexperiment
realtime Echtzeit
realtime clock Echtzeituhr, Systemuhr
realtime mode Echtzeitbetrieb, Realzeitbetrieb
realtime processing Echtzeitverarbeitung, Realzeitverarbeitung, schritthaltende Verarbeitung
realtime programming Echtzeitprogrammierung, Realzeitprogrammierung
realtime programming language Echtzeit-Programmiersprache, Realzeit-Programmiersprache
receive (to) empfangen
receive interrupt Empfangsunterbrechung
receive mode Empfangsbetrieb
receiving key Empfangsschlüssel
receiving terminal Empfangsstation
recognition Erkennung
recognize/act cycle Erkennen/Handeln-Zyklus
reconfiguration Rekonfiguration
record Satz
record chaining Satzverkettung
record linkage Satzverkettung
record locking Satzsperre
recording Aufzeichnung
recording density Aufzeichnungsdichte, Schreibdichte
recording format Aufzeichnungsformat
recovery Wiederherstellung
recovery block Wiederherstellungsblock
recursion Rekursion

recursive programming rekursive Programmierung
recursive relationship rekursive Beziehung
redesign Reorganisation
redesign (to) reorganisieren
redevelop (to) sanieren
redevelopment Sanierung
reducing redundancy Redundanz-Reduzierung
reduction of stock Bestandssenkung
reductionism Reduktionismus
redundancy Redundanz
redundancy check Redundanz-Prüfung
redundant redundant
redundant code redundanter Code
reeducation Umschulung
reevaluation Neubewertung
reference Bezug
reference chart Kurzbeschreibung
reference data base Referenz-Datenbank
reference monitor concept Referenz-Monitor-Konzept
reference value Sollwert
reference variable Führungsgröße
referential integrity Beziehungsintegrität
refinement Verfeinerung
reflection Reflexion
reflection factor Reflexionsgrad
reflective mark Reflektormarke
refresh Bildwiederholung
refresh (to) auffrischen
refresh frequency Bildwiederholfrequenz
refreshing rate Auffrischungsrate, Bildwiederholrate
refund of costs Kostenerstattung
registration fee Registrierungsgebühr
regression analysis Regressionsanalyse
regression test Regressionstest
regulation Vorschrift
rejection rate Rückweisungsrate
relation Relation, Beziehung
relation method Relationenmethode
relational data base relationale Datenbank
relational data base system relationales Datenbanksystem
relational model relationales Modell
relational query language relationale Abfragesprache
relational structure relationale Struktur
relations chart Datengitter
relationship Beziehung
relationship analysis Beziehungsanalyse
relationship map Beziehungsmappe
relationship type Beziehungstyp
relative autonomy relative Autonomie
relative figure Beziehungszahl
relative frequency relative Häufigkeit
relative strength of resource relative Ressourcenstärke
release Freigabe, Version
relevance to tasks Aufgabenbezogenheit
reliability Zuverlässigkeit
reliability date Zuverlässigkeitsangabe
reliability study Zuverlässigkeitsuntersuchung
relocatable verschiebbar
REM = Remark
remainder Rest
remark Anmerkung, Bemerkung
remote entfernt, fern
remote batch processing Stapelfernverarbeitung
remote cancellation Fernlöschung
remote computing Fernrechnen
remote concentration dezentrale Konzentration
remote control Fernwirken
remote data entry Datenferneingabe
remote data output Datenfernausgabe
remote data processing Datenfernverarbeitung
remote data transmission Datenfernübertragung
remote diagnosis system Ferndiagnosesystem
remote job entry Auftragsferneingabe, Fern-Stapelverarbeitung
remote maintenance Fernwartung
remote monitoring Fernüberwachung
remote programming dezentrale Programmierung
remote query Fernabfrage
remote station entfernt stehende Datenstation
remote supervision Fernüberwachung
removable disk memory Wechselplattenspeicher
removable winchester disk storage Wechsel-Winchester-Plattenspeicher
rename (to) umbenennen
renewal Erneuerung, Verlängerung
rent (to) mieten
reorder (to) nachbestellen
reorganization Reorganisation
reorganize (to) reorganisieren
repair (to) reparieren
repair time Reparaturzeit
repeat action key Wiederholtaste
repeat key Dauertaste
repeating frequency counting Multimoment-Häufigkeits-Zählverfahren

repeating time measurement Multimoment-Zeit-Meßverfahren
repetitive wiederholbar
replacement costs Wiederbeschaffungskosten
replicated data base mehrfache Datenhaltung
reply Antwort, Rückantwort
report Bericht
report date Berichtstermin
report file Berichtsdatei
report on need Bedarfsbericht
report program generator Berichtsgenerator
report specification Berichtsspezifikation
report system Berichtssystem
report writing Berichterstattung
reporting Berichterstattung
representation Darstellung
representative participation repräsentative Partizipation
reproducibility Wiederholbarkeit, Reproduzierbarkeit
reprogrammable read only memory mehrfach programmierbarer Festwertspeicher
reprogramming Umprogrammierung
REPROM = Reprogrammable Read Only Memory
request Anfrage
request (to) anfragen, auffordern
request for proposal Ausschreibung
request technique Anfrage-Technik
requirement Anforderung, Bedarf
requirements analysis Anforderungsanalyse
requirements definition Anforderungsdefinition, Pflichtenheft
requirements engineering Anforderungsanalyse
requirements profile Anforderungsprofil
requirements specification Anforderungsbeschreibung
requirements survey Erheben der Anforderungen
requirements validation Anforderungstest
requiry Anforderung
requiry mode Anforderungsbetrieb
research Forschung
research and development Forschung und Entwicklung
research finding Forschungsbefund
research methodology Forschungsmethodik
research on participation Partizipationsforschung
reserve (to) reservieren

reset (to) in Grundstellung bringen, in Wartestellung bringen
resident resident, ständig anwesend
resistance Widerstand
resistance to change Veränderungswiderstand
resolution Auflösung
resolving power Auflösungsvermögen
resource Betriebsmittel, Einsatzmittel
resource access security Betriebsmittel-Zugriffsschutz
resource allocation Zuteilung von Betriebsmitteln
resource scheduling Betriebsmittelplanung
resource sharing Betriebsmittelaufteilung, Betriebsmittelverbund, gemeinsame Betriebsmittelnutzung
respond (to) antworten
response Antwort
response time Antwortzeit, Beantwortungszeit, Reaktionszeit
response time distribution Antwortzeitverhalten
responsibility Verantwortung
restart Restart, Wiederanlauf
restart on seperate system externer Wiederanlauf
restart procedure Wiederanlaufverfahren
restriction Restriktion
restructuring Umstrukturierung
result Ergebnis
result-oriented ergebnisorientiert
result-oriented design ergebnisorientierter Entwurf
retail price Verkaufspreis
retention obligation Aufbewahrungspflicht
retention period Aufbewahrungsfrist
retraining Umschulung
retrieve (to) wiederauffinden
retrieval system Auskunftssystem
reusability Wiederverwendbarkeit
reusable wiederverwendbar
reusable prototype wiederverwendbarer Prototyp
reusable software wiederverwendbare Software
reuse (to) wiederverwenden
revenue Erlös
reverse rückwärts
reverse line feed Zeilenvorschub rückwärts
review Überprüfung, Nachprüfung
review (to) überprüfen, nachprüfen

REVS = Requirements Engineering and Validation System
RFI = Radio Frequency Interference
RFP = Request For Proposal
ribbon Farbband
ribbon cartridge Farbbandkassette
right aligned rechtsbündig
right justified rechtsbündig
right of codetermination Mitbestimmungsrecht
right of usage Nutzungsrecht
rigid magnetic disk starre Magnetplatte
rigidity Starrheit
ring network Ringnetz, Schleifennetz
ring topology Ringtopologie
RIP = Raster Image Processing
RISC = Reduced Instruction Set Computer
risk Risiko
risk analysis Risikoanalyse
risk assessment Risikoeinschätzung
risk factor Risikofaktor
risk management Risikomanagement
risk management model Risikomanagement-Modell
risk theory Risikotheorie
RIU = Ring Interface Unit
RJE = Remote Job Entry
RLL = Run Length Limited
RLS = Remote Link Service
ROA = Return On Asset
robot Roboter
robot programming language Roboter-Programmiersprache
robot workcell Roboter-Arbeitsplatz
robotics Robotik
robustness Robustheit, Unempfindlichkeit
rod diagram Stabdiagramm
ROI = Return On Investment
role Rolle
role conflict Rollenkonflikt

role description Rollenbeschreibung
role expectation Rollenerwartung
roller ball Rollkugel
rollover (to) abrollen
ROM = Read Only Memory
root event Top-Ereignis
root segment Kopfsegement
rotary dial telephone set Fernsprechapparat mit Nummernscheibe
round (to) runden
rounding Rundung
rounding error Rundungsfehler
roundoff error Rundungsfehler
routing Wegwahl, Weiterleitung
routing slip Laufzettel
RPG = Report Program Generator
RPC = Remote Procedure Call
RSL = Requirements Statement Language
rubber banding Gummiband-Verfahren
rule Regel
rule based knowledge representation regelbasierte Wissensdarstellung
rule based language regelbasierte Sprache
rule based program regelbasiertes Programm
rule based system regelbasiertes System
rule interpreter Regelinterpreter
rule oriented auditing regelorientierte Prüfung
ruler Zeilenlineal
run monitoring Ablaufbeobachtung
run time Bearbeitungszeit, Laufzeit
run time compression Lauf-Längen-Komprimierung
run time limit Bearbeitungszeitgrenze
runable system lauffähiges System
running costs Betriebskosten
running period Laufzeit
running time Betriebszeit

S

SA = Structured Analysis
SADT = Structured Analysis and Design Technique
safeguard Schutzvorrichtung
safety Sicherheit
safety engineer Sicherheitsingenieur
safety facility Sicherheitseinrichtung
safety factor Sicherheitsfaktor
safety hazard Gefahrenquelle
safety lock Sicherheitsschloß
safety measure Schutzmaßnahme
safety of operation Betriebssicherheit
safety official Sicherheitsbeauftragter
safety regulation Sicherheitsbestimmung, Sicherheitsvorschrift
safety stock Sicherheitsbestand
salary account Gehaltskonto
sales Absatz, Verkauf
sales data capturing Verkaufsdatenerfassung
sales information system Verkaufsinformationssystem, Vertriebsinformationssystem
sales promotion Verkaufsförderung
sales price Verkaufspreis
sales representative Vertriebsbeauftragter
sales territory Verkaufsgebiet
sales volume Absatzmenge
salespeople profile Verkäuferprofil
salesperson Verkäufer
SAM = Sequential Access Method
sample Stichprobe
sample contract Mustervertrag
sampling Samplingverfahren, Stichprobenverfahren
sampling inspection Stichprobenprüfung
SAS = Statistical Analysis System
satellite computer system Satellitensystem
satellite network Satellitennetz
satellite link Satellitenverbindung
satellite transmission Satellitenübertragung
satellite work center Satellitenbüro
satisfaction Zufriedenheit
satisfaction level Zufriedenheitsniveau
save (to) sichern
SBC = Single Board Computer
SBS = Satellite Business System
SBU = Strategic Business Unit
scale (to) normieren, skalieren
scale of measurement Meßskala
scaled goal production Zielwert
scan (to) absuchen, abtasten

scanner Abtaster, Bildabtaster
scanner data Scanner-Daten
scanning Abtastung
scanning field Abtastbereich
scanning technique Abtastverfahren
scenario Szenario
scenario technique Szenario-Technik
schedule Zeitplan
schedule (to) zeitlich planen
scheduled downtime geplante Stillstandzeit
scheduled maintenance zeitlich geplante Wartung
scheduler Ablaufplaner, Arbeitsplaner
scheduling Ablaufplanung, Terminierung, Zeitplanung
schema Schema
science Wissenschaft
scientific method wissenschaftliche Methode
scientific problem wissenschaftliches Problem
scope of activities Wirkungsbereich
scope of freedom Freiheitsspielraum
score Punktzahl
scoring Punktbewertung
scoring model Scoring-Modell
scoring procedure Punktbewertungsverfahren
scramble (to) verwürfeln
scrambler Verwürfler
scrapbook Album, Notizblock
scrapbook function Notizblockfunktion
scratch floppy disk Leerdiskette
screen Bildschirm
screen content Bildschirminhalt
screen display Bildschirmausgabe
screen form generator Bildschirmformular-Generator
screen layout Bildschirmmaske
screen size Bildschirmgröße
screen work area Bildschirmarbeitsplatz
screen working Bildschirmarbeit
scribophone Fernzeichner
script Schreibschrift
scroll (to) rollen
scrolling Aufrollung, Roll-Modus
scrolling device Abrollgerät
SCT = Systems Construction Tool
SD = Structured Design
SDM = Spatial Data Management
SE = **Software Engineering**
seal of approval Prüfsiegel
search (to) suchen
search key Suchschlüssel
search procedure Suchverfahren
search query Suchfrage

search strategy Suchstrategie
search tree Suchbaum
seasonal variation Saisonschwankung
seat reservation Platzbuchung
second normal form zweite Normalform
secondary data Sekundärdaten
secondary key Sekundärschlüssel
secret message Geheimbotschaft
secured file gesicherte Datei
security Sicherheit, Sicherung
security event logging Aufzeichnung von Sicherheitsvergehen
security file Kennwortdatei
security kernel Sicherheitskern
security management Sicherheitsmanagement
security measure Sicherungsmaßnahme
security need Sicherheitsbedürfnis
security officer Sicherheitsbeauftragter
security requirement Sicherheitsanforderung
security risk Sicherheitsrisiko
security software Sicherungssoftware
security standard Sicherheitsstandard
security system Sicherungssystem
security technology Sicherheitstechnik
SEE = Software Engineering Environment
SEES = Software Engineering Environment System
segment Segment, Abschnitt
segment (to) segmentieren, in Abschnitte zerlegen
select (to) auswählen
selecting mode Abrufbetrieb
selection Auswahl, Selektion
selection criterion Auswahlkriterium
selection method Auswahlmethode
selection of information Informationsselektion
selection procedure Auswahlverfahren
selection process Auswahlprozeß
selection rule Auswahlregel
selectivity Auswählbarkeit
selector channel Selektorkanal
self-adapting Selbstanpassung
self-adaptive user interface selbstadaptierende Benutzerschnittstelle
self-checking selbstprüfend, Prüfziffernrechnung
self-checking procedure Prüfziffernverfahren
self-controlling Selbstregelung
self-controlling group selbststeuernde Gruppe
self-design Selbstgestaltung

self-fulfilling prophecy selbsterfüllende Prophezeiung
self-knowledge Selbstwissen
self-management Selbstmanagement
self-motivation Selbstmotivation
self-organization Selbstorganisation
self-organizing system selbstorganisierendes System
self-realization Selbstverwirklichung
self-recording Selbstaufschreibung
self-reference Selbstreferenz
self-sufficiency Autarkie
self-test Selbsttest
selling Verkauf
semantic data integrity semantische Datenintegrität
semantic data model semantisches Datenmodell
semantic memory semantisches Gedächtnis
semantic network semantisches Netz
semantics Semantik
semi-autonomous group teilautonome Gruppe
semi-direct connection halbdirekte Verbindung
semi-dynamic instrumentation halbdynamische Instrumentierung
semi-structured dialog control hybride Dialogführung
semi-structured interview halb-standardisiertes Interview
semiconductor Halbleiter
Semiconductor Chip Protection Act Mikrochip-Schutzgesetz, Halbleiter-Schutzgesetz
semiconductor memory Halbleiterspeicher
semiconfusion inkonsistente Berichterstattung
semiformal description semi-formale Beschreibung
semigraphics Halbgraphik
semiotic triangle semiotisches Dreieck
semiotics Semiotik
sending mode Sendebetrieb
sending station Sendestation
sense (to) abtasten
sense system Sinnsystem
sensing station Abfühlstation
sensitive key sensitiver Schlüssel
sensitivity Empfindlichkeit, Sensibilität
sensitivity analysis Empfindlichkeitsanalyse, Sensibilitätsanalyse, Sensitivitätsanalyse
sensor Fühler, Geber, Meßfühler
sensor screen Sensor-Bildschirm
sensorics Sensorik

separate clause Trennsymbol
separation of functions
Funktionstrennung
sequence Ablauf, Reihenfolge
sequence checking Folgeprüfung
sequence code Zählnummer
sequence number Zählnummer
sequence Reihung, Sequenz
sequence of operations Arbeitsablauf
sequential sequentiell
sequential access sequentieller Zugriff
sequential access method sequentielle Zugriffsmethode
sequential control Ablaufsteuerung
sequential file sequentielle Datei
sequential file organization sequentielle Dateiorganisation
sequential memory sequentieller Speicher
sequential processing sequentielle Verarbeitung
sequential program sequentielles Programm
sequential search sequentielle Suche
serial seriell
serial access serieller Zugriff
serial access memory Speicher mit seriellem Zugriff
serial file serielle Datei
serial interface serielle Schnittstelle
serial mode serieller Betrieb
serial printer Serialdrucker
serial printing device serielles Druckwerk
serial transmission serielle Übertragung
series of jobs Auftragskette
serve (to) bedienen, warten
server Dienstleister
server processor Dienstleisterprozessor
service area Wartungsbereich
service center Dienstleistungszentrum
service information system Kundendienst-Informationssystem
service integration Dienstintegration
service level Dienstleistungsebene, Dienstleistungsgrad
service level concept Dienstleistungsebenen-Konzept
service market Dienstleistungsmarkt
service processor Dienstleistungsprozessor
service quality Dienstgüte
service unit Bedienungseinheit
serviceability Wartbarkeit
session control Sitzungssteuerung
session layer Sitzungsschicht
set Menge
set point Führungsgröße

setup instructions Installationsanweisung
setup time Rüstzeit
share (to) gemeinsam benutzen
share of costs Kostenanteil
shared access gemeinsamer Zugriff
shared file gemeinsam benutzte Datei
sheet Bahn, Blatt
sheet feeder Einzelblatteinzug
sheet width Bahnbreite
shell Metasystem, Schale
shell model Schalenmodell
shield (to) abschirmen
shielding Abschirmung
shift (to) umschalten
shift key Umschalttaste
shift operation Schichtbetrieb
shipping Versand
shipping cardboard Transportsicherung
shop-floor control Werkstattsteuerung
shop-floor data collection Betriebsdatenerfassung
shop-floor programming Werkstattprogrammierung
shop steward Betriebsrat
short circuit Kurzschluß
short dialling Direktwahl
short form precision normale Genauigkeit
short name Kurzname
short time memory Kurzzeitgedächtnis
short-range planning kurzfristige Planung
shrink-wrap licence Schutzhüllenvertrag
shunt Nebenanschluß
side effect Nebenwirkung
side function Nebenfunktion
sign-off Abmeldung, Abnahme
sign-on Anmeldung
signal Signal
signal converter Signalumsetzer
signature reader Unterschriftenleser
significant digit wesentliche Ziffer
SIMD = Single Instruction/Multiple Data
similarity of structure Strukturähnlichkeit
simplex data transmission einseitige Datenübertragung
simplex line einseitig gerichtete Leitung
simplex mode Simplexbetrieb
simplification Vereinfachung, Rationalisierung
SIMSCRIPT = Simulation Programming Language
SIMULA = Simulation Language
simulate (to) simulieren, nachahmen
simulation Simulation, Nachahmung
simulation experiment Simulationsexperiment

simulation language Simulationssprache
simulation model Simulationsmodell
simulation program Simulationsprogramm
simulation study Simulationsstudie
simulator Simulierer
simulmatics Simulmatik
simultaneous gleichzeitig, simultan
simultaneous documentation Simultandokumentation
simultaneous peripheral operations online simultane Peripheriesteuerung
simultaneous processing simultane Verarbeitung
single board computer Einplatinencomputer
single condition einfache Bedingung
single decision making behavior einfacher Entscheidungsstil
single error Einfachfehler
single linked file organization einfach gekettete Dateiorganisation
single precision einfache Genauigkeit
single program processing Einprogrammverarbeitung
single purpose computer Einzweckcomputer
single right of use einfaches Nutzungsrecht
single sheet feeding Einzelblattzuführung
single sided einseitig
single stepping Schritt-für-Schritt-Methode
single time measurement Einzelzeitmessung
single user software Individualsoftware
single user system Einplatzsystem, Einzelplatzsystem
single way ciphering Einwegverschlüsselung
single word recognition Einzelworterkennung
sink Senke
SIPO = Serial In Parallel Out
SISO = Serial In Serial Out
site preparation räumliche Vorbereitung
situation analysis Situationsanalyse
skill Fertigkeit
skip (to) übergehen
slack Pufferzeit
slave processor Sklavenprozessor
slave system Sklavensystem, untergeordnetes System
slide menu Gleitmenü
slot Steckplatz
SLSI = Super Large Scale Integration
SLT = Solid Logic Technology

smart card intelligente Karte, Chipkarte, Schlüsselkarte
SMTP = Simple Mail Transfer Protocol
social behavior Sozialverhalten
social efficiency soziale Effizienz
social impact soziale Auswirkung
social innovation soziale Innovation
social maturity soziale Intelligenz
social need soziales Bedürfnis
Social Sciences Sozialwissenschaft
social system soziales System
Sociobiology Soziobiologie
Sociology Soziologie
sociotechnical soziotechnisch
sociotechnical approach soziotechnischer Ansatz, konsensorientierter Ansatz
sociotechnical system soziotechnisches System
soft copy Ausgabe am Bildschirm, Bildschirmausgabe
soft facts nicht nachprüfbares Erfahrungswissen
soft function key programmierbare Funktionstaste
software auditing Software-Prüfung
software ciphering Software-Verschlüsselung
software compatibility Software-Kompatibilität, Software-Verträglichkeit
software configuration Software-Konfiguration
software configuration management Software-Konfigurationsmanagement
software crisis Software-Krise
software customizing Software-Anpassung
software deficiency Software-Mangel
software design methodology Software-Entwurfsmethode
software design principle Software-Entwurfsprinzip
software developer Software-Entwickler
software development environment Software-Entwicklungsumgebung
software development system Software-Entwicklungssystem
software engineer Software-Ingenieur
software engineering Software-Engineering, Software-Technik
software environment Software-Umgebung
software ergonomics Software-Ergonomie
software error tolerance Software-Fehlertoleranz
software generator Software-Generator
software house Software-Haus
software inspection Programminspektion
software interface Software-Schnittstelle

software liability Software-Haftpflicht
software licence Software-Lizenz
software life cycle model Software-Lebenszyklus-Modell
software life cycle principle Prinzip des Software-Lebenszyklus
software maintenance Software-Wartung, Software-Pflege
software market Software-Markt
software monitoring Software-Monitoring
software package Software-Paket
software pirate Software-Pirat
software product Software-Produkt
software project Software-Projekt
software protection Software-Schutz
software quality Software-Qualität
software quality assurance Software-Qualitätssicherung
software reliability Software-Zuverlässigkeit
software reusability Software-Wiederverwendbarkeit
software reuse Software-Wiederverwendung
software tailoring Software-Anpassung
software technology Software-Technologie
software theft Software-Diebstahl
software tool Software-Werkzeug
software virus Software-Virus
solicited message abgerufene Nachricht
solution Lösung
solution approach Lösungsansatz
solution method Lösungsmethode
solution procedure Lösungsweg
sort (to) sortieren
sort algorithm Sortieralgorithmus
sort criterion Sortierbegriff
sort key Sortierschlüssel
sound generating Tongenerierung
sound level Geräuschpegel
sound reflecting schallreflektierend
source Quelle
source area Ursprungsbereich
source data Primärdaten
source data medium Primärdatenträger
source document Eingabebeleg, Originalbeleg, Urbeleg
source key Primärschlüssel
source language Quellsprache
source library Primärbibliothek
source of fire Brandursache
source program Primärprogramm, Quellprogramm, Ursprungsprogramm
source requirements planning Primärbedarfsplanung
source statement Quellanweisung
space Leerschritt, Zwischenraum

space bar Leertaste
space condition Raumbedingung
space requirement Platzbedarf, Raumbedarf
spacing Zeilenabstand
SPAG = Standards Promotion and Application Group
spaghetti program Spaghetti-Programm
SPARC = Standards Planning and Requirements Committee
spare capacity Leerkapazität
spare part Ersatzteil
spatial data management räumliche Datenverwaltung
special brightness besondere Helligkeit
special character Sonderzeichen
special conditions of contract besondere Vertragsbedingungen
Special Economic Informatics Besondere Wirtschaftsinformatik
special task Spezialaufgabe
specialised journal Fachzeitschrift
specialist task Fachaufgabe
specialization Spezialisierung
specification Pflichtenheft, Spezifikation
specification certificate Spezifikationsschein
specification language Spezifikationssprache
specify (to) spezifizieren
specimen Muster
speech Sprache
speech analysis Sprachanalyse
speech annotation system Sprachannotationssystem
speech communications Sprachkommunikation
speech compression Sprachkompression
speech encoder Sprachcodierer
speech filing system Sprachspeichersystem
speech input Spracheingabe
speech output Sprachausgabe
speech output system Sprachausgabesystem
speech processing Sprachverarbeitung
speech retrieval Sprachwiedergabe
speech signal Sprachsignal
speech synthesis Sprachsynthese
speed call Direktruf
speed call network Direktrufnetz
spell check program Rechtschreib-Prüfprogramm
spell checker Rechtschreib-Prüfprogramm
sphere of actions Wirkungsbereich
spherical printhead Kugelkopf

spiderweb diagram Spinnennetz-Diagramm
split screen geteilter Bildschirm
Spool = Simultanuous Peripheral Operations Online
spool file Spooldatei
spreadsheet Arbeitsblatt, Tabellenkalkulation
spreadsheet system Tabellenkalkulationssystem
SPSS = Statistical Package for the Social Science
SPPS = Strategic Production Planning and Scheduling
square circle diagram Flächen-Kreisdiagramm
squaring diagram Flächendiagramm
squaring graphic Flächengraphik
SQL = Structured Query Language
SSADM = Structured Systems Analysis and Design Methodology
SSI = Small Scale Integration
stability Stabilität
stability analysis Stabilitätsanalyse
stack Keller
stack memory Kellerspeicher
stack pointer Kellerzähler
stacker Ablagefach
staff Personalbestand
staff allocation Personalzuordnung
staff association Betriebsrat
staff hiring Personalbeschaffung
staff planning Personalplanung
staff project organization Stabs-Projektorganisation
staff qualification Personalqualifikation
staff reduction Personalabbau
staff training Personalschulung
staff turnover Personalumschichtung
staffing Personalausstattung, Personalwesen
staffing table Stellenbesetzungsplan
stage hypothesis Stufenkonzept
stage model Stufenmodell
stagewise changeover stufenweise Umstellung, Teilumstellung
stagewise refinement stufenweise Verfeinerung
stand alone unabhängig arbeitend
standard Norm, Standard
standard application program Standardanwendungsprogramm
standard data format Standarddatenformat
standard digit Kennziffer
standard figure Kennzahl

standard figure analysis Kennzahlenanalyse
standard figure system Kennzahlensystem
standard of performance Leistungsnorm
standard price Einheitspreis
standard program Standardprogramm
standard report Standardauswertung, Standardbericht
standard setting Normenfestsetzung
standard software Standardsoftware
standard specification Normvorschrift
standard text Standardtext
standardization Normung, Standardisierung
standardization committee Normenausschuß
standardize (to) normen
standardized interview standardisiertes Interview
standardized programming normierte Programmierung
standardized user interface einheitliche Benutzeroberfläche
standby Reserve
standby computer Ausweichcomputer, Bereitschaftsrechner
standby equipment Ersatzgerät
standby power generator Notstromaggregat
standing journal entry Dauerbuchung
standing order procedure Bestellpunktverfahren
star network Sternnetz
star topology Sterntopologie
start (to) anlaufen, beginnen, ingangsetzen
start/stop operation Start/Stop-Betrieb
start date Beginntermin
start page number Anfangsseitennummer
start time Anlaufzeit
start up expense Anlaufkosten
state Zustand
state analysis Zustandsanalyse
state diagram Zustandsdiagramm
state key Zustandsanzeiger
statement Anweisung
statement of functions Funktionsbeschreibung
static statisch
static authorizing statische Autorisierung
static file statische Datei
static file backup statische Dateisicherung
static help system statisches Hilfesystem
static instrumentation statische Instrumentierung

static memory statischer Speicher
static program analysis statische Programmanalyse
static quality measure statisches Qualitätsmaß
static system statisches System
static testing statisches Testen
static topology statische Topologie
statistical analysis statistische Analyse
statistics Statistik
statistics interpreter Statistikinterpretierer
status Istzustand, Status
status indicator Statusanzeiger
status information Statusinformation
status quo portfolio Status-quo-Portfolio
steering committee Lenkungsausschuß
step Schritt
stepwise changeover schrittweise Umstellung
stepwise refinement schrittweise Verfeinerung
stewardship Verwaltung
sticker Aufklebezettel
stochastic stochastisch
stochastic heuristics stochastische Heuristik
stock Lager, Lagerbestand
stock control Lagersteuerung
stock inventory management system Warenwirtschaftssystem
stock on hand verfügbarer Lagerbestand
stock receipt Lagerzugang
stock replenishment Wiederauffüllung des Lagers
stock taking Inventur
stock turnover Lagerumschlag
storage Speicher
storage capacity Speicherkapazität
storage check Speicherkontrolle
storage device Speichergerät
storage function Speicherfunktion
storage hierarchy Speicherhierarchie
storage management Speicherverwaltung
storage medium Speichermedium
storage mode Speicherform
storage organization Speicherorganisation
storage partition Speicherbereich
storage technology Speichertechnik
storage unit Speicherwerk
store (to) speichern
store and forward switching Speichervermittlung
storing authority speichernde Stelle
strategic business unit strategische Geschäftseinheit

strategic early warning strategische Frühwarnung
strategic gap strategische Lücke
strategic goal strategisches Ziel
strategic information management strategisches Informationsmanagement
strategic information system strategisches Informationssystem
strategic information system component strategische Informationssystem-Einheit
strategic information system planning strategische Informationssystem-Planung
strategic key factor strategischer Schlüsselfaktor
strategic management strategisches Management
strategic planning strategische Planung
strategic success position strategische Erfolgsposition
strategic test planning strategische Testplanung
strategic thrust strategische Stoßrichtung
strategy Strategie
strategy planning Strategieplanung
streamer tape Sicherungsband
strength Stärke
strengths/weaknesses analysis Stärken/Schwächen-Analyse
strengths/weaknesses profile Stärken/Schwächen-Profil
stress Streß, Beanspruchung, Belastung
stress program Streßprogramm
stress stability Belastbarkeit
stressor Streßfaktor
string Zeichenfolge
string processing String-Verarbeitung, Zeichenfolgeverarbeitung
structure Struktur
structure (to) gliedern, strukturieren
structure block Strukturblock
structure diagram Strukturdiagramm
structure modelling tool Struktur-Modellierungswerkzeug
structure of program Programmaufbau
structure preserving strukturerhaltend
structured analysis strukturierte Analyse
structured box chart Struktogramm
structured data type strukturierter Datentyp
structured design strukturierter Entwurf
structured program strukturiertes Programm
structured program specification strukturierte Programmbeschreibung
structured programming strukturierte Programmierung

structured systems analysis strukturierte Systemanalyse
structured systems design strukturierter Systementwurf
structured testing ablaufbezogenes Testen
structured walk-through formale Programminspektion, strukturiertes Testen
structuredness Strukturiertheit
structuring Strukturierung
structuring concept Strukturkonzept
structuring method Strukturierungsmethode
stub card Abrißkarte
study of current system Istzustandsuntersuchung, Untersuchen des Istzustands
stylus Griffel
subfunction Teilfunktion
subject area Sachgebiet
subject data base Sachgebietsdatenbasis
subject dependent decision making style feldabhängiger Entscheidungsstil
subject goal Sachziel
subject independent decision making style feldunabhängiger Entscheidungsstil
subject index Sachverzeichnis
subjective subjektiv
subjective information requirement subjektiver Informationsbedarf
subjective job situation subjektive Arbeitssituation
submenu Untermenü
subordinate Untergebener
subphase Teilphase
subproblem Teilproblem
subprogram Unterprogramm
subproject Teilprojekt
subroutine Unterprogramm
subschema Teilschema
subscriber Teilnehmer
subscriber line Amtsleitung
subscriber station Teilnehmerstation
subscript Indexliste
subset Dialekt, Teilmenge
substantial organizing substantielles Organisieren
substitute due date Ersatztermin
substitution Ersatz, Substitution
subsystem Teilsystem, Untersystem
subtask Teilaufgabe
subtotal Zwischensumme
success Erfolg
success factor Erfolgsfaktor
success factor analysis Erfolgsfaktoren-Analyse
success positioning Erfolgsposition
success potential Erfolgspotential
suitability Eignung
sum (to) summieren
summation check Summenkontrolle
super computer Supercomputer
superior Vorgesetzter
supersmart card intelligente Chipkarte
supervisor Vorgesetzter
supplement Ergänzung
supplementary product Ergänzungsprodukt
supplier Lieferant
supplier's support Anbieterunterstützung
supply chain Versorgungskette
supply of software Software-Angebot
support Unterstützung
support (to) unterstützen
support activity Unterstützungsmaßnahme
support function Unterstützungsfunktion
support service Unterstützungsdienstleistung
support task Unterstützungsaufgabe
suppression Entstörung
survey Erhebung, Erfassung
survey finding Erhebungsbefund, Untersuchungsbefund
survey of current system Erheben des Istzustands, Istaufnahme, Istzustandserfassung
survey technique Erfassungstechnik, Erhebungsmethode
SUS = Software Update Service
SVA = Strategic Value Analysis
swap out (to) auslagern
swapper Zahlendreher
swapping Seiten ein- und auslagern
SWIFT = Society for Worldwide Interbank Financial Telecommunications
switch Schalter
switch (to) schalten
switchboard Vermittlungsstelle
switched connection Wählverbindung
switching algebra Schaltalgebra
switching center Vermittlungsstelle
switching technology Vermittlungstechnik
sx = simplex
symbolic address symbolische Adresse
symbolic computing symbolisches Rechnen
symbolic information processing symbolische Informationsverarbeitung
symbolic logic symbolische Logik
symbolic organizing symbolisches Organisieren
symbolic testing symbolisches Testen

symposion wissenschaftliche Tagung
symposium wissenschaftliche Tagung
symptom Symptom, Anzeichen
synchronization Synchronisierung
synchronization device Synchronisiereinheit
synchronous synchron, gleichlaufend
synchronous data transmission synchrone Datenübertragung
synchronous mode Synchronbetrieb
synectics Synektik
synergetics Synergetik
synergy Synergie, Zusammenwirken
synonym Synonym, sinnverwandtes Wort
syntax Syntax, Satzbau, Satzlehre
syntax diagram Syntaxdiagramm
synthesis Synthese
synthetic inferencing synthetisches Schlußfolgern
synthetic job synthetischer Job
synthetic thinking synthetisches Denken
systematization Systematisierung
system of tasks Aufgabensystem
system of terms Begriffssystem
systemic thinking systemisches Denken
systems analysis Systemanalyse
systems analyst Systemplaner
systems approach Systemansatz
systems architecture Systemarchitektur
systems auditing Systemprüfung
systems auditor Systemrevisor
systems availability Systemverfügbarkeit
systems behavior Systemverhalten
systems boundary Systemgrenze
systems call Systemaufruf
systems certificate Systemschein
systems check Systemprüfung
systems command Systemkommando
systems component Systemkomponente
systems configuration Systemkonfiguration
systems crash Systemabbruch, Systemausfall, Systemzusammenbruch
systems date Systemdatum
systems default Systemstandard
systems design Grobprojektierung, Systementwurf
systems designer Systemgestalter
systems development Systementwicklung
systems documentation Systemdokumentation
systems engineering Systemtechnik
systems environment Systemumgebung
systems error report Systemfehlermeldung
systems exit Systemausgang
systems failure Systemausfall
systems generating Systemgenerierung
systems house Systemhaus
systems implementation Systemeinführung, Systemimplementierung
systems integration Systemintegration
systems layout Systemauslegung
systems load Systembelastung
systems log-off Systemabmeldung
systems log-on Systemanmeldung
systems logging Systemaufzeichnung
systems maintenance Systempflege
systems operator Systembediener
systems outage Systemausfall
systems parameter Systemparameter
systems planning Systemplanung
systems planning methodology Methodik Systemplanung
systems program Systemprogramm
systems programmer Systemprogrammierer
systems programming language Systemprogrammiersprache
systems recovery Systemwiederherstellung
systems research Systemforschung
systems selection Systemauswahl
systems sign-off Systemabmeldung
systems sign-on Systemanmeldung
systems software Systemsoftware
systems structure Systemstruktur
systems teachings Systemlehre
systems test Systemtest
systems theory Systemtheorie
systems thinking Systemdenken
systems unit Systemeinheit
systems usage Systemnutzung

T

TA = Technology Assessment
TA = Terminal Adapter
table Tabelle
table control Tabellensteuerung
table generator Formulargenerator
table header Tabellenkopf
table of entity type attributes Objekttypen-Attribute-Tabelle
table of entity types Objekttypen-Tabelle
table of factors Faktorentabelle
table oriented planning modelling language tabellenorientierte Planungssprache
table plotter Tischplotter
tactical management taktisches Management
tactical plan Aktionsplan
tactile taktil, tastbar, den Tastsinn betreffend
tactile feedback taktile Rückmeldung
tactile man-machine interface technology taktile Schnittstellentechnik
taking the order Auftragsannahme
tangible erfaßbar, quantifizierbar
tangible benefits erfaßbarer Nutzen, quantifizierbarer Nutzen
tangible costs erfaßbare Kosten
tap (to) abhören
tap-proof telephone set abhörsicheres Telephon
tape Band
tape archive Bandarchiv
tape capacity Bandkapazität
tape density Banddichte
tape error Bandfehler
tape file Banddatenbestand
tape speed Bandgeschwindigkeit
tape spool Bandspule
tapping method Abhörmethode
target Ziel
target analysis Zielanalyse
target concept Sollkonzept
target data processing Zieldatenverarbeitung
target date geplantes Fertigstellungsdatum
target portfolio Soll-Portfolio, Ziel-Portfolio
target statement Zielanweisung
target system Sollzustand
target system-based approach sollzustandsorientierter Ansatz
task Aufgabe
task assignment Aufgabenzuordnung
task characteristic Aufgabenmerkmal

task description Aufgabenbeschreibung
task force Planungsgruppe, Projektgruppe
task force group reine Projektorganisation
task force in staff function Einfluß-Projektorganisation
task management Prozeßmanagement, Prozeßverwaltung
task modification Aufgabenwandel
task planning Aufgabenplanung
task scope Aufgabenumfang
task specific aufgabenspezifisch
task structuring Aufgabenstrukturierung
task synthesis Aufgabensynthese
task type Aufgabentyp
tasks of systems planning Aufgaben der Systemplanung
taxonomy Klassifizierung
TBF = Time Between Failures
TBT = Technology Based Training
TBx = Telebox
TCAM = Telecommunications Access Method
TCP = Transport Control Protocol
TCS = Telecommunications System
TDM = Time Division Multiplexing
TDMA = Time Division Multiplexing Access
team oriented inspection strukturiertes Gruppengespräch
teamwork Gruppenarbeit
technical and office protocol Schnittstelle für Fabrik- und Büroautomatisierung
technical data protection technischer Datenschutz
technical design technischer Entwurf
technical regulation technische Vorschrift
technical service technischer Kundendienst
technical specification technische Spezifikation
technical support technische Unterstützung
technics Technik, Ingenieurwissenschaft
technique Methode, Verfahren
technocentric approach technozentrischer Ansatz
technological change technologischer Wandel
technological constraint technische Beschränkung, technische Grenze
technological determinism technologischer Determinismus
technological innovation technische Innovation

193

technological integration

technological integration technische Integration
technological system Techniksystem
technology Technik, Technologie
technology assessment Technologiefolgen-Abschätzung
technology assessment research Technologie-Wirkungsforschung
technology forecasting Technologievorhersage
technology impact analysis Technologiewirkungsanalyse
technology management Technologiemanagement
technology strategy Technologiestrategie
technology transfer Technologietransfer
technometry Technometrie
Technovation = techno(logy and inno)vation
teleboard Fernzeichner
telebox service Telebox-Dienst
telebridge Fernbrücke
telecommunications Telekommunikation
telecommunications engineering Fernmeldetechnik
telecommunications equipment regulation Fernmeldeanlagen-Gesetz
telecommunications jurisdiction Fernmeldehoheit
telecommunications line Fernmeldeweg
telecommunications network Telekommunikationsnetz
telecommunications order Telekommunikationsordnung
telecommunications service Fernmeldedienst, Telekommunikationsdienst
telecommunications system Telekommunikationssystem
telecommuting Büroarbeit außer Haus, EDV-Heimarbeit, Telearbeit, informationstechnik-gestützte Heimarbeit
teleconference Telekonferenz, Fernsprechkonferenz
telecredit card Telephon-Kreditkarte
Telefax = Teleprinter Facsimile Exchange
telefax service Telefax-Dienst
telehome working Teleheimarbeit
teleletter service Telebrief-Dienst
telematics Telematik
telemessage Fernschreiben
telemetering Fernmessen, Telemetrie
telemetry Telemetrie
telephone Fernsprecher, Telephon
telephone channel Fernsprechkanal

telephone connection Fernsprechanschluß, Telephonanschluß
telephone exchange Fernsprechamt, Fernsprechvermittlung, Telephonvermittlung
telephone monitoring Telephonüberwachung
telephone network Fernsprechnetz
telephone subscriber Fernsprechteilnehmer
telephony Telephonie, Fernsprechen
telepost Telepost
teleprinter Fernschreiber
teleprinter exchange Fernschreibverkehr
teleprocessing Datenfernverarbeitung, Fernverarbeitung
teleprogram Teleprogramm
teleprogramming Teleprogrammierung
teleservice Teledienst, Teleservice
teleshopping Heimkauf, Telekauf
telesoftware Telesoftware
Teletex = Teleprinter Text Exchange
teletex service Teletex-Dienst
teletext Fernsehtext, Teletext
teletype code Fernschreibcode
teleworker Heimarbeiter, Telearbeiter
teleworking EDV-Heimarbeit, Telearbeit
teleworkplace Heimarbeitsplatz
telewriter Fernschreiber
Telex = Teleprinter Exchange
telex Fernschreiben
telex network Telexnetz
telex service Telex-Dienst
telex traffic Fernschreibverkehr
TEMEX = Telemetry Exchange
temex service Temex-Dienst
TEMPEST = Temporary Emanation and Spurious Transmission
tempest device Tempest-Gerät
template Schablone
template programming Schablonen-Programmierung
temporary data medium Datenzwischenträger
ten keypad Zehnertastatur
tendency Tendenz
tender Angebot
tender analysis Angebotsanalyse
tender evaluation Angebotsbewertung
tendering Angebotseinholung
terminal Endgerät, Terminal
terminal interface Endgeräteschnittstelle
terminal ready Datenstation bereit
terminal security Datenstationsschutz
terminal type Art der Datenstation
termination Beendigung
terminology Fachsprache, Terminologie

test Test, Versuch
test (to) prüfen, testen
test data Testdaten
test data generator Testdaten-Generator
test documentation Testdokumentation
test driver Testtreiber
test installation Testinstallation
test of hypothesis Hypothesenprüfung
test of structure Strukturtest
test pattern Testmuster
test program Testprogramm
test coverage Testabdeckungsgrad
test report Testbericht
test result Testergebnis
test run Probelauf, Testlauf
testability Testbarkeit
testcase Testfall
testcase matrix Testfallmatrix
testing Prüfung, Testen
testing device Prüfgerät
testing environment Testumgebung
testing method Testmethode
testing plan Testplan
testing productivity Testproduktivität
testing rate Testrate
testing resistance Testresistenz
testing schedule zeitlicher Testplan
testing strategy Teststrategie
testing system Testsystem
text communications Textkommunikation
text page Textseite
text processing Textverarbeitung
text processor Textprozessor
text reducing mechanism Text-Reduktionsmechanismus
textfax service Textfax-Dienst
textline grouping Absatzgestaltung
theory of bargaining Theorie des Verhandelns
thermo printer Thermodrucker
thermo transfer printer Thermo-Transfer-Drucker
thesaurus Thesaurus
thin film memory Dünnfilmspeicher
third normal form dritte Normalform
threat Bedrohung
threat analysis Bedrohungsanalyse
three-dimensional model dreidimensionales Modell
three-dimensional system dreidimensionales System
three-level concept Drei-Schema-Konzept
threshold Barriere
throughput Durchsatz
throughput time Durchsatzzeit
throw-away prototype Wegwerf-Prototyp
time analysis Zeitanalyse

time analysis report Arbeitstagebuch
time and attendance terminal Zeiterfassungsstation
time and motion measurement System vorbestimmter Zeiten
time and motion study Zeit- und Bewegungstudie
time between failures Zeit zwischen Fehlern
time comparison Zeitvergleich
time critical operation zeitkritischer Arbeitsgang
time determination Zeiterfassung
time division multiplexing Zeitmultiplexing
time estimate Zeitschätzung
time estimate report Tätigkeitsbericht
time horizon Zeithorizont
time management Arbeitstechnik
time measurement Zeitmessung
time measurement unit Vorgabezeit-Einheit
time multiplexing procedure Zeitmultiplex-Verfahren
time need Zeitbedarf
time oriented sequential control zeitgeführte Ablaufsteuerung
time out Zeitbegrenzung
time requirement Zeitanforderung, Zeitbedarf
time sharing Time-Sharing, Zeitaufteilung
time sharing computer center Time-Sharing-Rechenzentrum
time sharing mode Teilnehmerbetrieb
time sharing system Teilnehmersystem
time slice Zeitscheibe
time slicing Zeitteilung
time span Zeitraum
time study Zeitaufnahme, Zeitstudie
time study sheet Zeitaufnahmebogen
time theft Zeitdiebstahl
time/costs/progress diagram Zeit/Kosten/Fortschrittsdiagramm
timeliness Rechtzeitigkeit
timer Realzeituhr
tissue filter Gewebefilter
TMO-Technology = Thermo-Magnetic-Optic Technology
TMU = Time Measurement Unit
token Marke
token passing procedure Token-Passing-Verfahren
toll-free number gebührenfreie Telephonnummer
toner Farbpulver
tool Werkzeug

tool interface Werkzeugschnittstelle
tool kit Werkzeugkasten
TOP = Technical and Office Protocols
top down design Top-down-Entwurf
top down strategy Top-down-Strategie
top down test Top-down-Test
top event Top-Ereignis
top management Führungsspitze
top of forms Blattanfang
topicality Aktualität
topography Topographie
topology Topologie
total breakdown Totalausfall
total changeover Gesamtumstellung, Totalumstellung
total costs Vollkosten
total processing time Gesamtbearbeitungszeit
total sum Endsumme
totalizer Addiermaschine
touch sensitive panel Fingerspitzen-Tablett
touch sensitive screen berührungsempfindlicher Bildschirm, Kontaktbildschirm
TP = Teleprocessing
TP-Monitor = Teleprocessing Monitor
tpi = tracks per inch
trace Ereignisverfolgung
tracer Ablaufverfolger
tracing Ablaufverfolgung, Pfadverfolgung
tracing procedure Tracingverfahren
track Spur
track density Spurdichte
track width Spurbreite
tracker ball Ballroller, Rollkugel
tractor Traktor
trade Gewerbe, Handel
trade directory Firmenverzeichnis
trade discount Rabatt
trademark protection Warenzeichenschutz
traffic analysis Verkehrsanalyse
traffic quality Verkehrsgüte
trailer Nachsatz
train (to) schulen
trainee program Trainingsprogramm
training Schulung
training requirement Schulungsanforderung
training schedule Schulungsplan
transaction Bewegung, Vorgang, Transaktion
transaction analysis Transaktionsanalyse
transaction data Bewegungsdaten

transaction diagram Transaktionsdiagramm
transaction driven mode Teilhaberbetrieb
transaction driven system Teilhabersystem
transaction file Bewegungsdatei
transaction mode Transaktionsbetrieb
transaction number Transaktionsnummer
transaction pricing transaktionsorientierte Kostenverrechnung
transaction rate Transaktionsrate
transaction routing Transaktionswegleitung
transaction system Transaktionssystem
transfer of control Ablaufsprung
transitive transitiv
transitive dependency transitive Abhängigkeit
translator Übersetzer
transmission Übermittlung, Übertragung
transmission capacity Übertragungskapazität
transmission channel Übertragungskanal
transmission key Sendeschlüssel
transmission line Übertragungsleitung
transmission medium Übertragungsmedium
transmission mode Übertragungsmodus
transmission property Übertragungseigenschaft
transmission rate Übertragungsrate
transmission speed Übertragungsgeschwindigkeit
transmission technology Übertragungstechnik
transmit (to) übermitteln
transparency Durchschaubarkeit, Transparenz
transport (to) transportieren
transport layer Transportschicht
transposition Vertauschung
transposition error Drehfehler, Vertauschungsfehler
tree Baum
tree computer Baumrechner
tree structure Baumstruktur
tree topology Baumtopologie
trend Tendenz, Trend
trend analysis Trendanalyse
trend identification Trendermittlung
trial and error Versuch und Irrtum
trial installation Probeinstallation
trial mode Versuchsbetrieb
trigger Auslöser
trigger chain Vorgangskette
trigger concept Vorgangskonzept
trigger event auslösendes Ereignis

trigger oriented data processing
aktionsorientierte Datenverarbeitung,
vorgangsorientierte Datenverarbeitung
trigger oriented system
aktionsorientiertes System,
vorgangsorientiertes System
trouble report Fehlerbericht
troubleshooting Fehlersuche und
Fehlerbeseitigung
truncate (to) abschneiden, abstreichen
trunk line Fernleitung
TSS = Telephone Software Service
TSS = Time Sharing System
TTC = Teletype Code
Ttx = Teletex
TTY = Teletype Terminal
tumbling Torkeln
tune (to) abstimmen
tuning Tuning, Abstimmung
tupel Tupel
turn Umdrehung
turn off (to) abschalten
turn-key system schlüsselfertiges System
turnover Umsatz, Umschlag,
Umschichtung
turnover rate Umschlagshäufigkeit
tutorial program Lehrprogramm,
Tutorialprogramm
TV blank Austastlücke
twin printer Zwillingsdrucker
two-dimensional model zweidimensionales
Modell
two-dimensional system
zweidimensionales System
typamatic key Dauerfunktionstaste
type Typ, Drucktype
type band printer Typenbanddrucker
type declaration Typenvereinbarung
type face Schriftbild
type of benefits Nutzenart
type of end-user Benutzertyp
type of implementation
Implementierungsart
type of strategy Strategietyp
type printer Typendrucker
type size Schriftgröße
type wheel Typenrad
typewriter Schreibmaschine
typing error Schreibfehler, Tippfehler

U

UDC = Universal Decimal Classification
UHSIC = Ultra High Speed Integrated Circuit
UL = User Language
ultra computer Ultracomputer
unattended printing bedienerloses Drucken
unauthorized access unbefugter Zugriff
unauthorized deciphering unbefugte Entschlüsselung
unblocked record ungeblockter Satz
unbundling Entbündelung
uncertainty Ungewißheit
unciphered data unverschlüsselte Daten
unconstrained criterion Extremalkriterium
unconstrained goal Extremalziel
underload Leerkapazität
understandability Verständlichkeit
undo Widerruf
unfair competition unlauterer Wettbewerb
unformatted data unformatierte Daten
unic selling position einmalige Verkaufsposition
uniformity Einheitlichkeit
uninterruptable power supply unterbrechungsfreie Stromversorgung
uninterruptable power supply system Notstromaggregat
union-controlled approach gewerkschaftlicher Gegenmachtansatz
unipolar transistor unipolarer Transistor
unit costs Stückkosten
unit of information Informationseinheit
univariable forecasting univariable Prognose
Universal Decimal Classification Universelle Dezimalklassifikation
universal product code Einheitliche Artikelnumerierung
universal programming language universelle Programmiersprache
unjustified text Flattersatz
unscheduled ungeplant, außerplanmäßig
unscheduled downtime ungeplante Stillstandzeit
unscheduled maintenance ungeplante Wartung
unstructured program Spaghetti-Programm
unstructured task unstrukturierte Aufgabe
unusual end Absturz, Systemabbruch
unusual end of program Programmabbruch

UPC = Universal Product Code
update Änderung, Pflege
update (to) aktualisieren, ändern, fortschreiben, pflegen
update anomaly Mutationsanomalie
updating Stammdatenpflege
upgradability Verbesserungsfähigkeit
upgrade Aufrüstung, Verbesserung
upgrade (to) nachrüsten, verbessern
UPL = Universal Programming Language
upload Hinaufladen
upper case character Großbuchstabe
UPS = Uninterruptable Power Supply
uptime Benutzerzeit
upward communication Aufwärtskommunikation
upward compatible aufwärtsverträglich
upward compatibility Aufwärtskompatibilität
upward compilation Aufwärtsübersetzung
usability Benutzbarkeit, Verwendbarkeit
usage Nutzung
usage capability Benutzungsmöglichkeit
usage convenience Benutzungsfreundlichkeit
usage costs Nutzungskosten
usage duration Nutzungsdauer
usage permission Nutzungsbewilligung
usage regulation Benutzungsrecht
usage right Werknutzungsrecht
use (to) benutzen, anwenden
user Anwender, Benutzer, Nutzer
user acceptance Benutzerakzeptanz
user adequance Benutzeradäquanz
user analysis Benutzeranalyse
user area Fachabteilung
user area memory Benutzerspeicher
user authority Benutzerberechtigung
user consulting Benutzerberatung
user controlled benutzergesteuert
user controlled dialog benutzergesteuerter Dialog
user data Benutzerdaten
user data model externes Datenmodell
user design Benutzerentwurf
user dialog Benutzerdialog
user dictionary Benutzerkatalog
user division Fachabteilung
user driven benutzergesteuert
user driven computing benutzergesteuerte Datenverarbeitung
user error Benutzerfehler
user exit Benutzerausgang
user field Benutzerfeld
user file Benutzerdatei
user friendliness Benutzerfreundlichkeit

user group Anwendergruppe, Benutzergruppe
user guidance Benutzerführung
user identification Benutzeridentifizierung
user identification and verification Benutzeridentifizierung und -überprüfung
user interface Benutzeroberfläche, Benutzerschnittstelle
user interface technique Dialogtechnik
user involvement Benutzerbeteiligung
user language Benutzersprache
user liaison officer Fachabteilungskoordinator
user load Benutzeranzahl
user message Benutzernachricht
user model Benutzermodell
user monitoring Benutzerkontrolle
user objective Benutzerziel
user orientation Benutzerorientierung
user participation Benutzerbeteiligung
user profile Benutzerprofil
user program Benutzerprogramm
user query Benutzerabfrage
user requirement Benutzeranforderung
user report Benutzerbericht

user research Benutzerforschung
user satisfaction Benutzerzufriedenheit
user service center Benutzerservice-Zentrum, Informationszentrum
user support Benutzerunterstützung
user support service Benutzerservice
user terminal Benutzerstation
user test data Testdaten des Benutzers
user training Benutzerschulung
user transaction Benutzertransaktion
user view Benutzersicht
user's documentation Benutzerdokumentation
user's guide Benutzerhandbuch
user's illusion Benutzerillusion
user's manual Benutzerhandbuch
user's skill Benutzerfertigkeit
USP = Unic Selling Position
usufructuary right Nutzungsrecht, Werknutzungsrecht
utility Nützlichkeit
utility program Dienstprogramm
utilization Nutzung, Verwertung
utilization goal Verwertungsziel
utilization ratio Nutzungsgrad

V

valid gültig
validity Gültigkeit, Meßtauglichkeit, Validität
validity of content inhaltliche Validität
validity test Validitätstest
valuator Wertgeber
value Wert
value activity Wertaktivität
value added network Mehrwertnetz
value added service Mehrwertdienst
value analysis Wertanalyse
value analysis job plan Wertanalyse-Arbeitsplan
value assurance Wertgestaltung
value benefit analysis Nutzwertanalyse
value chain Wertkette
value chain analysis Wertketten-Analyse
value data Wertdaten
value engineering Wertgestaltung
value improvement Wertverbesserung
value of benefit Nutzwert
value of information Informationswert
value system Wertsystem
VAN = Value Added Network
VANS = Value Added Network Services
VAR = Value Added Reseller
variable Variable, Veränderliche
variable costs variable Kosten
variable data variable Daten
variable length record Satz variabler Länge
variance Abweichung, Schwachstelle, Varianz
variance analysis Abweichungsanalyse
variance report Abweichungsbericht
VAS = Value Added Service
VDT = Visual Display Terminal
VDU = Visual Display Unit
vector Vektor
vector computer Vektorrechner
vector graphics Vektorgraphik
vector processor Vektorprozessor
vendor Lieferant
vendor proposal Lieferantenvorschlag
vendor selection Lieferantenauswahl
vendor support Lieferantenunterstützung
Venn diagram Venn-Diagramm
verbal description verbale Beschreibung
verification Überprüfung, Verifikation
verification of speaker Sprecherüberprüfung
verify (to) überprüfen, verifizieren
version Ausführung, Modell
version planning Versionsplanung
versioning evolutionäres Prototyping

vertical parity Querparität
VHLL = Very High Level Language
VHSIC = Very High Speed Integrated Circuit
viability Lebensfähigkeit
vibrating mirror display Schwingspiegel-Bildschirm
video communications Bewegtbild-Kommunikation
video conference Bewegtbild-Konferenz
video digitizer Bewegtbild-Digitalisierer
video disk Bewegtbild-Platte
video editing system Bewegtbild-Aufbereitungssystem
video memory Bewegtbild-Speicher
video refresh memory Bewegtbild-Wiederholspeicher
video screen Bewegtbild-Sichtgerät
video teleconference Bewegtbild-Telekonferenz
video transmission Bewegtbild-Übertragung
videophone Bewegtbild-Fernsprecher
4GL = fourth generation language
view data Sichtdaten
virtual virtuell
virtual address virtuelle Adresse
virtual communications virtuelle Kommunikation
virtual connection virtuelle Verbindung
virtual line virtuelle Leitung
virtual machine virtuelle Maschine
virtual map virtuelle Mappe
virtual operating system virtuelles Betriebssystem
virtual periphery virtuelle Peripherie
virtual storage virtueller Speicher
virtual terminal virtuelles Endgerät
virus Virus
virus program Virus-Programm
visibility Durchschaubarkeit
visual display terminal Sichtgerät
visual file Sichtkartei
visual symbol Bildzeichen
visualization Visualisierung
visualization of process Prozeßvisualisierung
visualization technique Visualisierungstechnik
VLAN = Very Local Area Network
VLSI = Very Large Scale Integration
vocoder = vo(ice and)coder
vocoder Sprachcodierer
voice Sprache
voice box Sprachbox
voice coder Sprachcodierer
voice communications Sprachübertragung

voice message exchange system
Sprachnachrichtensystem
voice message service
Sprachspeicherdienst
voice recognition Spracherkennung
volatile memory flüchtiger Speicher
volume Datenträger
volume cleanup Datenträger löschen

volume model Volumenmodell
VTAM = **Virtual Teleprocessing Access Method**
VTOC = **Volume Table of Contents**
vulnerability Verwundbarkeit
vulnerability analysis
Verwundbarkeitsanalyse

W

walk-through Programmtest
WAN = Wide Area Network
warehouse Lager
warm backup computing center warmes Ausweich-Rechenzentrum
warm restart warmer Wiederanlauf
warm systems restart Warmstart
warning device Melder
warning indicator Warnanzeige
warning message Warnmeldung
warning system Warnsystem
warranty Gewährleistung
waste paper Altpapier
watchdog Wachhund
waterfall model Wasserfallmodell
weakness Schwäche
weighted crossfoot gewichtete Quersumme
weighted ratio method Gewichtungsmethode
weighting Gewichtung
well structured problem gut strukturiertes Problem, wohlstrukturiertes Problem
what/if analysis Was/Wenn-Analyse
wheel network Sternnetz
wheel printer Raddrucker
wheel topology Sterntopologie
white box Weißer Kasten
white box principle Prinzip des Weißen Kastens
white box test Weißer-Kasten-Test
white box testing programmbezogenes Testen
white line skipping Bildkompression
why-technique Warum-Technik
wide area network Weitverkehrsnetz
wideband Breitband
wild card universelles Ersatzzeichen
wild growth Wildwuchs
winchester disk Winchester-Plattenspeicher
winchester disk drive Festplattenlaufwerk
window Fenster
windowing Fenstertechnik
wire tapping Abhören einer Leitung
word Wort
word editing Textbearbeitung
word processing Textverarbeitung
word processing equipment Textautomat
word processing system Textverarbeitungssystem
word processor Textautomat, Textverarbeitungssystem
word stem analysis Wortstammanalyse

work area Arbeitsbereich
work condition Arbeitsbedingung
work dissatisfaction Arbeitsunzufriedenheit
work element Tätigkeit
work environment Arbeitsumgebung
work file Arbeitsdatei
work measurement Arbeitszeiterfassung
work on (to) bearbeiten
work organization analysis Arbeitsorganisationsanalyse
work program Arbeitsprogramm
work sampling Multimomentstudie
work satisfaction Arbeitszufriedenheit
work sequence Arbeitsfolge
work session Arbeitssitzung
work standard Arbeitszeitvorgabe
work study Arbeitsstudie
workbench Arbeitstisch, Werkbank
workgroup Arbeitsgruppe
workgroup computing Arbeitsgruppen-Verarbeitung
working capacity Arbeitskapazität
working condition Arbeitsbedingung
working hypothesis Arbeitshypothese
working intensity Arbeitsintensität
working memory Arbeitsspeicher
working method Arbeitsverfahren
working process Arbeitsablauf, Arbeitsprozeß
working strain Arbeitsbeanspruchung
working style Arbeitsmethode
working system Arbeitssystem
working technique Arbeitsverfahren
working temperature range Betriebstemperaturbereich
working time measuring Arbeitszeiterfassung
workload Arbeitsbelastung, Arbeitslast, Lastprofil
workload projection Arbeitslast-Prognose
workplace Arbeitsplatz
workplace computer Arbeitsplatzcomputer
workplace evaluation Arbeitsplatzbewertung
workplace for telecommuting Heimarbeitsplatz, Telearbeitsplatz
workplace layout Arbeitsplatzgestaltung
workplace level Arbeitsplatzebene
worksheet Arbeitsblatt
workshop manager Betriebsleiter
workstation Arbeitsstation
workstation system Arbeitsplatzsystem, Arbeitsplatzcomputer
workteam Arbeitsgruppe
WORM = Write Once Read Mostly
write head Schreibkopf

write protection Schreibschutz
write protection ring Schreibring
write/read memory Schreib-/Lese-Speicher
written questioning schriftliche Befragung
WS = Work Station
WSI = Wafer Scale Integration
WYSIWYG = What You See Is What You Get

X

XPS = Expert System
XTEN = Xerox Telecommunications Network

Y

year plan Jahresplan

Z

zero Null
zero check Nullkontrolle
zero divide Division durch Null
zero suppression Nullunterdrückung
zip code Postleitzahl

Französischsprachige Abkürzungen

AFCET = Association Francaise pour la Cybernetique Economique et Technique
AFIN = Association Francaise des Informaticiens
AFNOR = Association Francaise de Normalisation
ANTIOPE = Acquisition Numérique et Televisualisation d´Images Organisées en Page d´Ecriture
CCITT = Comité Consultatif International Télégraphique et Téléphonique
CEN = Comité Européen de Normalisation
CENELEC = Comité Européen de Normalisation Electrotechnique
CEPT = Conférence Européenne des Administrations des Postes et des Télécommunications
ETSI = Européen Telecommunications Standards Institute
NETS = Normes Européennes de Telecommunication